Educational Management and Leadership

Word, Spirit, and Deed
for a Just Society

Douglas J. Thom

Detselig Enterprises Ltd.
Calgary, Alberta

Canadian Cataloguing in Publication Data

Thom, Douglas J. (Douglas John), 1946-
  Educational management and leadership

  Includes index.
  ISBN 1-55059-048-0

  1. School management and organization –
  Canada.   2. Educational sociology – Canada.
  I. Title.
  LB2890.T56 1993   371'.00971   C93-091664-6

Detselig Enterprises Ltd.
210, 1220 Kensington Rd. N.W.
Calgary, Alberta T2N 3P5

Printed in Canada   SAN 115-0324   ISBN 1-55059-048-0

Acknowledgements

The following groups contributed to the research and development of this book: the Social Sciences and Humanities Research Council of Canada (SSHRC), Lakehead University, Brock University, the University of Saskatchewan, the Canadian Society for the Study of Education, the Ontario Institute for Studies in Education, the Ontario Ministry of Colleges and Universities, the Saskatchewan School Trustees' Association, and the University of Hong Kong. This support is gratefully acknowledged.

Certain individuals were significant in realizing this publication. Input on law, which inspired the book, came from David Mullan (Queen's University), Lynn Campbell (Carleton University), Howard McConnell (University of Saskatchewan), Greg Dickinson and Wes Raynor (University of Western Ontario), Bruce Thom, Dr. J.T. Angus, D. Bates, and Dr. Robin H. Farquhar. Thank you to these people and special thanks to the late Dr. William G. Walker (Australia), Dr. Richard E. Ripple (Cornell University), James Scali, Dr. Daniel Klassen, Edythe Thom, Dr. T.J. Harvey, Dr. Fentey Scott, Sheila Wilson, Eleanora Bailey, Terry Noble, and Uta Hickin for their general support.

Further, the assistance of Dr. T.E. Giles, Detselig Enterprises Ltd., and reviewers is gratefully acknowledged. Finally, to my wife Susan and children Jade and Wesley, I express my thanks.

Douglas J. Thom

Contents

Tables

Figures

Financial support provided by the Alberta Foundation for the Arts, a beneficiary of the Lottery Fund of the Government of Alberta.

Financial assistance from the Department of Communications for the 1993 publishing program is also appreciated.

Preface

This book is for those who wish to learn about education, how and why it changes in society, and how it can be effectively managed and led. Canada is emphasized but much of the contents has wide applicability.

Essential themes of this book are:

(a) society is in a turbulent state of moving toward a fully multicultural, fair, and just society;

(b) the education system is pervaded by this same turbulence;

(c) as a result, people at all levels of society and education increasingly are taking action as groups/collectives to voice their wishes and are obtaining positive results more often than used to be the case;

(d) the effective educational leader considers the needs and requests of those he/she serves, together with his/her formal responsibilities as leader, and then uses conscience in making decisions; and

(e) educational law and educational finance are very important areas.

This inspired the book's title – *Educational Management and Leadership: Word, Spirit, and Deed for a Just Society.*

The format of the book is to first discuss the changing social order in society and education, then to discuss the practice and theory of educational management and leadership, past and present, and finally to present an appropriate original postpositivistic model for the future called "Educational Leadership with CONSCIENCE." The book has a sociological flavor. The Conscience-based model is rooted in law and its values and a recognition that effective leadership is considerably culture-specific. Moreover, leaders are recognized as spiritual in their relationship with followers, giving new images and meanings to things from their power and influence base. Inevitably the book's contents include the topics of bureaucracy, finance, politics, and religion. Also, personal profiles of successful leaders are presented. The book is intended for wide readership and for use particularly in colleges and universities at the undergraduate and graduate levels. It has specific relevance for theory, practice, and training with respect to the educational administration discipline. Further, the appendices provide information and tools which are useful for education students at all levels.

My point of view derives from my experience in education and educational administration East and West in Canada and abroad. This includes secondary school teaching and being a professor of educational administration at the University of Saskatchewan, the University of Hong Kong, and Lakehead University, Thunder Bay, Ontario. Further, I have held membership in the Commonwealth Council for Educational Administration (CCEA) since 1972, am a former editor for The Canadian Society for the Study of Education, and am a member of the Canadian Society for Studies in Educational Administration (CASEA) and the American Education Finance Association. My research, writing, and other scholarly work is on values and organizational culture surrounding bureaucracy, including finance, and on taxonomy with respect to the educational administration discipline. Interorganizational linkages and path analysis methods are particular interests of mine. The material in this book is based on my research and development over the years, much of it supported through Social Sciences and Humanities Research Council of Canada (SSHRC) programs.

I began my scholarly work in Educational Administration at the Ontario Institute for Studies in Education (OISE), Toronto in 1971. At that time the discipline was relatively young and was dominated by the structured systems approach (e.g., Daniel Griffiths). As with any relatively new discipline, a general theory was being sought. Taxonomic research and development was prevalent and I became involved. I published several bibliographies including *A Selected Bibliography of Educational Administration: A Canadian Orientation* (with E.S. Hickcox, Canadian Education Association, CEA, Toronto, 1973) and *A Teaching Bibliography for Educational Administration* (Commonwealth Council for Educational Administration, CCEA, Australia, 1984). With my concern for quality teaching and my taxonomic background, I produced "Perspectives on the Teaching of Educational Administration" which was presented to the Convention Program of the University Council for Educational Administration (UCEA), University of Virginia, U.S.A. in 1987.

While at OISE I was fortunate to have had involvement with individuals who were developing the phenomenological perspective on educational administration which revolutionarized thinking internationally beginning, with T.B. Greenfield, in 1974. Thus, I gained first-hand insights into the movement away from the original systems paradigm toward an ethnographic/human participant base. With this and my experience as Course Director, Advanced Studies in Educational Management at the University of Hong Kong (1980-84), I grasped the transition in ways of understanding educational administration from impersonal bureaucracy, to human relations, to structuralism, to open systems, ethnography, contingency theory, organization development, and critical thinking, through to the renewed emphases on leader beliefs and ethics and the redefinition of educational administration as a moral science. This led to the publication of, among other things, "Questioning Bureaucracy" (1981), "Educational Administration Theory Development into the 1980s" (1984), "The Spiritual Factor in Educational Administration" (1984), "On Improving Society and Schools" (1986), and the text *Education and Its Management: Science, Art, and Spirit* (1988) (with D. Klassen) which explores the common conceptual ground shared by the field as a whole. While at the University of Hong Kong, I and my graduate students initiated the formation of the Hong Kong Council for Educational Administration (HKCEA). It gives me pleasure to see HKCEA doing so well, and seeing that former students are now contributing to the discipline of educational administration including, notably, Cheng Kai Ming, in his innovative development of East-West cultural factors and rethinking theories and research. The Council hosted the Seventh Regional Conference of the CCEA, "Educational Administrators - Facing the Challenges of the Future," in 1992, with support from Australia's Drs. B. Taylor and W. Mulford.

In recent years we have witnessed the promotion of "excellence" and a resurgence of concern for effectiveness, efficiency, and accountability within education. This has sparked a call for reform from various levels. The reform takes time but its presence is evident in the general shift to the direction of more "power to the people" (collectivism). In effect, this shift characterizes the latest phase of what began as the human relations approach in organization so many years ago. Over the years the concern for the workers involved has escalated in the belief that true democracy is headed for full potential.

However, in organizations we have both labor and management. The workers and those in charge form collective agreements as to responsibilities of each of the parties. Educational leaders, as all leaders, need to lead with conscience so that fairness and justice are followed in these arrangements. This book explores this.

Some of the ideas in this book are provocative and controversial, as with any original scholarly contribution. I do my best in using my unique interdisciplinary and comparative experience and insights to analyze and explain the happenings in society, education, and leadership which continue to be witnessed. Scientific and philosophical interpretations are included. Finally the moral-ethical dimension of things is being recognized as very important, in word and deed. Readers are encouraged to adopt this spirit and conscience in their involvement with society and the education system.

Douglas J. Thom
Thunder Bay, Ontario
August, 1993

Part One

Sociological Perspectives on Society and Education

The world has well-nigh become a great aggregation of democracies. No democracy will rise very far above the level of its average thinking capacity, and no aggregation of democracies will rise very far above intellectual abilities of its members. In short, democracy has come to its great trial, and the verdict will depend largely on its capacity to make men think. It is not enough to say that other systems by their very nature discourage men from thinking because they aim to provide organizations at the top to do their thinking for them. That may be true, but it is no answer to the proposition that if democracy is to succeed it must deserve success by proving that it can inspire the race of common men to serious, continuous, effective consideration of the problems of common men.

On democracy
by Warren G. Harding, U.S. president
July 1922

Part One includes two chapters, the first on society and education and the second on bureaucratic theory.

1

Society and Education

General

There are many groups involved in the educational enterprise within our democratic society. Among them are students, parents, teachers, trustees, administrators, and teacher federations. Further, there are the ministries and departments of education and broader-spectrum groups such as the Canadian Education Association. Giles and Proudfoot (1990) refer to such groups as "publics" which are served in the system and they provide a detailed discussion of them. With the teacher at the centre, in essence we have the following:

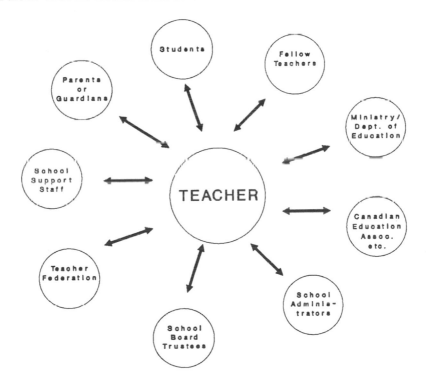

Figure 1-1

"Teacher - Other Education Groups" Relationships

These various groups broadly define what one terms a "sociology of education" – they form the basis for "the systematic study of the development, structure, and function of human groups conceived as processes of interaction or as organized patterns of collective behavior" (Webster's Dictionary). There is variation in the nature and extent of involvement among the groups. Chapters throughout this book and Appendix B elaborate information on them. Within this context several high profile subgroups have emerged in more recent years. These include women, natives, and special students (e.g., handicapped, gifted, etc.) and their concerns have greatly influenced the complexion of the entire school system. Over the years, imbalances with respect to these interest groups have been growing and now they are being corrected through improved accessibility and special programs. To fully understand, one must examine our changing society at large as it grapples with a "consideration of the problems of common men."

The Multicultural Just Vision

Society is in a state of considerable change. Ours is increasingly multicultural. If asked to define Canada, many people would mention ideas such as the following: predominantly French and English; multicultural; conservative; tolerant; cautious; dull; the Canadian flag; the Canadian Charter of Rights and Freedoms; the Mountie; the beaver; the lumberjack; hockey; a good banking system; a good overseas image; democratic; free; "just"; ruled by law; a good welfare system; the Canadian Broadcasting Corporation; native unrest; regional inequalities and power struggles, especially with respect to resources such as oil; and a federal, provincial, municipal operating structure. Many look at this society in bewilderment, unable to keep up with the change, and astounded as to how different it is from years ago. It is considered to be modern, enlightened, and very democratic. John Porter (1965) in *The Vertical Mosaic* depicted Canada as a pillar of groups, with the groups on top dominating those below in a delineation of social statuses. The lower, middle, and upper classes were clear. However, since the 1960s the country has been into a plan of equality and equity such that we now have a society in which there is less of a middle class *per se* and a large gap between the rich and the poor. The Canadian Charter of Rights and Freedoms introduced in 1982 has created a new tolerance of all groups. The Section 15 clause on equality rights is particularly relevant. The original goal set years ago by Prime Minister Pierre Elliott Trudeau was to create a just society in which all groups, including children, were to live in harmony with a guarantee of equal rights and freedoms. Society was to be a model for the rest of the world, free from discrimination and racism. That society is now closer to being, yet some would disagree on the last point concerning racism. In the United States the social structure has been described as a "melting pot" or "tossed salad" in which various ethnic groups assimilate into the grander society, all becoming patriots (Lipset, 1991). However, recently there has been an effort to alter this viewpoint. For example, professor Gary Nash of UCLA discusses a society which better recognizes blacks, natives, Asian Americans, Hispanics, women, and the disabled as significant by presenting U.S. history not solely through the eyes of male, Christian Europeans.

Society is now characterized by special attention to women, natives, and other distinct groups. The argument is that historically the needs and interests of these groups have been downplayed. So now there is attention to the battering of women, the return of land to the Indians, and special facilities for individuals with impairments. Further, there is an increased acceptance of all religions and languages. Canada is no longer grappling with just the traditional schisms between English/French and Protestant/Roman Catholic. The ideal of this society – all groups living in harmony – is a commendable one, but there are problems. (William G. Gairdner's *The Trouble With Canada*, 1990, is insight-ful.)

Growing Pains

Our society is complex and to many it seems to be in a confused mess. Canada appears to be in a state of endless debating on its very social fabric and many see the future as highly multicultural and East/West divided – the breakdown of unity. Ultimately no one knows what will result, but the situation can be understood in terms of the country's goal to become a just society. In these terms, what is being experienced now in society, education, and all sectors are growing pains.

History may show that Canada led the world in the proper development of things. Canadians are termed idealists and peacemakers and "laid back" by many. They are liked abroad and our country is viewed as beautiful, peaceful, and as a desired place to live. Trudeau effected the beginning of the just society dream when the Canadian Charter of Rights and Freedom was put in place. The ideal is a society with fairness and justice applied to all. Consider Section 15.(1) of the Charter:

Equality Rights

15.(1) Every individual is equal before and under the law and has the right to the equal protection and equal benefit of the law without discrimination and, in particular, without discrimination based on race, national or ethnic origin, colour, religion, sex, age or mental or physical disability.

(2) Subsection (1) does not preclude any law, program or activity that has as its object the amelioration of conditions of disadvantaged individuals or groups including those that are disadvantaged because of race, national or ethnic origin, colour, religion, sex, age or mental or physical disability.

This is a beautiful vision! Canada could lead in the development of a multicultural, peaceful, just, global village – is this not what the world should be? Campbell (1988) refers to welcoming "a mighty multicultural future." Maybe Canada should not be criticized so much. Time will tell if the country is on the right track.

Charles Dickens once wrote: "it was the best of times; it was the worst of times." At the moment our country is more into the best of times than the worst – it is a matter of having a positive attitude. On the surface there do appear to be serious problems. In 1993 the general situation in the country was as follows: Quebec was in debate about separating and preserving culture. Other provinces were considering the benefits of doing away with the Federal tier of government. In fact, one suggestion was to collapse the Federal and Provincial governments into *one* government in Ottawa comprised of MPs elected from across the country. The farmers in Canada were suffering; the loggers and fishermen were suffering; so too the autoworkers. The Federal government appeared to have ruined global markets through such things as the Free Trade deal with the United States and general controls. Further, wealth was being redistributed – in this case through Federal government transfer payments from central coffers back to the provincial governments. A national referendum on the Charlottetown constitutional accord on October 26, 1992 saw Canadians vote by 54.4% to 44.6% to reject an elected senate, an increase in provincial powers, and self-government for native peoples. Recession recovery then became the focus, with "social contract" activity.

There is a growing dislike of politicians. Canadians object to the Goods and Service Tax (GST). Traditionally, Ontario, as one of the strong "have" provinces, has helped to carry the "have-not" provinces. Increasingly Ontarians are objecting to providing for the "good of Canada." Ontario taxes are high, there is resentment, and the Federal government politicians try to appease the powerful and wealthy interests. Alberta feels that it does not need Ottawa but Ottawa feels that Alberta is needed (for its resource revenues). Finally, environmental and animal rights activists are busy and the natives are unhappy. Too much diversity in the country? Too much social, political and intellectual fragmentation? There are many continuing issues.

This does sound complex and a disintegration of unity appears to be inevitable! What ever happened to those pleasant accounts of our great Canadian country with our vast landscapes and our abundant natural resources spread from coast-to-coast with each province contributing uniquely, e.g., lumber, oil, wheat, minerals, and fish, to the total mosaic held together by the strong monarchy of England? Oh Canada, glorious and free! Times definitely seem to have changed. Many people would say that if our country were periodically evaluated as a family, with Ottawa as the head and the provinces as children, we would fail miserably. The family is "dysfunctional." But, again, these could be growing pains on the way to the glorious ideal. Support for this thought comes when one considers how relatively comfortable people in our country are, how volunteerism for worthy causes is at such a high, and how strongly the principles of justice and fairness are being applied. The education system *per se* is caught up in the same complexity as described above, yet at the same time it provides unprecedented choice, innovation, and excitement to students and does produce some excellent graduates. It will take some time for enlightened emerging goals for society and education to be realized. Meanwhile, reform continues.

In the enthusiasm for equality on all fronts, there is a danger that a firm, direct philosophy for the country is absent. Canada (and the United States) has moved from a long-standing base of Judaeo-Christianity to a base of many religions. Historically, societies which create tolerance of many groups and their customs ultimately have problems with breakdown of communication/ understanding across the groups. One might suggest that the scenario begins with a single predominant interest group, such as Judaeo-Christians, agreeing to relinquish the predominant role in favor of permitting other groups to form, and to participate and influence – to establish their own strong groups. The predominant group is willing to give up its monopoly, persuaded that to culturally predominate and to reinforce their unique identity (customs, norms, values, and so on) is not all that important. Yet, the many other groups who enter the scene, on equal terms, begin asking for increased acceptance and predominance in the scheme of things. That is, special rights and freedoms are requested and eventually the original predominant group realizes just how important unique identity can be and that it should not necessarily and easily be given up. Interestingly, England has been witnessing a new wave of racism and rejection – it was thought that Asians and other groups would assimilate, but they have not done so. Some people believe that the multicultural thrust in any country is a ploy by the rich and powerful to create a feeling of equality for lesser-status groups. However, some groups are satisfied with nothing short of infiltrating the rich and powerful circle.

Our society risks experiencing some specific difficulties. For instance, with so many choices and little clear direction, money may become the "religion." This seems to have happened in places such as Hong Kong. With the great emphasis on machines, particularly computers, there is a risk that people are developing as robots. Children seem to be imitating without a great deal of understanding. In fact, our contemporary society possibly does not nurture enough the future generation – children. Are adults themselves too selfish – too interested in "me first"? Perhaps it takes a war such as in the Persian Gulf to sort out a country's real goals.

Also, there is a "new order" of politicians, men and women who seem particularly anxious and uncontrolled much of the time. Toffler (1990) refers to them as the "shabby gentility." He sees them as greedy individuals, most of them, lacking the gentility of solid politicians of old and intent on making personal fortunes for themselves (p. 10). Further, the media speak of how advocates of "political correctness" drive in a "relentless pursuit of inoffensiveness," which is creating a situation of tolerance over truth as elimination of bias against members of minority groups is sought. There is a tremendous lack of confidence in contemporary politicians – they are often referred to as continually "talking out of both sides of their mouth." There appears to be a spiritual sickness within politics.

It is difficult to determine exact cause and effects, but leaders in this society just described are finding that their daily work involves many highly-charged factors. Figure 1-2 summarizes the breadth of this activity in the education system (this is elaborated on later). Confrontation is common.

Particularly, a knowledge of the entire human rights area is necessary. Knowledge concerning grievances is required. A prime issue is how much "special consideration" should be given to particular interest groups, and the bottom line is "just" treatment.

In society at large, one sees regional breakdowns (e.g., Western versus Eastern provinces) and clamoring by the grassroots populace. Authority is challenged often and the authorities do not always like to be challenged. One sees a society stressing fairness and justice more than ever before. Equity everywhere is an issue. Many individuals have an attitude that they "want it all" for themselves. Yet, not all want to put out effort or be responsible. Many want continually to have "a good time." The fallacy is that man has always sought personal control and discipline within freedom. Life cannot be continuous fun.

The context is one of varying expenditures of effort but everyone expecting to look the same. However, Canada is a relatively conservative society which espouses traditional virtues. Thus, on the positive side, there is more openness in people, "volunteerism" is widespread, and there is a genuine concern for the environment.

The evolution of society is evident everywhere.

Of course, the complexion of the broader society relates to that of the education system, a discussion to which this book now turns.

Education within a Broader Society

Sociologists believe that reality results from individuals and groups coming together and forming a *shared definition* of reality; depending on the people, the definition may differ. Further, changes in education tend to lag behind changes in society by a few years; movements in our society later are reflected in the education system, for example, new courses and changes in methods. However, since the 1960s, education increasingly has been an agent of social change as many of those educated move out into society and promote reform.

To clearly and comprehensively define modern-day education is virtually impossible. Thus, what is now presented consists of a broad overview which highlights points important to the theme of this book.

The contemporary education system is complex and superficially confusing. It can be characterized as stressing humaneness, flexibility, accessibility, accountability, and the ideal of equality of educational opportunity. The attempt is to individualize instruction and thus cater to the needs, abilities, and interests of each student. This emphasis began with the release of reports such as Ontario's *Living and Learning* (1968), and Alberta's *A Future of Choices, a*

Choice of Futures (1972). Many provinces have some form of separate and private schools. (See Appendix A – "Provincial Arrangements for Choice in Schooling.")

Broad Social Trends				
Elements of School Systems	Information-Based Society	Aging Population	Increased Cultural Diversity	Equal Rights
Education Goals	- more ambitious - self-directed problem solving	- pressure to address much broader range of goals	- increased ambiguity - broadened range of non-intellectual and intellectual goals	- all goals considered accessible to all clients
Educational Means or Tasks	- more flexible - more efficient	- more flexible - more efficient - more client-controlled	- more flexible - increased variety - more client-controlled	- more flexible - increased variety - elimination of discriminatory strategies (e.g., streaming)
Fiscal Resources	- increased value placed on education	- more competition for tax dollars	- more pressure to fund "non-public" schools	- pressure for increased funding
Organizational Structures	- greater diversity - greater local control - greater rational coordination	- pressure to collaborate with other education agencies - more market-oriented	- increased pressure for culturally homogeneous schools	- more minorities and women in positions of responsibility - greater diversity
Personnel Policies	- increased need for continuous staff development	- increased need for continuous staff development	- personnel selection criteria need to reflect diversity - increased need for staff sevelopment	
Information Collection and Decision-Making	- more information readily accessible for decision-making	- greater participation in decision-making by clients	- decisions based on wider set of criteria	- decisions based on wider set of criteria (especially human rights criteria)

Figure 1-2:
Social Trends and Education

From: *The Canadian School Superintendent,* by J.W. Boich, R.H. Farquhar, and K.A. Leithwood, 1989, p. 171. Copyright 1989 by OISE Press, Toronto, ON. Reprinted by permission.

An effective school system begins with a statement of goals. These goals generally fall into the following four categories:
the basics – developing reading, writing, and arithmetic skills;

vocation – preparing for a job;

socialization/citizenship – fitting into society; included in here are goals concerning proper behavior and physical activity to maintain one's

health;

aesthetic appreciation – developing an appreciation for cultural activities such as in art and music.

In essence, ideal goals of secondary school education are saleable skills, good health, citizenship (democratic) skills, ethical values, family life skills, consumer expertise, scientific method understanding, the capacity to appreciate beauty, leisure time use skills, and the general ability to think rationally. Some systems emphasize specific religious goals as well. Thom (1978/1979; 1987) examined high school goals. The strong emphasis in elementary education is on basic skills (Thom, 1986, 1987). Appendix A contains a typical goal statement for a school system.

Many sociological groups have contributed to the formation of the education system. Historically, missionaries settled the country and established the first schools; thus there is a formidable religious base. Evidence of this is at many universities where various colleges have a religious-affiliated name, e.g., Knox College, University of Toronto and St. Thomas More College, University of Saskatchewan. Queen's University has a Presbyterian base. Further, across the country many elementary and secondary schools are named after religious figures. Since the mid-1980s there has been a movement to remove the Judaeo-Christian emphasis from the public schools. For Ontario schools, the Lord's Prayer was removed by 1990. Considering the long tradition, it would take some time to completely discard such an emphasis. Figure 1-3 indicates when schooling began in Canada.

Education is a provincial responsibility through the *British North America Act, 1867,* section 93 (Education). In this decentralized, regional manner the various factors of religion, language, ethnicity, and provincial disparities with respect to items such as teaching certification, grade organization, taxation, and general resources can be better addressed. However, the education of groups such as native Canadians, the children of Armed Forces personnel, and those training in vocational and technical education is a Federal government responsibility.

Frederick Turner (of "Turner's Frontier Thesis") has explained how original settlement patterns determined the complexion of the education system in the United States. For instance, the pioneers who migrated to California for the goldrush were innovative and adventuresome, and one could argue that schools there over the generations became characterized as such. So too, in Canada the principle applies. For example, a variety of explorers from Europe docked at Newfoundland and set up churches and schools, which helps to explain the current multitude of such institutions, e.g., Newfoundland has several school system bases – Roman Catholic, Integrated (United Church, Salvation Army,

Anglican), and Pentecostal, as compared to the other provinces which have just a few.

Canadian schools have progressed through several important broad stages. Originally they were established for children of elite families, then they were open to all with a fee payable, next they were free of charge, and, finally, education to a certain age was made compulsory. Further, grammar, secondary, and normal schools each had unique stages of development.

[Date Province admitted to Confederation
indicated in brackets.]

Figure 1-3
Beginning of Schooling in Each Province/Territory (Dates)

At Confederation (1867), of Canada's 3.8 million population, 61 and 31 percent were of British and French origin, respectively. In 1992, of 27 million, the corresponding figures were about 41 and 27 percent (Royal Bank of Canada, 1992).

The following is a summary of the key ideas underlying the Canadian education system:

Principle: The settlement pattern of the country helps to explain the observable education system
– education is a provincial (as opposed to federal) responsibility

– separate and private school systems exist in many provinces
– schools originally were for the elite
– education is now compulsory (to a certain age), free, and open to all
– religion and language factors have always been important
– administration is relatively centralized
– school boards comprised of elected trustees oversee operations (in recent times there has been talk of replacing school boards with some less costly form of educational authority)
– the underlying ideal is equal educational opportunity for all (although it is difficult to attain)
– the system is characterized by humaneness, flexibility, accessibility, and accountability.

Brady (1992) outlines some growing trends regarding native trustee school board representation.

Not everyone agrees that school systems are doing well. The media tend to highlight negative aspects such as the general decline in standards, as evidenced by the failure of the system to inculcate sound moral values in graduates and to adequately prepare them with skills (e.g., reading, writing, and numerical) to fit into the working world. Culture-fair standardized testing is difficult with the changing societal ethnic mix. The education system gets blamed for many of society's complexities.

To some extent these arguments are valid. Yet, on the positive side, the education system is exciting and vibrant with more and more varied programs and opportunities then ever before. From the perspective of many of the students, parents, and educators themselves, the schools are wonderful, effective, and enjoyable. One should not deny this. Often those in the media (and educators) are too cynical and perhaps somewhat out of touch.

The role of one of the key sociological actors – the teacher – definitely has changed. Years ago, to be a teacher implied a very submissive, conservative existence. Consider the following "Rules for Teachers" circa 1872 (Quinte Education Museum and Archives, Bloomfield, Ontario):

1. Teachers each day will fill lamps, clean chimneys, and trim wicks.

2. Each teacher will bring a bucket of water and a scuttle of coal for the day's session.

3. Make your pens carefully. You may whittle nibs to the individual tastes of the pupils.

4. Men teachers may take one evening each week for courting purposes, or two evenings a week if they go to Church regularly.

5. After ten hours in school the teachers should spend their remaining time reading the Bible or other good books.

6. Women teachers who marry or engage in uncomely conduct will be dismissed.

7. Every teacher should lay aside from each pay a goodly sum of his earnings for his benefit during his declining years so that he will not become a burden on society.

8. Any teacher who smokes, uses liquor in any form, frequents pool or public halls, or gets shaved in a barbershop, will give good reason to suspect his worth, intentions, integrity, and honesty.

9. The teacher who performs his labors faithfully and without fault for five years will be given an increase of 25 cents per week in his pay providing the Board of Education approves.

Obviously teachers have come a long way in pay scales, from females not being able to marry, and so on, but even today a basic conservative expectation remains. The overall image of the teacher has improved as professionalism has increased.

The characteristics of a profession are as follows (Giles & Proudfoot, 1990):

1. A profession serves a unique, essential, service to mankind.

2. A profession is based on a body of knowledge which has taken a long period of time to develop, and active, planned efforts are made to understand this knowledge and further it for the betterment of mankind.

3. Members of a profession undertake a long training period plus an internship period before being recognized by their particular association, and the public, as being competent to practice.

4. The public accepts and respects the opinions and practices of the members of the profession.

5. The life-style of the members of the profession reflect an above-average standard educationally and culturally. Usually, this is accompanied by an above-average monetary entitlement.

6. Members of professions organize into closed-shop associations which protect the public from "unprofessional" practices and protects the profession from unscrupulous members of the public. (p. 310)

Teaching is thought by many not to be as much of a profession as medicine or law, partly because it does not have as lengthy an internship nor as mystical terms/jargon surrounding it. Regardless, the job has become multi-faceted with a variety of roles such as subject specialist, counsellor, mediator, and public relations person involved. Despite the changes, great teachers still lead by example – they are organized, are great motivators, and are firm but fair.

Projections of Enrolments and Staffing

The Canadian Teachers' Federation predicts that almost 300 000 elementary and secondary teachers will be needed by the year 2001. Elementary school enrolment will increase from the current 2.9 million to 3.1 million by 1997.

Secondary school population will rise to 1.91 million in 2001. Tables 1-1 and 1-2 include these figures.

Teacher education programs have been under review in recent years. The following Ontario-based discussion highlights issues and attitudes which generally apply across the country. The Fullan and Connelly report of 1987 delved into enrolment prerequisites and selection procedures, evaluation of pre-service programs, the induction period after teacher training, and the nature of in-service programs. A specific recommendation was for a lengthy internship in the schools after a faculty of education program. A focus of the review was on the relationship between reflective practice and career development and on determining the role to be played by various institutions with respect to improving teacher education (Fullan & Wideen, 1987).

Table 1-1

Projection for Canadian School Enrolments

Elementary		Secondary	
Now	1997	Now	2001
2.9 million	3.1 million	1.7 million	1.9 million

Table 1-2

Projection for Number of Full-time Canadian Teachers

Elementary		Secondary	
Now	2001	Now	2001
148 000	165 000	106 000	119 000

The Ontario Teachers' Federation (OTF) has been concerned about teacher shortage. Secretary-Treasurer Margaret Wilson says:

> Despite the availability of accurate information on the increased number of teachers retiring, despite government policies reducing class size in the primary division, despite a number of other indicators that the supply/demand situation was changing, we are facing a shortage of teachers. (OTF Seeks Measures . . . 1989, p. 5)

Emergency measures are needed to fill the supply gap. For instance, in 1988-89 over 2 500 Letters of Permission were granted. Teacher shortage in such specialty areas as Technological Education has been particularly acute.

One measure is the teacher "apprenticeship" program which contains the use of non-certificated teachers in the classroom with teacher training to follow later. Some individuals predict a revival of a six-week summer course for training.

OTF had asked both the Ministry of Colleges and Universities and the Ministry of Education to increase funding for training teachers, with an emphasis on attracting males to teach in the Primary/Junior divisions. Further, there is a concern that admission requirements for Ontario education faculties may be too high.

With respect to the establishment of "apprenticeship" pre-service programs, OTF has requested teacher education institutions and school boards to involve them from the outset in the interests of quality control. Important matters are those of certification, letters of permission, pension considerations, workload, equity, and compensation (Ibid., p. 6).

Greater enrolments in the schools are attributed to the high fertility rate of the baby boomers and the number of immigrant children. Greater need for teachers will grow faster because of a trend toward decreasing pupil-teacher ratios (CTF, 1989).

B.Ed. Student Survey

There has been a range of studies of teaching and teacher trainees. The following study was conducted using a sample of 180 B.Ed. year students at Lakehead University.

The students completed a thirty-minute questionnaire. As well as background information items, one third of the items assessed Awareness of Demands/Limitations of the Teaching Profession, one third assessed Extrinsic Factors as Motivators to Teach, and one-third assessed Intrinsic Factors as Motivators to Teach. All questions employed a Likert response scale. The questionnaire was adapted from research by P.E. Griffin at the Faculty of Education, University of Hong Kong and G.A. Postiglione, State University of New York. L. Zorzes assisted.

It was found that teacher trainees are well aware of demands/limitations of the profession (Table 1-3). 96% believed that teacher burn-out is a reality. 80% were aware of the lack of job security. 77% believed that teaching is highly stressful in comparison to other occupations. 50% were aware of teacher's limited status within society.

Extrinsic factors were found to be of limited significance as motivators (Table 1-4). 90% stated that teacher surplus was not an important factor regarding their decision to enter the teaching profession. Only 40% believed that teachers were well paid. Further, 71% would give up the opportunity to make more money elsewhere in order to become a teacher. Teaching year (summers off) was a motivator to only 20%; in addition, 85% of students expressed a willingness to teach during summer vacations. The perceived short working day was attractive to only 25%. Parents were cited as an important factor in entering the teaching profession by only 40%. Former teachers were cited as an important influence by 63%. Past experience with teachers remained significant, but not as much so as in findings from previous studies. Often former teachers are identified as the most important influence on students to enter the teaching profession.

Intrinsic factors were found to be the dominant determinants (Table 1-5). 94% felt it was an honor to be a teacher. 100% believed that teaching is a "caring" profession. 99% stated presenting a good lesson as a very rewarding experience. 99% stated teaching to be a very satisfying profession.

There was further evidence of intrinsic motivation. 92% would alter a personal habit, e.g., smoking, in order to set an example for their students. 97% would teach a subject other than their specialty. 91% would teach at an inferior school. 94% would take a class with discipline problems. 70% would question orders from the principal if they did not agree. 83% would *not* favor the wishes of the parent over the child.

Table 1-3
Awareness of Demands/Limitations of the Teaching Profession

Item	Percentage Aware
Teacher burnout is a reality	96
Lack of job security in teaching	80
Teaching is highly stressful	77
Teacher's limited status within society	50

Table 1-4
Extrinsic Factors as Motivators to Teach

Item	Percentage Motivated by
Teacher surplus	10
Teacher salaries	40
Summers off	20
Short working day	25
Parents' encouragement	40
Former excellent teachers	63

Table 1-5
Intrinsic Factors as Motivators to Teach

Item	Percentage Motivated by
Honor of being a teacher	94
Teaching is a "caring" profession	100
Teaching well is rewarding/satisfying	99

Also, the sample indicated a high regard for equal treatment of students, an adherence to high professional standards, an enthusiasm for working with dedicated students, and a desire to continue personal professional development.

The findings may be summarized as follows: Those entering the teaching profession are aware of demands and limitations of the profession. They are willing to make most any sacrifice in order to become a teacher. Intrinsic motivators are much more important than extrinsic.

These findings generally support those of the previous separate Korteweg and Stephenson surveys of the 1980s in the Lakehead University School of Education. Korteweg found that students entered the profession with little feelings of "repayment to society." They entered teaching because "I wanted to do it." Both surveys also established that the opportunity to impart knowledge, be around children, and to utilize creative skills were by far more important motivators than working conditions, salaries, or job security.

A strong indication is that the contemporary graduates of teacher training are highly committed and have noble attitudes with respect to the career of teaching (Osborn-Seyffert, 1992, generally confirms this). The love of children, eagerness to impart knowledge, and the desire to maintain high professional standards are main priorities. Also, the desire is to be a good example to students especially in the area of imparting sound values and attitudes. Wilson and Cowell (1989) present a theme congruent with these trends.

From this research, given the trainees' desire to be creative and the fact that they place a much greater emphasis on their perceived needs of the child as opposed to the parent, there may be considerable difficulty in implementing curriculum changes that involve an increase in structure, such as back to the basics.

The number of prospective teachers who have expressed a willingness to work at times not usually associated with school instruction would allow different approaches to be used regarding enrichment or extra-curricular activities. The possibility exists for schools to operate in some form on a seven day per week, twelve month per year basis.

The findings have implications specifically for educational management and leadership. Given the importance of intrinsic factors to teachers, the school's organizational structure should be examined. If a bureaucratic top-down model of management is being used, changes could be made to establish a more collegial, shared decision-making environment. In addition, greater accountability for providing quality education would rest with the individual schools. Teachers want the opportunity to be creative and have expressed a willingness to take whatever steps are needed in order to produce a quality educational program for their students. More insight into teacher absenteeism problems and required cures (Ponder, Scott, & Welsh, 1992) comes from considering the findings with respect to teacher motivation. Rather than constraining teachers through increased centralization, individual schools might be given both the responsibility of effective program delivery and the authority to take whatever actions are necessary to ensure its success.

References

Alberta (1972). *A future of choices, a choice of futures.* Edmonton, AB: Queen's Printer.

Boich, J.W., Farquhar, R.H., & Leithwood, K.A. (Eds.). (1989). *The Canadian school superintendent.* Toronto, ON: OISE Press.

Brady, P. (1992). Individual or group representation: Native trustees on boards of education in Ontario. *Canadian Journal of Native Education, 19*(1), 67-72.

British North America Act, 1867 (amended to *Constitution Act, 1867* in 1982).

Campbell, J., with Meyers, W. (1988). *The power of myth.* New York, NY: Doubleday.

Canadian Charter of Rights and Freedoms. Part I of *Constitution Act, 1982,* Schedule B to *Canada Act 1982* (U.K.), U.K. Stats. 1982.

Canadian Teachers' Federation (1989). *Elementary and secondary enrolment and the teaching force in Canada 1987-88 to 2006-07.* Ottawa, ON: CTF.

Dickens, C. (1970). *A tale of two cities.* Middlesex, England: Penguin.

Fullan, M., & Connelly, F.M. (1987). *Teacher education in Ontario: Current practice and options for the future.* Toronto, ON: Ontario Ministry of Education.

Fullan M., & Wideen, M. (1987). Reform of teacher education in Canada. Presentation at the Canadian Society for the Study of Education annual conference, McMaster University, Hamilton, ON.

Gairdner, W.D. (1990). *The trouble with Canada: A citizen speaks out.* Toronto, ON: Stoddart.

Giles, T.E., & Proudfoot, A.J. (1990). *Educational administration in Canada* (4th ed.). Calgary, AB: Detselig.

Korteweg, L. (mid-1980s). Student survey. School of Education, Lakehead University, Thunder Bay, ON.

Lipset, S.M. (1991). *Continental divide: The values and institutions of the United States and Canada.* New York, NY: Routledge.

Ontario Department of Education (1968). *Living and learning.* The Hall-Dennis Report. Toronto, ON: Queen's Printer.

Osborn-Seyffert, A. (1992). Student survey. School of Education, Lakehead University, Thunder Bay, ON.

OTF seeks measures to counter teacher shortage. (1989, November). *OTF/FEO Interaction, 16*(2), 5-6.

Ponder, A., Scott, F., & Welsh, R. (1992, February). Teacher absenteeism in Canada. Critique. *The Canadian School Executive, 11*(8), 27-31.

Porter, J. (1965). *The vertical mosaic: An analysis of social class and power in Canada.* Toronto, ON: University of Toronto Press.

Royal Bank of Canada (1992, Spring). *The royal bank reporter.* Toronto, ON.

Stephenson, G. (mid-1980s). Student survey. School of Education, Lakehead University, Thunder Bay, ON.

Thom, D.J., & Klassen, D. (1986, December). Study examines students' attitudes. *Teacher Education News,* p. 3.

Thom, D.J. (1979). Hockey participation as a factor in the secondary school performance of Ontario students: An effects study for administrators (Doctoral dissertation, University of Toronto, 1978). *Dissertation Abstracts International, 40,* 2, 600A.

Thom, D.J. (1986, October). On improving society and schools. *Comment on Education, 17*(1), 7-12.

Thom, D.J. (1987). School administrators discuss students. *Orbit 83, 18*(3), 16-17.

Thom, D.J. (1992, November). Teacher trainees' attitudes toward the teaching career. Research report. *The Canadian School Executive, 12*(5), 28-29+.

Toffler, A. (1990). *Powershift: Knowledge, wealth, and violence at the edge of the 21st century.* New York, NY: Bantam Books.

Turner, F.J. (1961). *Frontier and section: Selected essays.* Englewoods Cliffs, NJ: Prentice-Hall.

Wilson, J., & Cowell, B. (1989). *Taking education seriously.* London, ON: Althouse Press, University of Western Ontario.

2

Bureaucratic Theory

Premises

When one considers sociological theories applied to education, such works as Homans' *The Human Group* (1950), Willard Waller's *The Sociology of Teaching* (1961) and Coleman et al.'s *Equality of Educational Opportunity* (1966) necessarily come to mind. Homans focused on "in" and "out" groups and their importance. Waller gave a comprehensive overview of the total system. The Coleman work improved understanding of equal educational opportunity. Mifflen and Mifflen (1982) provide an excellent summary of the key theories in the sociology of education when they cover the following: social stratification/class differences, the functionalism/consensual model, the conflict model (Marx, Weber), critical functionalists, and interactionists/micro analysts. Inevitably their classification of these theories and the discussion may not find agreement among other sociologists; however, their point of view is well presented. Their text goes on to discuss in detail the important concepts of socioeconomic status and educational opportunity, the family, socialization and educational achievement, and educational achievement and economic success. The following are important summary ideas from any discussion of this sociological perspective:

a. through "social reproduction," individuals and groups who have status and power advantages in society and education tend to pass these on to their offspring;

b. children of higher socioeconomic status (SES) tend to have more educational opportunity and achievement and, eventually, increased economic success; and

c. critical theorists tend to interpret society in terms of power elites suppressing the masses.

The development of these ideas can be understood in the context of broad theories of social change. Such theories range from evolutionary (e.g., Hegel), to structural functionalists (e.g., Parsons), to modernistic (e.g., McClelland), to human capital (e.g., Schultz) through to conflict (e.g., Marx) in character. All attempt to describe, explain, and predict societal change. All have their use and the conflict interpretation based on dialectics (Hegel) is of high profile, for as soon as we begin to consider things in their motion we become involved in the study of contradictions (Evers & Lakomski, 1991, p. 145). Dialectics involves thesis and antithesis (opposites) resulting in synthesis (thus class conflict results in change in social structure). The various theories have varying degrees of emphasis on preserving the status quo and transforming things. The neo-Marx approach in which the purpose of education is to raise the consciousness of exploited societal groups is popular for it appears to have elements which speak to what is happening in multiculturalistic societies such as Canada. The approach is characterized by conflict and suggests revolutionary outcomes (often motivated by anger) more than do the other social change theories. It is true that reality presents contradictions.

Since the 1960s, the apparent emphasis in education has been on making formal education more accessible to all individuals. Yet many argue that social class differences and social reproduction are too entrenched. New developments in the theory and practice of democracy and bureaucracy provide insights into this.

To further understand contemporary education from a sociological perspective, bureaucratic theory can provide a most fruitful approach.

Questioning Bureaucracy

Most of the literature on bureaucracy begins with some reference to Max Weber's "ideal-type" construct. Over fifty years ago Weber stated that the following organizing principles maximize rational decision-making and administrative efficiency: the use of a division of labor and specific allocations of responsibility; a well-defined hierarchy of authority; administrative thought and action based on written policies, rules, and regulations; an impersonal, universalistic application of the bureaucratic environment to all inhabitants ("formalistic impersonality"); and promotion and selection based on technical competence (Gerth & Mills, 1946). Over the years many have criticized Weber's ideas, claiming inconsistencies and conflicting tendencies in his presentation. His failure to discuss dysfunctions, and the informal relations and unofficial patterns which develop in formal organizations, have been highlighted in particular (Gouldner, 1954; Merton, 1968; Parsons in Weber, 1947; Selznick, 1948).

Weber's academic and well-expressed ideas have become the basis of the literature, but it is important to realize that bureaucracies existed and were described well before Weber's time. The Dynasties of China, the armies of earlier civilizations, and the Roman Catholic Church are some examples (Steinberg, 1975). Despite the weaknesses in Weber's conceptions, he has made an outstanding contribution simply by stimulating further analyses of bureaucracy. Some individuals feel that analyzing such organizations as contemporary Chinese government and the Mafia yields the most profound insights.

Today, the study of bureaucracy incorporates a multitude of elements: goal-setting, structure, power, authority, control, influence, communication, decision-making, motivation, leadership, team-building, conflict, effectiveness and efficiency, contracts, evaluation, change, climate, inter-organizational relationships and the institution-society interface. Basic approaches abound, as well, such as the scientific management, human relations, structuralist, systems, and phenomenological approaches. Finally, many "catch phrases" have emerged to describe bureaucratic processes – line and staff, the Peter Principle, time-motion, satisficing (Simon), MBO (Management by Objectives), Murphy's Law, "Those who can't . . . ", zone of indifferences (Bridges), disentanglement, and the halo, Groupthink, and Doppelganger effects – to list a few.

Many people believe that bureaucratic structures are problematic for today's society, and there is no lack of evidence to support this belief. Entire countries sometimes break down under the weight of their own bureaucracies; there are frequent stalemates in organizational collective bargaining; but, what is more meaningful and important, a great many individual employees arrive home each day feeling frustrated, angry, and helpless because of what "my job is doing to me." Some probing questions must be asked in order to gain some insight into how the well-being of people working in bureaucracies, including educational institutions, can be protected.

Question 1: *Is bureaucracy the inevitable organizational structure which individuals will form?*

It is intriguing to consider the question as to whether bureaucratic structures are inherent in man's nature or whether there are other, more natural organizational patterns. Without a doubt, bureaucracy involves some individuals leading and others being led. It involves competition, the application and enforcement of rules and regulations, and the emphasis by management on logic and on being motivated by rational, economic considerations in order to attain efficiency and effectiveness. Under this type of system the individual receives concrete guidance as to his or her responsibilities, and a steady, known remuneration. Direction and security are provided.

Indeed, it is difficult to find a group of people who are organized in other than a bureaucratic fashion, which is to say without a hierarchy of authority, without job specialization, and without rules and regulations. It might be argued that certain religious societies such as the Hutterites deviate from the norms of the typical bureaucracy, but even here its processes can be identified. The elders of the community constitute the authority, rules and regulations are contained in the Bible and in the traditions of the society, and job specialization exists in a general sense, though dependent on the needs of the community rather than on the skills of the individual.

In 1971 the author researched social structure possibilities though a group of Canadian Natives and Inuit. The native group was asked to imagine that they had been involved in a plane crash over a lake, as a result of which they all arrived on an island where they could expect to remain for a long time. The question was posed: "What would you do as a group?"

Initially, the group indicated that they would structure themselves more or less bureaucratically, forming committees to satisfy various personal and communal needs. These included a committee to hunt for food, a firewood committee, a water committee, a housing committee, a social committee, and later on, an education committee. Some suggested that there would have to be a specific set of rules for behavior and a police force so that members would not shirk work. It was felt that a defence force, good foreign relations, and some plan of conservation of resources were necessary. [Many of these ideas can be tied to theories of human needs, motivation and informal organization (Etzioni, 1964; Lane, Corwin, & Monahan, 1971; Maslow, 1962; Thom, 1990).]

Gradually however, the group showed a potential for organizing non-bureaucratically. One member spoke of not having a leader, on the somewhat peculiar grounds that this could prevent mutiny later on. Others mentioned that they would not necessarily have a hunting committee; if one person killed an animal, all would share it as food. One member said "I don't think we would really set up the society like we did. Indians would just *know* how to survive under these conditions." Yet, in the main, the suggested organization was bureaucratic in nature.

Blau (1962) explains that there are particular historical conditions within a given social structure which push men toward bureaucratic structures. A money economy with its payment of regular salaries creates a combination of dependence and independence in employees which is conducive to perpetuating bureaucracy. The sheer size of an organization and the emergence of special, complex administrative problems encourages the development of bureaucracies. Further, capitalism and religion both encourage it: the former, to be effective, requires governments to maintain order and stability; the latter, with its basis of rational discipline, fuels bureaucratic structure. And if men seek optimum efficiency in organization, which they ideally do, they will lean toward bureaucracy if Weber's view is valid.

In the final analysis it remains unclear whether bureaucracy is inherent in man's nature or whether it is the result of centuries of socialization. In either case, the fair answer to a question about the inevitability of bureaucratic structure seems to be, "Yes, it is inevitable."

Question 2: *Are there significant relationships between the concepts of bureaucracy and democracy?*

On the surface it might appear that the broad, democratic society, with its emphasis on human freedom and the rights of the individual, is irreconcilable with the regimentation, the restrictions, and the impersonality of bureaucracy.

Bennis and Slater (1968) give an opinion on the question. They argue that democracy is inevitable but that bureaucracy is not "[E]very age develops an organizational form appropriate to its genius, and . . . the prevailing form . . . bureaucracy . . . is out of joint with contemporary realities" (p. 54). Thus, there is an incongruency which these authors suggest must be remedied. In somewhat of a contrast, Blau (1962) states that the free enterprise system of democracy fosters the development of bureaucracy. "The interest of capitalism demands . . . the establishment of governments strong enough to maintain order and stability" (p. 38). Further, it is often argued that the climate of impersonal detachment within bureaucracy engenders equitable treatment of all persons, thus fostering democracy (Ibid., p. 30). An example here would be the practice of the administrator who tells any employee who approaches him asking for resources to try out a creative idea, "No, if I do it for you then I'll have to do it for everyone else who comes along." However, many would say that this does not represent democracy – treating others the "same" is neither treating them "fairly" nor "democratically." Democracy in spirit is positive.

Many would disagree that democracy is inevitable; in fact, they might say that the opposite is true. From the discussion under Question 1 we would infer that bureaucracy is inevitable. It is suggested that bureaucracy and democracy in juxtaposition are seemingly at odds, and yet bureaucracy does exist within democracy. It flourishes, in fact, as it has flourished throughout history in every conceivable form of government, from communist dictatorships to absolute monarchies to anarchy-syndicalist collectives. It seems, then, there is no significant relationship between bureaucracy and any type of government. It is perhaps true that democracy functions within bureaucracy rather than the other way around. Democracy, communism, monarchies, and so forth are not all-pervasive, whereas bureaucracy is, and it might well be that the survival of any type of government is dependent on its ability to function within a framework of bureaucracy.

Finally, bureaucrats of communist countries, of course, might explain the relationship between democracy and bureaucracy in terms of strong bureaucratic institutions being necessary for control in an interim stage leading to a true democratic society.

Question 3*: How possible are the ideals of the human relations approach, such as autonomy, self-realization, trust, and openness, in the typical organization?*

The general flavor of the administration literature in the last two decades has been of the "humanistic approach." Sergiovanni and Carver (1979) and Hoy and Miskel (1991) are cases in point. Argyris (1966) emphasizes the need to integrate the individual and the organization. Yet in the day-to-day operation of our institutions (bureaucracies) a multitude of workers are frustrated by the lack of humane and fair treatment. Many would say that the human relations approach is not realistic in today's organizations. In fact, some would argue that the principles of Taylor's impersonal, mechanistic, scientific management (1923) still abound. Bendix (1965) looks at Taylor.

Just how possible human relations are would seem to depend on the purposes (and technology) and size of an organization. Blau and Scott (in Carver & Sergiovanni, 1969) describe various purposes for formal organizations: economic, political, religious, educational, public service, and so on (p. 13). Logically, one would expect a more humanistic climate in the service/people oriented institutions as opposed to the production/object oriented. Hodgkinson (1991) supports this in his "Education is Special" presentation. One would also expect a correlation between the size of the institution and the extent of bureaucratization and hence the amount of depersonalization, as for example when the individual worker becomes increasingly remote from the head of the organization. Further, in these times, greater size of institution implies more continuous evaluation of staff and activities, which in turn is often associated with "dehumanization." On the other hand, in very large bureaucracies, increased humanism is possible within smaller subdivisions, especially through the impact of informal groups.

These informal groups are vital to the operation of schools, especially with respect to the democratic process. Bureaucracies have both formal and informal organizations which exist side by side (Lane, Corwin, & Monahan, 1971). The formal organization of a school is its administration. The informal organization is often referred to as "shadow organization." This forms within the school as well. As the term implies, informal organization grows up in the shadow of the formal structure of administration.

We see many examples of the shadow organization within the school bureaucracy – the staff room, the secretarial staff, the janitorial staff subcultures. These shadow groups are very important because they affect the quality of output and the pace of work in the school. This is why sometimes a new school teacher gets tapped on the shoulder and is asked to slow down. "Don't be so keen; don't work so hard because it is making the established members of the staff look bad."

The benefits of the informal organization within the school are substantial. Informal organization can help support organization goals. It is an additional means of communication or it provides a "grapevine." Also, it can provide a means of social satisfaction for members of the organization. Further, it can bolster or compensate for leaders who lack ability.

However, there are drawbacks to the informal organization as well. Informal groups start rumors, they can provide resistance to change, and they may foster too much group conformity. School staff rooms often display this.

To answer the question posed, it must be appreciated that different degrees of the human relations approach are possible at different levels of the organization, and a distinction must be made between the hypocritical "window-dressing" type of humanistic practices and those of the sincere, pervading type. (Drucker, 1980, elaborates.)

Question 4: *What about bureaucratic organization and change and innovation?*

Many argue that the very character of bureaucracy makes it resistant to change and innovation. For instance, Abbott (1965) and Hanson (1991) state that an organizational hierarchy has a natural tendency to slow down the process of change. Kimbrough and Todd mention that school bureaucracies generally lack the willingness to expand and to probe the unknown (p. 418). Several specific points about this bureaucracy are listed: the inability to legitimize differences in ideas among personnel depresses creativity; new ideas generated from within are often vetoed by members of the official hierarchy, especially if they are in conflict with perceived rational teaching behavior; there is an inadequate structure and process for the review of decisions in the bureaucracy;

the extrinsic reward system stimulates conformity rather than innovations; the prior commitments of organizational resources to subunits within the organization make it difficult to develop innovative solutions for new problems; and the lines of communication are often closed because of hierarchical divisions (p. 420). Many theorists believe that until tendencies such as these are reversed, change and innovation will be difficult.

However, other individuals believe that in recent years the educational bureaucracy has been amply open to, and involved in, change and innovation. Witness the pluralism, the collegial relations in decision-making, the community participation, and the general decentralization/school-based thrusts in school systems. "Grassroots" curriculum development is a good example. The level of the bureaucracy on which we are focusing again becomes important in considering whether bureaucracy stimulates or inhibits change and innovation.

Again, real (sincere) and seemingly real intentions and results must be carefully distinguished.

Question 5: *How is the study of bureaucracy useful for the educational practitioner?*

Bureaucratic theory provides the practitioner with a tool for the understanding of his or her environment. One is able to dissect situations and to become more aware of where one fits in the hierarchy. The theory includes discussion of roles, change, morale, power, leadership, climate, communications, and decision-making; it provides the practitioner with ideas to sharpen his/her skills.

The historical development of bureaucratic theory enlightens the practitioner as to the various possible approaches to managing and leading: Scientific Management, Human Relations, Structuralist, Systems, and so on. One can learn in which situations to use which approach. Moreover, one learns through the theory how one is socialized into organizational roles. Thus, there is an increase in self-awareness.

On the value of a systems approach to a school administrator, Griffith (1979) says the following:

> It is a model or conceptual analogue for examining the way a school functions.
> It indicates that a school is a suprasystem composed of interrelated and interdependent subsystems and that the boundaries of these subsystems must be clearly demarcated to prevent duplication and waste . . .

Systems theory is also a theory base for research, a framework around which an investigator can organize observations and thinking. It is a guide by which school personnel can bring about curricular change and improve the quality of a school's service to its students and community. Finally, it is a method of budgeting and evaluation, of determining the financial needs of each component, and of assessing the relationships between input and output (pp. 31-32).

So, the systems component of bureaucratic theory would seem to be potentially very useful. Generally, the study of bureaucracy brings understanding for the practitioner, resulting in valuable insights into worker morale, accountability phenomena, and style. The theory helps the practitioner to formulate questions to be answered about one's organization, and knowing the questions is usually more than half the battle. Directions about how to change and innovate emerge. Also, important ideas appear about what is sometimes referred to as "coping effectively with difficult people."

Considering the school bureaucracy in specific terms helps to answer Question 5.

By legal mandate our schools are supported, in various ways, from three levels – the federal, the provincial, and the local or municipal level. Federal responsibilities for education in Canada include the education of the children of armed forces personnel, native Canadians, and those in manpower training programs. Further, there are many ways in which the federal government supports education through the provision of resources such as materials used in the health classes in high schools. A provincial ministry/department of Education is of high profile. Its mandate includes the setting of standards for schools, the certifying of administrators and teachers, and providing services such as library, health, and transportation. The local boards of education appoint teachers, provide facilities, support staff and maintenance, and set standards of health and safety.

Roles, Needs, and Satisfaction

Under our legal, bureaucratic framework, responsibility for school administration is through several major positions. There is a formal organization and line of authority. Directors of education are in the overall position of serving the school board. They oversee the entire educational process, implementing the Education Act. They are concerned with effectiveness and efficiency in our schools. Superintendents of education work closely with the director and often these personnel can feel a "role ambiguity." Many superintendents were once school principals and knew very clearly what their responsibilities in the school system were, but once principals become superintendents usually their role is not as clearly defined. According to the Education Act, the formal responsibilities of superintendents are the inspection of new teachers, the provision of school facilities, and the development of professional development programs. Also, they have a responsibility for certain business affairs of the board (including dealing with school trustees who represent the community's interests), and for the general support of the teachers, administrators, and students in the system. Superintendents should be especially gifted in the area of school and community relations.

Principals are probably the most important people in the education system. They are charged with maintaining order and discipline, providing good facilities, implementing and improving educational programs, and selecting and developing personnel. Frymier (1987) discusses their importance. Principals of schools must work closely with the community. Also, they have management and leadership of the school as a major responsibility. Further, pupil records are their responsibility. Principals are often referred to as administrative and instructional leaders. They, too, should possess outstanding public relations skills.

The role of the high school department head is to assist the school principal with such activities as budgeting, coordinating curriculum and developing staff. Finally, there is the classroom teacher – last but not least. In the main, the teacher is charged with maintaining and controlling the class environment. He/she has an overall responsibility for classroom teaching and learning.

Jacob Getzels and Egon Guba have developed a model that depicts two important dimensions of a social system such as a school and that elaborates roles. First is the personal, or idiographic, dimension referring to the personalities and needs of the individual involved in the system. Second is the institutional dimension (nomothetic) which refers to the formal duties described for the people in the system by the institution. It is not always the case that these two dimensions are congruent (Argyris again). Sometimes the needs of individuals in the system do not match the formal expectations of the institution. Abraham Maslow (1962), an American psychologist, developed a hierarchy of human needs that very neatly connects to the Getzels/Guba model. Maslow theorized that every individual has the same needs. There are lower-order and higher-order needs and, as one grows psychologically, the lower-order needs emerge first and then the higher-order needs. What are the lower-order needs?

First, there are physiological needs which must be satisfied – the needs for such things as food, shelter, and sex. These are first to emerge. As one moves up the hierarchy, the need for security emerges. Then, the area of social needs appears, then ego/esteem needs, and finally the level called self-actualization-type needs. Self actualization has been stated as a prime goal of schools. "Responsible" self actualization is a good way to view it. Later, Maslow categorized two other needs above self-actualization that people experience. What possibly could be above and beyond self-actualizing for a person? He identified the category of "sense of wonder" – type needs that one wishes to satisfy and that was topped by a "sense or order" – type, the need to look beyond oneself to some real meaning for everything.

The important point about the Maslow theory is that *an unsatisfied need is a motivator of a person*. Thus, if a need is not satisfied then that is what is motivating an individual. This is important for teachers, administrators, and schools to understand. Often when someone is behaving a particular way, Maslow's scheme helps to identify what is motivating that individual and this can aid the teacher or administrator in interacting with the person.

Another theorist, Frederick Herzberg, looked at worker satisfaction in terms of satisfiers and dissatisfiers. Thomas Sergiovanni applied Herzberg's ideas to teachers. Examples of satisfiers are things such as a good salary and pleasant working conditions. Examples of dissatisfiers are a lack of autonomy or harassment from fellow-staff. The aim in all of this is to maintain motivation of people in the organization. Understanding of roles, needs, and satisfaction is important and comes from a study of bureaucracy.

School Leadership

Leadership has been studied from many different points of view. What is found in all of the theories of leadership are two main dimensions – the task (initiating structure) dimension and the maintenance (consideration) dimension. An analogy can be drawn between the idea of bureaucracy and democracy and the idea of (a) task and maintenance and (b) control and freedom in organizations. Bureaucracy implies control, whereas democracy implies freedom. The real challenge for leaders, not just in schools but in every sector, is to balance the control and freedom concepts. How does one lead in a school such that there is enough control for things to occur in some kind of a logically ordered sequence, and yet freedom to learn? It is a big challenge and it is something of which education leaders are not always enough aware – the fact that they are trying to balance bureaucracy and democracy at the same time. Again, the leader displays two aspects, one is task related (or related to getting the job done in the education setting), the other relates to maintenance or looking after the needs and emotions of the people who are being led.

Another theorist from the 1950s, Robert Bales, suggests that, in any human group, there are two types of leaders: a task-oriented and a maintenance- or people-oriented leader. But sometimes one person can capsulize both dimensions of leadership. One individual might be both leaders. Mr. Art Warwick, a secondary school principal, gives a practical appreciation of leadership:

> A school is an educational institution and is part of the total educational bureaucracy. As a result, controls are imposed upon schools by the province through the Ministry of Education's *Education Act* requirements and grants, and by municipalities through the boards of education in the areas of staffing, administration, and curriculum. Controls and structures are essential because they identify and make the members aware of the organization and indicate to members what ought to be achieved. However, there is freedom within the structures in achieving the goals of the organization. The school as a culture or mini-society has goals, regulations, and expectations which allow for the smooth operation of the school. The people within that school culture have freedom to do what they want to do and freedom to do what they ought to do. The new OSIS document has become very prescriptive vis-à-vis content and evaluation. However, within that, there is a degree of freedom on how teachers achieve identified objectives, especially in the area of teaching strategies and resources.

> I cannot see using one particular style of leadership for all situations. The style of leadership used will depend upon the situation, and therefore emerges a situation-style leadership depending on the time available to make a decision and on the human resources available. This is a continuum of leadership which has a diagonal access that separates the authority of the leader from the freedom of the group (Note: see Appendix D, under Tannenbaum & Schmidt).

At one extreme we have then an *autocratic style* leadership which really maximizes the authority of the leader and minimizes the freedom of the group. In this style, the leader would identify an issue or concern, consider alternatives, choose one of those alternatives, and communicate the decision to others. In this style, there is no opportunity for participation in the decision-making process. There are times in normal operation on the school level when this leadership is used effectively. Another leadership style along the continuum is *democratic* or *participatory leadership*.

A cabinet comprised of department heads and others is a key component for many principals in the administration and operation of the school. In our cabinet meetings, participatory leadership is used. It is important to define parameters. A problem issue or concern is identified, opinions, feelings and expressions are requested, and a decision is made. A decision may be made by the leader, or may be made by the members of the group through consensus or in the form of a motion and voting. In this style, the authority of the leader has been reduced and the freedom of the group has been increased.

It is my feeling that the goals of an organization can be achieved by providing opportunities for growth, in fact, self-actualization for the members of the organization. It is a perception on my part that the leader advocates his/her responsibility by using this style of leadership. What better way to recognize and to rear talented people within your organization than to use this particular type of leadership! If this style is going to be used and an issue or concern is going to be identified, and parameters and timelines are going to be established, then the group will have the task to challenge him/herself to complete the task and to solve the problem. To me it is not a weakness on the part of the leader to transfer the responsibility of decision-making and authority to other leaders of the organization.

In summary, several styles of leadership are used and the effectiveness of the style used will depend upon the strength of the leader, the strength of the members of the group, and certain aspects of the situation such as the time available for decision-making and the magnitude of the decision to be made.

One theory of leadership depicts three types/styles; authoritarian, laissez-faire, and participatory/democratic. Mr. Warwick mentions Tannenbaum and Schmidt's continuum of leadership behavior that runs from boss-centred to subordinate-centred. Moving along the continuum from more authoritarian to less authoritarian, leadership is portrayed as a "telling" kind, a "selling" kind, a "testing" kind, a "consulting" kind, and finally a "joining" kind of leadership. In the last type, full cooperation exists between leader and subordinates. In contemporary education, a team building or teamwork style of leadership is most effective and efficient. Our society and our schools have become such that this team building approach is appropriate. Years ago it seemed acceptable to have an authoritarian or directive type of leadership, but times have changed and, now, educational leaders who use the authoritarian style to excess have difficulty. The prevalence of legal suits is a reaction to some of the authoritarian techniques that have been tried in more recent years. There is an entire technology called Organization Development (O.D.) which incorporates the team-building style. It is the type of approach worth endorsing and is outlined in Chapter 6 of this book.

Climate

Organizational climates are closely associated with the style of educational leadership. Administrative style will determine the climate within the organization. Researchers such as Andrew Halpin (1966) measured organizational climates, using two instruments – the organizational climate description questionnaire (OCDQ) and the leadership behavior description questionnaire (LBDQ). Using these instruments, school climate can be categorized as to one of the following: open; autonomous; controlled; familiar; paternal; or closed. Within contemporary education, these days,there should be very few examples of closed climates because of the character of society and how people in organizations think. They think in much more humanistic terms than people used to. So, in trying to apply Halpin's climate scales now, it becomes difficult to create a differentiation between closed and open climates. Most of the data would most likely indicate a heavy loading on open climate in schools.

Sometimes the mere look or feel of a school can tell a person which climate – closed or open – is in effect. Seasoned educators can walk into a school and tell something about the leadership style and climate. If students are around the building mid-morning, banging doors, and smoking cigarettes, immediately this says something about the school, in comparison to a school in which there is considerable order. When referring to school environments the question often comes up, "Is the noise in the school healthy or unhealthy?" Educators talk about healthy or productive noise versus unhealthy or unproductive noise. Ultimately, climate depends on the community and the leadership style.

Thus, the bureaucratic perspective provides a wealth of useful ideas to the educational practitioner. Again, the bottom line challenge is to create a proper balance between controlling and creating freedom.

Bureaucratic organization has been with us for some time and chances are that it will continue for some time to come. While it does provide order and a degree of efficiency, there are critical drawbacks to such a structure. The well-being of employees is not always what it should be. Bureaucracies may be admirably suited to those individuals who need clearcut directions and rewards in a work situation, but at the same time they can stifle the creativity and initiative of others. All bureaucracies, including the educational one, appear to be resistant to change and innovation.

Implications

Many employees do not enjoy their jobs. They get frustrated with the oppression of the bureaucracy. It is a problem of a deficient integration of the individual's needs, interests, and potentials with the goals of the organization (Argyris, 1966). C. Wright Mills explains the "floating paranoia" which sets into people who feel little control over their job situation. Specifically, there is often poor leadership; management holds too much power in too many organizations. As a result, we see insufficient communication, inappropriate reward systems, and poor morale. Too many people get into positions of management which they cannot handle and this sets off a multitude of difficulties: cutting of corners, too many meetings, temper tantrums, loss of sight of organizational goals and of sound, proven value bases from which to operate, loss of interest in employees' needs, and, generally, a resorting to personal survival practices. Many managers appear to become almost psychotic. And well-meaning, capable employees must suffer the consequences. Workers are often ordered to do as they are told and to not ask any questions. Most important, these kinds of things discourage excellent people from joining the organization. It is a complex situation which will not be overcome easily – but choosing excellent leaders is the starting point.

Several writers see the elimination of bureaucracy and the creation of an alternative organizational form as necessary. Bennis (1966) feels that rapid and unexpected change, overwhelming organizational size, the complexity of modern technology, and an enlightened managerial approach will lead to the following.

> Adaptive, problem-solving, temporary systems of diverse specialists, linked together by coordinating and task-evaluating executive specialists in an organic flux – this is the organization form that will gradually replace bureaucracy as we know it . . . I call this an organic-adaptive structure. (p. 265)

Argyris states that in the organization of the future "[T]he concept of directive authority or power will be expanded to include the influence of individuals, through rewards and penalties that minimize dependence, through internal commitment, and through the process of confirmation" (p. 273). Foucault (1980) elaborates power and knowledge phenomena. Toffler specifically addresses the educational bureaucracy:

> The present administrative structures of education, based on industrial bureaucracy, will simply not be able to cope with the complexities and rate of change . . . They will be forces to move toward ad-hocratic forms of organization merely to retain some semblance of control. . . . super-industrial education must prepare people to function in temporary organization – the Ad-hocracies of tomorrow. (p. 408)

Several books have attempted to explain deep, profound forces which are at work in society [*The Hidden Persuaders* (Packard), *Battle for the Mind* (Sargant), *The Brain Watchers* (Gross)] and others, such as *Brave New World* (Huxley) and *1984* (Orwell), have described a total society of the future. Andrews and Karlins (1971) envision a "psytocracy," a society where all things, including people "things," are subject to careful and precise technical manipulation (p. 53); they underestimate people.

It is not so hopeful that the broad bureaucratic structures of the future will be much different from those of today. However, specific changes within these broader structures are coming. Imaginative futurists and analysts stimulate our thinking. Most importantly, people have basic needs, especially the need for security, and they will not accept extended oppression and manipulation passively.

Bennis and Slater (1968) missed something very crucial in their projections about the future organic/temporary work situation. They did not anticipate that employees in the 1970s and 1980s would become militant and take initiatives to protect their job security through collective agreements. This is the reality nowhere mentioned in many futurists' arguments. Granted, such things as automation and computers will alter – in fact, are already beginning to alter – the nature of bureaucracies, but people are bound to protect their self-interest. Assertiveness by Polish workers (Solidarity) and the peoples of China, Roumania, the Soviet Union, East Germany, and Denmark are more recent examples of the growing "collectivism" reality. Changing the ownership of organizations from private to public, including having employees as owners, is another alteration we are seeing in bureaucracies (Doig, 1975). This is more conducive to worker self-interest, yet it is doubtful whether the change produces an alleviation of the common organizational problems (Argyris, 1966, p. 277). The particular purposes and ownership of a bureaucracy influence its general internal climate and the extent to which the aforementioned problems are present.

Unlike business organizations, educational organizations have a "guaranteed existence" through society's tax money and support. This may result in less caring about inefficiencies and poor leadership in the system. Serious, immense problems for schools and universities are possible as indicated by the following:

• There is not enough agreement on the purpose of education. Wastage and a proliferation of programs result;

• Too many administrators work from a business base rather than from an academic base. Term appointment of new faculty, rationalized by declining student enrolments, is an example of a business practice. It exploits people, effects poor morale, and works against academic freedom;

• Current promotion and tenure systems tend to foster misunderstanding, jealousy, and disagreement about criteria. As a result, many good educators are frustrated and find it difficult to participate;

• The educational bureaucracy of today often contributes to poor health in its employees. There appears to be a lack of insight and sensitivity concerning the way experience and stress take their toll on a normal employee. The bureaucracy often fails to provide enough security for seasoned employees; and

• The "gloom and doom" attitudes and the adherence to undesirable value bases in educational bureaucracies are contagious. Again, this can keep good people from participating.

Woodrow Wilson, in his essay "The Study of Administration" (1887), argues that executive method should be based on stable principles rather than empiricism. Currently this is not enough the case in our institutions. Bureaucracies need to hire the very best people they can get. There is a great need for disciplined, decent leaders who apply common sense and have a deep regard for their employees. We need leaders of expert vision who are capable of courageous acts (Perrow, 1973, p. 13). Leaders are needed who believe that the great majority of workers *want* to do well, *are* responsible, and, if the organizational situation is just, *will* perform well. A sense of community is enhanced by leadership with this type of conscience.

We are an organizational society (Presthus, 1978). We have become a collective bargaining and legalistically oriented society. With our expanding knowledge in such areas as organizational psychology, organization development, and career development (e.g., Mayer, 1978; Schein, 1978), it is possible to make bureaucracies enjoyable places for people to work, and let's face it, work is a very important aspect of one's life. Currently, many institutions are breaking the spirit of workers and harming families. At work the onus seems to be on the employee to save himself. Obviously this is wrong.

The potential is with us to put our knowledge to work so as to revitalize our institutions, especially the educational ones. True humanizing requires a continual questioning of bureaucracy.

The Growing Collectivism

Worldwide one witnesses a challenging of those in charge by those who are being led. There is less now of "follow the leader." Entire countries are changing as the populace pressure for reforms and fundamental shifts in power result. This growing emphasis on collective action and development of community pervades society. It results from distrust of politicians and the belief that they are looking after themselves first. This has been growing over the years. Penner (1978-79) captures the essence in his reference to collective bargaining in universities:

> the rapid growth of Canadian universities in number and in enrolment led almost inevitably to the growth of an employer bureaucracy which, becoming increasingly alienated from the professoriat, developed hard-nosed administrative responses to faculty concerns. In the process such bureaucratic responses shattered the illusions of many academics about collegiality as the guiding ethos of university life. Beginning with the termination of open-ended Federal funding for higher education in 1972, the long downhill run of financial restraint led to increasing out-of-hand administration rejections of faculty association salary briefs. As one member of the Collective Bargaining Committee of CAUT [Canadian Association of University Teachers] put it, the era of "binding supplication" was at an end. (p.72)

He goes on to say that the situation has been confounded by the fact that, traditionally within the university, professional schools such as law and dentistry have enjoyed a favored status with respect to salary increases and job conditions (workload, promotion, etc.) generally. "Old boy networks" often are at work. The overall effect has been one of conflict and a new challenging.

The collectivism approach is here and it is a critical factor in understanding contemporary educational management and leadership at all levels. Among other things, collective bargaining in education systems has created an improved model for professional unionism, one which moves toward harmonizing control and freedom. More will be said on this later in the book.

Conclusion

In this Part One, Sociological Perspectives on Society and Education, the following have been discussed:

- contemporary society (with some of its associated difficulties)
- education (highlighting goals, publics, history, and attitudes), and
- sociological theories applied to education.

It is evident that although certain things such as goals and structures tend to remain unchanged, the very mix of society is changing. Our democracy has many new faces, including the added intellectual abilities of its diverse multi-cultural newcomers.

In Part Two, Essences of Educational Management and Leadership:

- the applied management areas of educational law and educational finance are discussed, using bureaucratic and democratic ideas to elaborate
- beginning with an overview of the historical development of educational management and leadership thought, the importance of values, beliefs, and ethics to education and its leadership is discussed, and
- an organizational framework is presented through reference to theology, the Organization Development (O.D.) technology (with a focus on personal skills development) is summarized, and the organizational realities of education politics and power are discussed. Comments from excellent educational leaders are included.

This sets the stage for the presentation of an original leadership model in the latter part of the book.

References

Abbott, M.G. (1965). Hierarchical impediments to innovation in educational organizations. In M.G. Abbott & J. Lovell (Eds.), *Change perspectives in educational administration* (pp. 41-45). Auburn University, School of Education.

Andrews, L.M. & Karlins, M. (1971). *Requiem for democracy?* New York, NY: Holt, Rinehart and Winston.

Argyris, C. (1966). *Integrating the individual and the organization.* New York, NY: John Wiley and Sons.

Bendix, R. (1965). Taylor and Mayo compared. In *Work and authority in industry.* New York, NY: John Wiley and Sons.

Bennis, W.G. (1966, November/December). The coming death of bureaucracy. *Think Magazine*, pp. 30-35.

Bennis, W.G., & Slater, P.E. (1968). *The temporary society.* New York, NY: Harper and Row.

Blau, P.M. (1962). *Bureaucracy in modern society.* New York, NY: Random House.

Blau, P.M., & Scott, W.R. (1969). The nature and types of formal organizations. In F.D. Carver & T.J. Sergiovanni (Eds.), *Organizations and human behavior: Focus on schools.* Toronto, ON: McGraw-Hill.

Bridges, E.M. (1967). A model for shared decision-making in the school principalship. *Educational Administration Quarterly, 3*(1), 49-61.

Coleman, J.S., Campbell, E.Q., Hobson, C.J., McPartland, J., Mood, A., Weinfield, F.S., & York, R.L. (1966). *Equality of educational opportunity.* Washington, DC: U.S. Government Printing Office.

Doig, J. (1975). Germany puts factory workers in the boardroom. Democracy on the Job Series. *The Toronto Star*, p. C3.

Doig, J. (1975). Swedish employers balk at boosting labor's power. Democracy on the Job Series. *The Toronto Star*, p. B3.

Doig, J. (1975). British workers pressure Wilson for a voice in managing industry. Democracy on the Job Series. *The Toronto Star*, p. B3.

Drucker, P.F. (1980). *Managing in turbulent times.* New York, NY: Harper and Row.

Etzioni, A. (1964). *Modern organizations.* New Jersey, NY: Prentice-Hall.

Evers, C.W., & Lakomski, G. (1991). *Knowing educational administration: Contemporary methodological controversies in educational administration research.* Oxford, England: Pergamon.

Foucault, M. (1980). *Power/knowledge: Selected interviews and other writings 1971-1977.* New York, NY: Pantheon.

Frymier, J. (1987, September). Bureaucracy and the neutering of teachers. *Phi Delta Kappan.*

Gerth, H.H., & Mills, C. (Trans. and Eds.). (1946). *Max Weber: Essays in sociology.* New York, NY: Oxford University Press.

Gouldner, A.Q. (1954). *Patterns of industrial bureaucracy.* Glencoe, IL: Free Press.

Griffith, F. (Ed.). (1979). *Administrative theory in education: Text and readings.* Midland, MI: Pendell.

Gross, M.L. (1963). *The brain watchers.* New York, NY: New American Library.

Halpin, A. (1966). *Theory and research in administration.* New York, NY: Macmillan.

Hanson, E. M. (1991). *Educational administration and organizational behavior* (3rd ed.). Toronto, ON: Allyn and Bacon, Inc.

Hodgkinson, C. (1991). *Educational leadership: The moral art.* Albany, NY: State University of New York Press.

Homans, G.C. (1950). *The human group.* New York, NY: Harcourt, Brace and World.

Hoy, W.R., & Miskel, C.G. (1991). *Educational administration: Theory, research, and practice* (4th ed.). New York, NY: McGraw-Hill.

Huxley, A. (1932). *Brave new world.* New York, NY: Doubleday.

Interview with Mr. Art Warwick, secondary school principal. Thunder Bay, ON, Spring 1989.

Kimbrough, R.B., & Todd, E.A. (1970). Bureaucratic organization and educational change. In J.E. Heald, L.G. Romano, & N.P. Georgiady (Eds.), *Selected readings on general supervision.* Toronto, ON: Collier-MacMillan.

Lane, W.R., Corwin, R.G., & Monahan, W.G. (1971). *Foundations of educational administration.* Toronto, ON: Collier-MacMillan.

Maslow, A. (1962). *Toward a psychology of being.* Princeton, NJ: Van Nostrand.

Mayer, N. (1979). *The male mid-life crisis: Fresh starts after 40.* Scarborough, ON: New American Library.

Merton, R.K. (1968). *Social theory and social structure.* Glencoe, IL: Free Press.

Mifflen, F.J., & Mifflin, S.C. (l982). *The sociology of education: Canada and beyond.* Calgary, AB: Detselig.

Orwell, G. (1949). *1984.* New York, NY: Harcourt.

Packard, V.O. (1958). *The hidden persuaders.* New York, NY: Pocket Books.

Penner, R. (1978-79). Faculty collective bargaining in Canada: Background, development and impact. *Interchange, 9*(3), 71-86.

Perrow, C. (1973). The short and glorious history of organization theory. *Organizational Dynamics, 2*(1), 2-15.

Peter, L.J., & Hull, R. (1969). *The Peter principle: Why things always go wrong.* New York, NY: William Morrow and Co.

Presthus, R.V. (1978). *The organizational society: An analysis and a theory* (rev. ed.). New York, NY: St. Martin's Press.

Sargant, W.W. (1961). *Battle for the mind: A physiology of conversion and brainwashing.* Baltimore, MD: Penguin Books.

Schein, E.H. (1978). *Career dynamics: Matching individual and organizational needs.* Reading, MA: Addison-Wesley.

Selznick, P. (1948).Foundations of the theory of organization. *American Sociological Review,* 13, 25-35.

Sergiovanni, T.J., & Carver, F.D. (1979). *The new school executive: A theory of administration* (2nd ed.). New York, NY: Harper and Row.

Sergiovanni, T.J., & Starratt, R.J. (1971). *Emerging patterns of supervision: Human perspectives.* New York, NY: McGraw-Hill.

Simon, H.A. (1957). *Administrative behavior* (2nd ed.). New York, NY: MacMillan.

Steinberg, R. (1975). *Human behavior: Man and the organization.* New York, NY: Time-Life Books.

Tannenbaum, R., & Schmidt, W.H. (1958). How to choose a leadership pattern. *Harvard Business Review.*

Taylor, F.W. (1923). *The principles of scientific management.* New York, NY: Harper and Bros.

Thom, D.J. (1971). Democracy and the indian. Paper, Department of Educational Administration, Ontario Institute for Studies in Education, University of Toronto, Toronto, ON.

Thom, D.J. (1981). Questioning bureaucracy: Beyond Weber, Argyris, and Bennis. *McGill Journal of Education, 16*(2),199-210. Reprinted in *Studies in Educational Administration* (March, 1981), *Comment on Education* (December, 1981), and *The Hong Kong Manager* (January, 1982).

Thom, D.J. (1990). Bureaucracy, informal systems, and school leadership. *The Saskatchewan Educational Administrator, 22*(2), 25-33.

Toffler, A. (1970). *Future shock.* Toronto, ON: Bantam Books.

Waller, W.W. (1961). *The sociology of teaching.* New York, NY: Russell and Russell.

Weber, M. (1947). *The theory of social and economic organization* (A.M. Henderson & Talcott Parsons, Trans.). Glencoe, IL: Free Press and Falcon's Wing Press.

Wilson, W. (1987). The study of administration. *Political Science Quarterly, 2*(2).

Part Two

Essences of Educational Management and Leadership

A distinction should at the outset be drawn between two classes of political inconsistency. First, a statesman, in contact with the moving current of events and anxious to keep the ship on an even keel and steer a steady course, may lean all his weight now on one side and now on the other. His arguments in each case, when contrasted, can be shown to be not only very different in character, but contradictory in spirit and opposite in direction: yet his object will throughout have remained the same. His resolves, his wishes, his outlook may have been unchanged, his methods may be verbally irreconcilable.

We cannot call this inconsistency. In fact it may be claimed to be the truest consistency. The only way a man can remain consistent amid changing circumstances is to change with them while preserving the same dominating purpose.

Consistency in leadership
by Winston Churchill, British statesman, prime minister
January 1936

Part Two includes four chapters on the following themes, respectively – educational law, educational finance, values, and organizational framework.

3

Educational Law

Introduction

In this chapter important educational law knowledge is presented. Included are four cases – one from a school setting, one from a community college, and two pertaining to universities.

In the contemporary culture extra skills and knowledge are required by educators and increasingly will be required in the future. Administrators, teachers, and professors alike must be well versed in educational law. We live in a legalistically oriented society where lawsuits are very prevalent. At all levels an understanding of negligence, in loco parentis, standard of care, adequate supervision, reasonable man, vicarious liability, assumption of risk, and rights and freedoms generally, as they apply to educators and students, is required.

negligence –

Negligence consists in the omission to do something a prudent and reasonable man (person) would do, or the doing of something which a prudent and reasonable man (person) would not do, and is actionable whenever as between the Plaintiff and the Defendant, there is a duty cast upon the latter not to be negligent, and a breach of this duty which causes damage to the Plaintiff.

In education, the test is whether or not the educator (teacher, administrator) failed to use that care for the pupil which a reasonably careful parent would exercise in respect of his/her own children.

in loco parentis –

This means that a person stands in the position of parent as unofficial guardian. This concept allows a teacher some of the privileges of a parent, but also brings with it added responsibilities for the protection of students. The educator is to act as a kind, judicious parent would act. The disdain for improper touching of students can be understood in this context. For example, section 146 of the Canadian Criminal Code defines sexual exploitation as follows:

> Every person who is in a position of trust or authority towards a young person or is a person with whom the young person is in a relationship of dependency and who, for a sexual purpose, touches, directly or indirectly, with a part of the body or with an object, any part of the body of the young person, is guilty of an indictable offence and liable to imprisonment for a term not exceeding five years. ["young person" means a person 14 to 18 years of age.]

Of interest is that in other cultures, such as Hong Kong, penalties are harsher if a teacher harms a female rather than a male student.

standard of care –

The educator is obliged to follow a commonly accepted standard of care for students. For example, the teacher is to take precautions to avoid accidents from happening. Lighting in the gymnasium, thickness of tumbling mats, safety of chemicals and gas in science classes, safety of furniture and playground equipment – all of these are issues. Another important issue is that of having adequate liability insurance (school board and personal) with respect to transporting students in one's vehicle and in being a science or physical education teacher.

adequate supervision –

The following have been accepted as indications of adequate and sufficient supervision:

• Discipline was good

• Students were carrying on in orderly fashion

• Rules had been formulated for the guidance of the students

• The supervisor was competent

• The supervisor was present

• Practices had been adopted generally, and

• Practices had been followed successfully in the past

Assuming that a supervisor is capable, the problem becomes one of determining the amount of supervision and when it is to be given.

reasonable man –

This concept elaborates *in loco parentis*. The educator is expected to act as would a reasonable man (person) under similar circumstances. Turner provides a definition:

1. The reasonable man will vary his conduct in keeping with the circumstances.

2. The reasonable man will be made to be identical with the actor in the matter of physical characteristics. The man who is blind, lame or deaf is not required to do the impossible by conforming to physical standards.

3. The reasonable man is accorded no allowance for lack of intelligence short of insanity. For a defendant to do the best he knows is not enough.

4.The reasonable man is considered to be an adult. Children, therefore, are not required to meet the same standard of conduct as that of the reasonable man.

5. The reasonable man will be accorded special abilities and skills and will be held responsible for them when the circumstances so warrant. In other words, the law will take knowledge of the fact that some people are of superior knowledge, skill, and intelligence.

6. The reasonable man is required to maintain a higher degree of standard of conduct when he has had time to reflect on his course of action than when he must act in an emergency.

7. The reasonable man, under many circumstances, will be charged with the duty of anticipating and guarding against the conduct of others. For instance, where children are in the vicinity, greater caution and anticipation are required than if they were adults. (pp. 431-32)

Points 3 and 5 appear to be in conflict somewhat.

vicarious liability –

This is the notion that because the teacher works in a master-servant relationship with a school board, then, if the teacher is liable, then so is the board because of its responsibility for the teacher. Vicarious liability applies across all hierarchical levels of a system, e.g., principal, superintendent, board.

assumption of risk –

This is the notion that the student must assume added responsibility for adverse outcomes resulting from his/her participating in high-risk school activities, e.g., murder ball.

Though precedence is helpful, it is difficult to predict the outcomes from court proceedings with respect to a particular case. One must look to the particular facts and the particular circumstances, including the interplay of law from across various federal, provincial, and local sectors. For example, various legislation from the child day care and transportation areas come to bear on schools, e.g., licensing. Also, there are local school board policies.

Figure 3-1 summarizes important aspects of teacher legal liability with respect to students.

1. Knowing school law is important

2. Some divisions of law

CRIMINAL LAW		CIVIL LAW	
Court		Court or tribunal	
(arbitrator)		(arbitator)	
Plaintiff	Defendant	Plaintiff	Defendant
(society)	(person or organization)	(person or organization)	(person or organization)

3. Sources of law

Statutes	Common Law	Case Law	Regulations

4. The common law with respect to pupil control

the pupil	the teacher

– punctual	– courteous	– reasonable	– fair
– clean	– respectful	– fair	– firm
– tidy	– accountable	– foreseeing	– judicious
– diligent	– conforming	– knowledgeable	– in loco parentis
– kind			

Criminal Code	"Reasonable" force
It is lawful for every parent or person in place of a parent, school-master or master, to use force by way of correction towards any child, pupil or apprentice under his care, providing such force is reasonable under the circumstances.	– used for cause – used for correction and without malice – not cruel, not excessive – no permanent injury or risk of permanent injury results – suited to age and sex – not protracted – instrument of punishment suitable – administered to appropriate part of anatomy

5. Criteria for negligence

(a) Duty of care exists

Type of entrant	Duty of care
Trespasser Licensee Invitee (pupil)	No traps Protect from known dangers Protect against known dangers and dangers that should be known

(b) There is negligence (failure to provide duty of care)

> Negligence consists in the omission to do something a prudent and reasonable man would do, or doing of something which a prudent and reasonable man would not do.

(c) There is loss of comfort, property, health, or life

(d) The negligence caused the loss

6. Liability

A court may award damages to a plaintiff as compensation for loss of earnings, medical expenses, pain and suffering, or for loss of consortium and social life. However, if the teacher was acting within the scope of his employment, the school board becomes vicariously liable for the damages. The limitations on the Board recovering from the teacher vary with the province.

A School Act

Where the board, the principal, or the teacher approves or sponsors activities during the school hours or at other times, the teacher or other person responsible for the conduct of the pupils shall not be liable for damages caused by pupils to property or for personal injury suffered by pupils during such activities. (However, be careful – was the teacher acting within his/her capacity as a teacher?

Note: The school board must carry adequate liability insurance, but the teacher should also investigate his/her own coverage.

Figure 3-1

The Teacher, Students, and Legal Liability

It is important to understand the Education Act of the relevant province – particularly the duties and powers of teachers, school principals and school boards (certain Regulations which accompany the Education Act and local board bylaws also contain information on these). Special education, hitting students, assault and abuse generally, teaching prejudice, freedom of information and Boards of Reference are key areas. Further, the educator should know cases and their outcomes and must know when and how to obtain legal counsel if cases arise in his/her work.

The following four cases are presented, with considerable analysis on the fourth. Settings include a school, a college, and two universities. Together these cases cover a multitude of educational law concepts (basic and advanced).

Case 1: A School

The "Govan" Case (Saskatchewan)

On February 12, 1963, an accident occurred in which a boy fell from the end of parallel bars. The boy sustained permanent crippling injuries which paralyzed him from the waist down leaving only partial use of his arms. A civil action was launched by the boy and his father against the teacher who was in charge of the physical education class.

In October, 1963, the legal firm retained by the Saskatchewan Teachers' Federation (S.T.F.) applied for a judgment from the Chief Justice to strike out the action on the basis of section 225 (later section 242) of the School Act (on scope of authority). The Chief Justice held that the teacher was acting within the scope of his authority as a teacher and these allegations would be struck out. However, with regard to the allegations that the teacher was acting beyond the scope of his authority as a teacher and beyond the directions given to him by the School Board, the action could be maintained against the teacher.

The implication in this decision concerns the question of implied instructions from the School Board to the teacher. The other factor is that the School Board admitted that the teacher was acting in the scope of his authority as a teacher.

In the meantime, the plaintiff pleaded an alternative claim, namely that in the event that the teacher was not acting within the scope of Section 225(a), that is, outside of school hours, he could still be found liable, and Section 225(a) was not a defence to such a claim. Defence counsel then launched an application of claim over against the Board of the School Unit, to the effect that in the event any liability was found against the teacher, the Board should be liable. The Board denied any liability and moved to have this claim struck out. Defence counsel appeared again before the judge to oppose the Board's motion, whereupon the motion against the teacher was dismissed, with costs to follow the event. Defence counsel then served the Insurance Company under which the Board of the School Unit was insured with a notice to admit that 1) the teacher was a properly employed teacher, and 2) that he had acted on that day in question as a servant of the School Unit and was properly authorized by the School Unit to instruct the boy who had been injured. When the Insurance Company finally admitted the notice to Admit Facts, defence counsel launched another application to the Court of Queen's Bench to have the teacher released from the action since it was now clearly established that he was acting within the scope of his employment, and that Section 225(a) did apply. It was eventually agreed to by the solicitors for both the plaintiff and the defendant School Unit that an order be granted releasing and dismissing the case against the teacher subject to the approval of the Judge. This is where the action stood in September, 1964. The teacher was still under subpoena to attend the trial set for the January sittings, where a solicitor would be present to protect his interests inasmuch as his integrity and ability as a teacher were still in issue.

In February, 1965, a Court of Queen's Bench jury found the School Unit liable on a charge that it was negligent in instruction of gymnastics.

The jury found that the School Unit failed in its duty of care to the plaintiff and listed six reasons: (1) lack of competent coaching on the parallel bars; (2) insufficient care and attention to "spotting"; (3) insufficient demonstrations on the bars; (4) progressive movements on the bars were rushed; (5) the instructor was not sufficiently qualified; (6) and there were inadequate safety precautions.

In June, 1967, the majority Judgment of the Court of Appeal stated, after quoting Section 225(a) of the School Act, "This section (meaning Section 255(a)) is a defence to the teacher on the present facts" and the action against him was properly dismissed. Counsel argued, however, that the section also granted immunity to the appellant (school board) from claims against it stemming from the acts of the teacher. In other words, it was contended that, if the teacher was relieved of liability, he could not be the source of vicarious liability to his employer. The section refers to the board, the principal, and the teacher, but exempts only the teacher. To exempt the board from responsibility for the acts of the teacher would require very clear language. On its plain meaning, the section excuses the teacher from liability in certain circumstances. It makes no such concession to the board.

This case illustrates concepts, procedures, and argument in law. It contains the elements of negligence, in loco parentis, standard of care, adequate supervision, reasonable man, vicarious liability, and assumption of risk. Lawyers on such a case would combine these elements in their arguments in a way which they believed would win for them.

Other important areas of educational law include the following: tribunals, fairness and natural justice, bias, arenas for appeal, collective agreements, arbitration, jurisprudence, employment equity, workplace disputes generally, privacy and freedom of information, human rights commissions, the Canadian Charter of Rights and Freedoms, negotiation, and judicial review. These areas come into play across the following cases:

Case 2: A University

A "Student Discipline" Case (Ontario)

Aylward v. McMaster University

After a professor lodged complaints of academic dishonesty against a graduate student, a tribunal constituted by the faculty committee was convened. When the professor advised that he was withdrawing the complaints, the tibunal continued the hearing and called him as a witness. The senate resolutions on academic dishonesty set up a code of procedure to be initiated by the instructor.

On an application for prohibition by the student, **held,** Killeen J. dissenting in part, the application should be granted.

Per Flinn J., Donnelly J. concurring: The issue to be decided by the tribunal was within its jurisdiction, and judicial review was precluded unless the tribunal lost jurisdiction by making a patently unreasonable decision. It did so in continuing once the complaints were withdrawn. There was no prescribed procedural framework to enable the board to continue as a prosecutor or to embark on an investigative or inquisitorial proceeding. Therefore, the decision was beyond its *quasi*-judicial role and its authority. The decision constituted a structural defect in the proceeding, giving rise to the reasonable apprehension that the tribunal would not act in an entirely impartial manner and was in excess of jurisdiction and in violation of the rules of natural justice. In the circumstances, the discretion of the court should be exercised to grant prohibition to prevent the tribunal from proceeding.

Per Killeen J., dissenting in part: The remedy proposed was too narrow, as it is addressed only to the currently constituted hearing tribunal. The procedures established by the senate to deal with academic dishonesty constitute a self-contained code. Once the instructor withdrew his complaints, no one within the university could pursue them against the applicant.

Case 3: A Community College

A "Student Loan" Case (Ontario)

Sometimes, in the course of making informal inquiries, new information is uncovered which results in a government ministry reconsidering its original decision. In this case, the Ontario ombudsman assisted a student who was denied financial assistance under the Ontario Student Assistance Program (OSAP) to complete his studies.

In 1988 the complainant applied for OSAP to attend Community College. However, the financial aid office advised the complainant that he was placed on the "restricted list" due to the fact that he defaulted on a previous OSAP loan in 1987. The complainant had explained that he had made regular payments and had to the best of his knowledge repaid his previous loan. The complainant submitted an appeal but the decision was unchanged. Further, he was advised that he would remain on the restricted list for a period of one year. Without a loan, the complainant indicated that he would be unable to continue in his program at the college.

The complainant indicated that he had last made payments in 1987 through a private collection agency. When advised he had $95.00 outstanding to repay the account, the complainant asked for an explanation from the collection agency for this figure. The agency agreed to provide him with an explanation. Nonetheless, it appears the collection agency closed the account and contacted Central Collection Services (of the Ministry of Government Services) that the debt was uncollectable and that they advised CCS to write off the account. However, the complainant was not notified by either the private collections agency or by Central Collection Services (CCS) that the account was written off and that the student would be placed on the restricted list, which in effect, would prevent him from obtaining future student loans.

Central Collection Services confirmed that the complainant had made regular payments up to March 1987 and that he had paid a total of $1 045.00 to the private collection agency. CCS also verified that the account was closed without notifying the complainant or giving him an opportunity to pay the balance before placing him on the restricted list. Furthermore, CCS indicated that the private collection agency had an obligation to confirm with the complainant the exact amount owing before closing the account. This apparently was not done. Finally, CCS acknowledged that before April 1988 the Ministry did not have procedures in place to adequately monitor the practices of private collection agencies who are responsible for collecting government-related debt.

In light of this information, the Student Awards Branch agreed to reconsider its original decision. Following its review, the Ministry determined that the complainant had acted in good faith and removed him from the restricted list. This resolved the complainant's problem and resulted in him being awarded a loan of $1 800.00 and a grant of $3 140.00 As a result, the complainant was able to complete his studies.

Case 4: A University

A "Tenure" Case (Nova Scotia)

Thomas v. Mount Saint Vincent University

A university faculty member, appointed on a probationary contract, was denied tenure by the president after a negative recommendation of the committee on appointment, rank, promotion and tenure. An ad hoc appeal committee was established in accordance with the appeal process in the faculty manual. That process was adopted as a regulation by the university senate pursuant to the Mount Saint Vincent University Act, 1966 (N.S.), c. 124, which permits the senate to make regulations regarding academic qualifications of the academic staff. The ad hoc appeal committee was made up of a nominee of the president and of the faculty member and a chairman chosen by these nominees. Hearings were held, and, as permitted by the procedure, both the faculty member and the president attended and participated in the hearing. The president was also a witness. The committee recommended the granting of tenure but the president refused to accept the recommendation and denied tenure. On an application for certiorari [a writ of a superior court to call up the records of an inferior court or a body acting in a quasi-judicial capacity] to quash the decision, held, the application should be granted.

The decision of the president to refuse tenure was subject to certiorari proceedings. The university is a creature of statute and is a public institution. The faculty manual, which sets out the tenure procedure, has the force of law so as to attract the remedy of certiorari even though the manual is a body of regulations passed by the senate, for the regulations were passed pursuant to an authorizing statute.

The participation of the president in the tenure appeal process gave rise to a reasonable apprehension of bias. Moreover, the appeal process set out in the faculty manual itself raised a reasonable apprehension of bias, because it permitted the president to sit on appeal of her own decision, as well as to participate as an advocate and witness in the hearing to determine whether she was right and then to accept or reject the ad hoc appeal committee's recommendation concerning her original decision. No provision in the Act permits such a scheme. There was no waiver of any objection by the faculty member in signing an employment contract requiring observance of the regulations in the faculty manual. Therefore, the president's decision should be set aside and the faculty member reinstated in employment for such time as it takes for further consideration of an appeal in accordance with the requirements of procedural fairness from the original decision by the president to deny tenure. Compensation for loss of salary and benefits should be made.

Broad Implications

This tenure case illustrates some of the advanced legal knowledge which is required. Following are some important points:

(1) universities and many other organizations, through their manuals, collective agreements, etc., have created "internal laws" which are sometimes at odds with broader societal laws, such as with respect to natural justice and discrimination. The legal community has hesitated to interfere much with these internal agreements, leaving these institutions to look after their own

affairs. The university is viewed as a society unto itself. However, circumstances are changing, with lawyers and human rights personnel increasingly calling for systemic reviews of institution's decisions – reviews based on such principles as fairness;

Figure 3-2:
Grievance: Avenues of Appeal

(2) criteria in such things as collective agreements should be applied properly;

(3) an applicant has several progressive avenues of appeal once a grievance begins. The Mount Saint Vincent case involved largely an ad hoc appeal committee tribunal. Figure 3-2 illustrates the appeal avenues, internal and external to a university, which typically apply. A requirement is that the appeal process be exhausted at a lower level before there is an appeal at a higher level;

(4) for fairness in a tribunal hearing there are *bias, consistency,* and *information* requirements. Improperly biased members (those involving a reasonable apprehension of bias) must not sit, applicants with the same qualifications applying over the past few years must be treated similarly, and the applicant is entitled to know any case against him/her and be given the opportunity to respond to all information brought forward;

(5) jurisprudence (re "procedures previously followed with success") is often used as the counter-argument in a grievance which is challenging the status quo, e.g., a challenge to how stated criteria in documents are applied;

(6) an applicant for tenure/promotion has specific considerations to make:

(a) the process will involve arguments and counter-arguments;

(b) to grieve, the applicant should have a strong case and decide how much satisfaction is being sought;

(c) care should be taken in trusting lawyers, and in deciding when to proceed no further;.

(d) tenure/promotion decisions may be very "arbitrary." Different appraisers use the same criteria differently. However, decision-makers changing these criteria as they "go along" is unfair. If an arbitrator is eventually utilized, his/her decision may be affected by something as basic as family interaction that morning;

(e) applicants for tenure/promotion are not always successful on their first attempts; reapplication at a future date is a possibility;

(f) overall, if a case such as Case 4 is pursued to the courtroom (in a judicial review), the applicant would expect to be awarded at least a new, fair hearing. The applicant may hire his/her own lawyer and press to have an improperly biased member removed from any tribunal before the hearing. There would be jurisprudence counter-arguments to overcome. The applicant may charge his/her faculty association under a labor relations act (re "failure to fairly represent" the member); if the association loses, its status is lessened.

Other Implications

There is "more than meets the eye" in a case as just described. One would do well to understand the principles in Wing's *The Art of Strategy* (1988) for such situations, particularly concerning tactics and strategies. Similarly, Canadian civil liberties activist M. Borosky suggests publication, dislocation (lawful disruption), and coalition/alliance as effective tactics in very tough situations.

University politics is strong. Tenure and promotion can be particularly complex and, for those involved, valuable experience for expanding one's range of abilities required to operate in "hardball" situations is provided. A case such as Case 4 reveals the intricacies of relationships among the various interest groups in a university. It teaches lessons regarding commitment, goals, negotiation, timing, and character. Most important, it educates about justice and fairness.

Overall, cases such as Case 4 help post-secondary institutions. Democracy is enhanced. Tribunals are used considerably now and fairness and justice must be protected. Within education, some of the more interesting cases which are arising pertain to the extent of access to our educational institutions for students directly from other countries, whether in loco parentis fits with the fact that students *must* attend schools, and the view that in working for a school board, teachers "contract away" some of their rights. Appendix C contains another case of interest from a school setting – a student drug search.

In conclusion, a challenge for educators is to know law but to not let it take away from their spontaneity too much in performing their job. Finally, one caution is that law varies across districts, provinces, and countries; the educator should know general concepts and principles, such as in this chapter, but, if actually involved in a case, one must also know the specifics of the law in the pertaining context.

References

"Aylward v. McMaster University." (1991). *Dominion Law Reports (4th). 79:119-129.*

Borosky, M. (1990, Fall). Speech on effective lobbying strategies. Thunder Bay, ON.

Canadian Charter of Rights and Freedoms.

Canadian Criminal Code.

Education acts and regulations (provincially).

Govan case (Saskatchewan).

Ontario. (1989). *The ombudsman of Ontario annual report 1988-89.* Confidential Summary no. 4, p. 9. Toronto, ON: Queen's Printer.

"Thomas v. Mount Saint Vincent University." (1986). *Dominion Law Reports* (4th). 28.

Turner, R.A. (1955). The principles of school law with applications for Alabama's public school system (Ed.D. dissertation, Alabama Polytechnic Institute).

Wing, R.L. (1988). *The art of strategy: A new translation of Sun Tzu's classic, the art of war.* New York, NY: Dolphin/Doubleday.

Further Readings

Dickinson, G. (1991). The legal dimensions of teachers' duties and authority. In R. Ghosh, & D. Ray (Eds.), *Social change and education in Canada* (2nd ed.) (pp. 217-237). Toronto, ON: Harcourt Brace Jovanovich.

Gall, G.L. (1990). *The Canadian legal system* (3rd ed.). Toronto, ON: Carswell.

Giles, T.E., & Proudfoot, A.J. (1990). *Educational administration in Canada* (4th ed.). Calgary, AB: Detselig.

Hurlbert, E.L., & Hurlbert, M.A. (1992). *School law under the charter of rights and freedoms* (2nd ed.). Calgary, AB: University of Calgary Press.

Manley Casimir, M.E., & Sussel, T.A. (1986). *Courts in the classroom: Education and the charter of rights and freedoms.* Calgary, AB: Detselig.

McConnell, H., & Pyra, J. (1989, Winter/Spring). The impact of some aspects of the constitution and the charter of rights and freedoms on education. *The Saskatchewan Educational Administrator, 21*(1), 1-36.

Mullan, D.J. (1975). Fairness, the new natural justice. *University of Toronto Law Journal,* 25.

Ontario Secondary School Teachers' Federation. (1990). *School law: A reference guide for educators.* Toronto, ON: OSSTF.

O'Reilly, R. (1992). A review and analysis of case law on the integration of exceptional pupils into regular classrooms. Toronto, ON: Ontario Ministry of Education.

Zuker, M.A. (1988). *The legal context of education.* Toronto, ON: OISE Press.

4

Educational Finance

Introduction

To operate well in modern bureaucracy, a person needs knowledge not only of educational law, but also of educational finance. Everywhere costs are a concern. In recent years the funding of Canadian elementary and secondary schools has undergone rigorous review, and this will continue in the future. Reform continues and fairness/equity is the guideline. Educators should be versed in terminology, processes, and issues within this context: recognized expenditure, average daily enrolments, equalized assessment, equity, mill rate, grants, and so on. Following is a report on educational finance in the province of Ontario which provides a good basic understanding. It is based on the author's research which was conducted with support from the Social Sciences and Humanities Research Council of Canada (SSHRC). Allowing for differences in terminology, the information has applicability to educational systems anywhere. Among other things, the report considers the philosophy underlying the finance system, and highlights some of the important current issues in education. Some of the suggested reforms for the future are inspired by the ideas of 1991 Nobel Peace Prize laureate in Economics, Professor Ronald Coase.

Financing Elementary and Secondary Education:

Values, Needs, and a Fair View of the Future

This chapter examines effective methods of financing elementary and secondary schools in the province of Ontario, Canada. The current education funding model provided a framework from which to describe, expand, and revise. A description of the basic funding model for Ontario is described, as well as the results of a research study.

The broad issues considered were: (a) Is the current model too complex?; (b) What is the appropriate split of control between provincial and municipal governing bodies?; and (c) How adequate are the established expenditure ceilings?

Thirteen research questions were addressed under the headings of governance of education, revenue (taxation, provincial grants), budgeting, expenditures, and issues for the future (Lawton, 1987). These questions reflect the concerns of those working "hands-on" in educational finance. Using a Delphi technique, a sample of 20 individuals experienced in the practice and study of educational finance were asked to reach a consensus on the "best" future scheme for financing through addressing the research questions. The results are presented and discussed under Lawton's headings. Ontario's review of education funding addresses such key issues as the expansion of the separate (Catholic) and independent school systems, pooling of commercial and industrial assessment, ceiling limits, tax bases, retirement gratuities, busing, sharing of control, federal/provincial transfer payments, auditing, and the provision of equality and equity. The current situation is one of considerable turbulence. The issues represent a mix of political, philosophical, and economic concerns – some technical, some broad – as would thus be expected. Increasingly, the issues are entering the public domain for discussion, especially with Canada's economic difficulties and changes in political parties in charge. The findings from this study indicate the importance of a fair and proper balance between political and educational motives in decisions, and highlight the need for more development of healthy public attitudes toward the value of education and schools. Several directions from these findings are presented. The findings and directions provide the reader with a modest systematic overview of a vital and rapidly altering situation. Further research into the issues and the development of appropriate fiscal models and policies is encouraged.

Background

Although some funding comes from federal sources, Section 93 of the *British North America (BNA) Act, 1867* (the *Constitution Act, 1867*) mandates the education of Canadians as a provincial responsibility. Also, local municipalities share with the provincial authorities in support. Figure 4-1 displays federal, provincial, and local jurisdictions. From this it is evident that the main impetus for elementary and secondary school financial support is within each province.

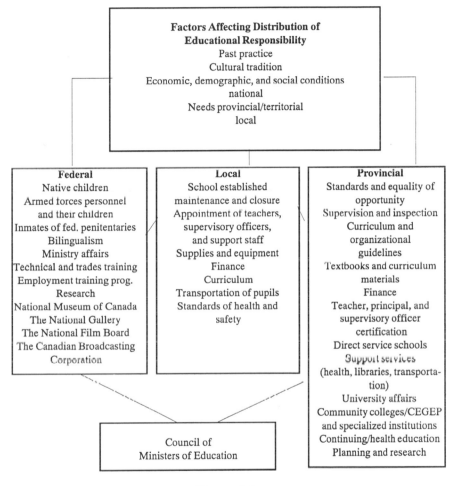

Figure 4-1:
Federal, Provincial, and Local
Responsibilities and Involvement in Education

From "Government Control of Education" by M.A. Awender and A.S. Nease, 1987, *Contemporary Educational Issues: The Canadian Mosaic*, p. 555. Copyright 1987 by Copp Clark Pitman, Toronto, ON. Reprinted by permission.

The Education Funding Model (Basics)

A mill rate equalization grant plan forms the core of elementary and secondary education financing in Ontario (Ontario Ministry of Education, 1991). The important components are recognized expenditures (ordinary and extraordinary), average daily enrolment, property assessments, mill rates, and a general consideration of centralized vs decentralized activity, ability, burden, need, effort, and equality and equity (horizontal: meaning "equal treatment of equals," and vertical: meaning "unequal treatment of unequals"). Overall, it is a plan consisting of block grants and conditional grants, some of which are equalized and some of which are not. Figure 4-2 shows the provincial funding model.

Broad

Education Funding in Ontario, 1991

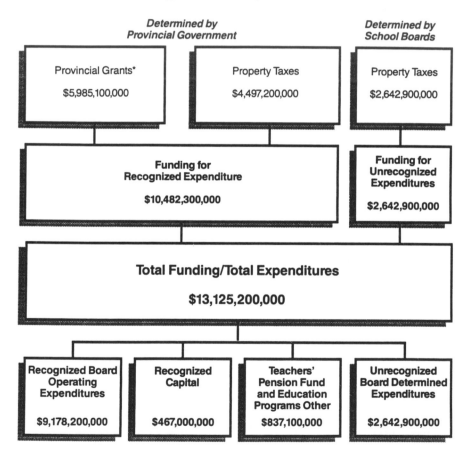

Specific
The Education Funding Model
Summary of Categories 1 to 5

Provincial Funding for Education (1991)	**$5,985.6 Million**
Category 1: Basic Per Pupil Grant	$3,307.6 Million
Category 2: Board-Specific Grants	$224.8 Million
Category 3: Program-Specific Grants	$1,284.1 Million
Category 4: Capital Funding Grants	$332.0 Million
Category 5: Additional Provincial Support for Education	$837.1 Million

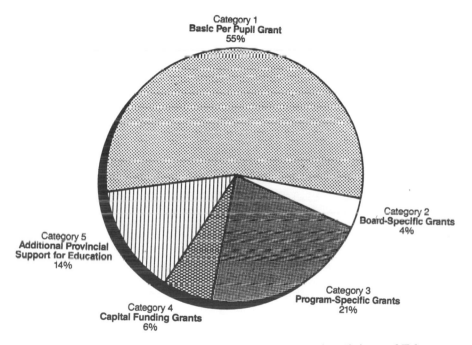

From *Education Funding in Ontario 1991* by Ontario Ministry of Education, Toronto, ON, March, 1991.

There are five major categories of funding (with subcategories *within* for the latter four) as follows: basic per pupil grant; board-specific grants (French as a First Language, Small Schools, Small Boards, Small Section, Goods and Services, Compensatory Education, and Declining Enrolment); program-specific grants (Other, New Initiatives, Language, and Special); capital funding grants (Program Update – including technological education, Renovation and Replacement, and Site Purchase and New Pupil Places – including child care and junior kindergarten); and additional provincial support for education (Education Programs Other and Teachers' Pension Fund Payments). The "Small Sections" grant refers to small English-language and/or French-language enrolments. "Other" grants pertain to the following: Assistance for En Block Transfers (re schools and programs from a public to a separate board), Secondary School Reorganization (re creating a French and an English secondary school), Change in Tax Revenue (re assessment change during the year), Special Assistance in Respect of Debentures, Special Support for Pooling, Isolate Boards, Board on Tax-Exempt Land, and Interim Financing. "Special Grants" (category 3) pertain to the following: Recognized Extraordinary Expenditure (including Transportation), Technological Education, Programs in Lieu of Provincial Services for Blind/Deaf Pupils, Education Programs in Care, Treatment and Correctional Facilities, Continuing Education, Secondary Summer School and Driver Education, Heritage Language, Cost of Education for Non-Resident Pupils, and Open-Access Tuition Fees. "Education Programs Other" (category 5) pertain to support for consultants, support for the Educational Computing Network of Ontario (ECNO) system with respect to school boards and the development and upgrading of administrative procedures generally, and support for Junior Kindergarten Classroom Equipment. The sum of a school board's various operating and capital monies is called the "General Legislative Grant (G.L.G)."

Over a period of years many of the themes which receive grants reflect changing interests and needs of society.

With respect to the detailed calculations of the various grants, each year the Ontario Ministry of Education publishes "Regulation, General Legislative Grants, Public, Separate and Secondary School Boards – made under the Education Act." This contains the definitions and formulas for use by the finance officers with the school boards.

Some of the grant calculations involve the concept of a sharing of expenditures between the province and the municipality. The category 1 basic per pupil block grant is an example. With this a school board applies Ministry-set standard mill rates (elementary and secondary) to equalized property assessment to raise tax dollars in support of the schools. This local share tax amount is subtracted from expenditure which is recognized by the Ministry as being necessary for the board to provide education of an adequate standard (calculated as the product of a per pupil recognized expenditure amount and average daily enrolment). This determines the grant to the board. Other grant types involve 100% provincial funding (no local sharing), e.g., the French as a first language grant and grants for small schools and small boards (under category 2) and the grant for reduction in class size in grades 1 and 2 (under category 3).

For program-specific grants (category 3), the level of provincial support varies from full funding to programs requiring a local share.

Generally underlying the grants whereby expenditures are shared is the concept:

Grant (G) = Recognized expenditure (R) – Local Taxes (T)

The Ministry defines two types of recognized expenditure:

Recognized Ordinary Expenditure (R.O.E.) – this is expenditure which is common to all school boards, e.g., expenditures for administration, instruction, plant operation and maintenance, non-capital furniture and equipment, non-capital renovations and repairs, current interest expense and bank charges, and special education expenditures ("built in" per pupil in 1989). For 1991, *R.O.E.* included $32 per pupil as support for the coterminous sharing or "pooling" of the commercial assessment base initiative being phased in over a number of years.

Recognized Extraordinary Expenditure (R.E.E.) – this expenditure includes pupil transportation, computer hardware, debt charges, and building costs.

Grant calculations involving *R.O.E.* and *R.E.E.* are done separately.

The *R.O.E.* per pupil (ceiling) is the fixed dollar amount per pupil as a standard for all school boards in Ontario, determined by the province each year. For the category 1 G=R-T calculation, total *R.O.E.* is the number of pupils of the school board X the provincial recognized ordinary expenditure per pupil. Average Daily Enrolment (A.D.E.) is used for pupil numbers (checked three times per year).

The *R.O.E.* used in this category 1 grant calculation (recognized for grant purposes by the Ministry) is different for elementary and secondary school students. Recognized ordinary expenditure (*R.O.E.*) for 1991 was $3 770 per elementary pupil and $4 710 per secondary pupil (Ontario Ministry of Education, 1991). A particular school board may calculate its *R.O.E.* below the provincial ceiling, and it will be entitled to just that amount in the G=R-T calculation.

Locally raised tax (T) is the second major component in calculations. Each year the province sets standard uniform mill rates (number of dollars per 1 000 dollars of equalized property assessment to be paid as tax support for education) for the province. In recent years three main pairs of mill rates have been used, one with *R.O.E.* and two (re levels) with *R.E.E.* There is also a pair of rates for operating expenditure. Each pair consists of an elementary and a secondary rate. The *R.O.E.* rates are used in the calculation of the category 1 basic per pupil block grant; the *R.E.E.* rates are used for category 3 calculations. In 1991 the standard mill rates for elementary and secondary were 5.628 and 4.635 mills, respectively. All boards have the same equalized mill rate for the same level of recognized ordinary expenditure per pupil.

There are recognized and unrecognized expenditures for school boards and thus a need to make a distinction between the equalized mill rate and the total mill rate. The local tax revenue to support the schools comes from applying the education mill rates to the applicable total equalized property assessment value in each community. Then G=R-T. In 1988, equalization factors were updated to reflect the changes in property valuation that have occurred since 1970. Further, there has been the provision of a better measure of the relative tax capacity at the local level. To better reflect the different residential/commercial assessment revenue generating capacity, residential assessment is reduced by a discount factor based on the Ontario wide average assessment practice.

Figure 4-3 shows how the per pupil block provincial grant (category 1) would be determined for three school boards with differing enrolments and property assessment bases (Ontario Ministry of Education, 1992). The rate of grant is calculated as G/R x 100% and indicates the extent of provincial government support.

	Board A	Board B	Board C
1. Recognized ordinary expenditure per pupil	4 000	4 000	4 000
2. Average daily enrolment	1 000	2 000	2 000
3. Total recognized ordinary expenditure (1x2)	$4 000 000	$8 000 000	$8 000 000
4. Provincial standard mill rate	5 mills	5 mills	5 mills
5. Board's equalized assessment	$200 000 000	$200 000 000	$1 000 000 000
6. Yield from provincial standard mill rate			
applied to board's equalized assessment (4x5)	$1 000 000	$1 000 000	$5 000 000
7. Provincial grant (3-6)	$3 000 000	$7 000 000	$3 000 000

Figure 4-3

Calculation of the Basic Per Pupil Block Grant

From *Toward Education Finance Reform 1992*, p. 10, by Ontario Ministry of Education, Toronto, ON, March, 1992.

Again, the category 1 block grant is an example whereby expenditures are locally shared. Other grants such as the French as a Second Language grant of category 3 follow the same basis, but an "eligible sum" for FSL (an approved amount per pupil) instead of recognized expenditure per se is used.

The grants for small schools and small boards, and goods and services (category 2) are examples of grants which utilize approved amounts per pupil but they are not on a locally shared basis. Generally, they apply to Northern boards. The capital funding grant (category 4) assists boards in financing capital projects, with higher rates of grant paid to school boards that have a more modest assessment base. The boards provide multi-year forecasts on capital expenditure to the Ministry each year.

Many of the grant funding formulas are very complex. Although the specifics may alter over the years, the 1989 calculation of "day school A.D.E. [Average Daily Enrolment] for grant purposes" itself indicates, generally, the calculation complexity involved:

"day school A.D.E. for grant purposes" means the sum of,

(a) the portion of the A.D.E. calculated under section 2 of Ontario Regulation 127/85, (Calculation of Average Daily Enrolment) that is in respect of resident-internal pupils of the board; and

(b) the amount in respect of declining enrolment that is calculated as follows,
E x [(A x C) + (B x D)], correct to two places of decimals, where,

E = the amount calculated in clause (a),

$$A = \frac{(\; ADE \; 88 \;)}{ADE \; 89 + ADE.EB.89} - 1 \qquad \text{correct to four places of decimals,}$$

$$B = \frac{(\; ADE \; 87 \;)}{ADE \; 88 + ADE.EB.88} - 1 \qquad \text{correct to four places of decimals,}$$

C = 0.6 if A is greater than zero and E is less than 4 000, or

    − 0.3 if A is greater than zero and E is equal to or greater than 14 000, or

$$= 0.6 \; x \; [1 - \frac{(E - 4 \; 000)}{20 \; 000}]$$ correct to four places of decimals, if A is greater

    than zero and E is greater than 4 000 but less than 14 000, or

= 1.0 if A is equal to or less than zero,

    D = 0.3 if B is greater than zero and E is less than 4 000

(Ontario Ministry of Education, 1989)

Overall, most of these formulas involve some combination of factors of student enrolment, approved amounts [e.g., from SELECTED GRANTS ($S PER PUPIL) and TRANSPORTATION tables in the back of the G.L.G. document], mill rates, and equalized assessment. In actually calculating overall expected revenue, a school business superintendent often first determines miscellaneous revenues (e.g., tuition fees), then grants, and then local taxes; "the lesser of" and fractional amounts enter into several grant formula calculations.

Philosophy Underlying the Model

The mill rate equalization plan is based upon the principles of equal yield for equal effort, i.e., all school boards with the same mill rate (effort) on their equalized property assessment will have the same financial revenues per pupil (yield) through a combination of local property tax revenues and provincial grants. School boards determine their own budgets and raise their share of costs from local property taxes. The various equalization grants to boards provided by the Ministry in general are unconditional and are made on a block funding basis. This means that school boards can use these funds to meet their own priorities and program delivery systems as long as they maintain provincially determined program standards and adhere to provincial guidelines (Ontario Ministry of Education, 1989).

With boards spending "over ceilings", the Ontario system has become a foundation grant program. This program exemplifies the fiscal equity principles of equality of educational opportunity and local tax equity such as the adequacy of its pre-pupil level allows. It can lead to grave inequities. Figure 4-4 indicates conceptually how the revenues needed to pay for a foundation unit of education are raised.

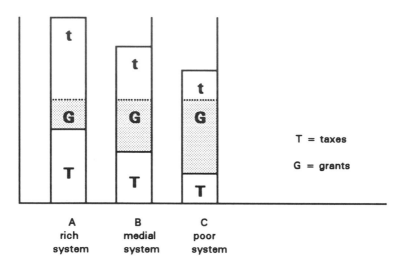

Figure 4-4
Revenue for a Foundation Unit of Education

A beginning assumption is that equal expenditure per pupil provides equal educational opportunity per pupil. Each school system A, B, and C, levy a uniform mill rate on an equalized assessment to raise an amount of revenue indicated by T. The government pays in the form of grants, G, the additional monies needed to pay for the foundation program. This program supports a minimum acceptable level of education indicated by the horizontal dotted line (. . . .) for each of A, B, and C. The tax burden in all systems is equal, but the poor district receives a relatively higher proportion of its revenues from grants. If supplementary revenues, t, in excess of the foundation program are required for local education priorities above the provincially established base of service, normally they must be raised 100 per cent from local taxation sources. Thus the local mill rate would be set above the provincial uniform one and, with application, the equalization principle is violated because one mill would raise less tax in a poor district than in a wealthy district. For equal per-pupil over-ceiling spending, the poor boards must use a higher tax rate.

It is the case that if an assessment-rich community wishes to invest more money in their system they are permitted to do so by increasing local mill rates above the level stipulated by provincial regulation. However, the province does not get involved and the school board becomes accountable to its local taxpayers for the added tax burden. In 1991, property taxes determined by Ontario boards to fund such "unrecognized expenditures" accounted for almost 40% of total property taxes for education. Some believe that this is unacceptable.

Throughout, the foundation system strives to provide *preservation of local autonomy, initiative, and awareness*, and *stimulation* and *control* (re increasing the consumption of educational services locally and making it possible for central government to alter provincial expenditures on education in accordance with fiscal capacity).

There are 170 school boards and communities within Ontario with diverse community socio-economic and assessment bases. Lawton (1989) notes that the great majority of school boards now spend over their grant ceilings and, in fact, "ceilings" have become "floors." He confirms that the Ontario plan has become a foundation grant plan (p. 7).

Annual Budgeting Timelines

Each year there are certain dates which are important in budgeting for Ontario elementary and secondary education. The fiscal year for school boards runs from January 1st to December 31st whereas the fiscal year for government is from April 1st to March 31st. The boards begin work on their budgets in September/October and have until March to file their budget reports for the succeeding year. The province sets its own budget in February. In a particular year the "Regulation, General Legislative Grants, Public, Separate and Secondary School Boards" is released in the Spring, usually sometime in March. Included in this are the equalized mill rates and recognized expenditures for the September 1st to August 31st academic year coming. The following is a budgeting plan for a typical Ontario board:

The Ministry requests school enrolment projections in the Fall (October) and these forecasts are finalized to produce the school board budget by the Spring (April 30th).

Plan for Budget Development

	Action	Completion Date
1.	Each department leader meets with department personnel to review the budget process and establish the responsibility of each individual in the preparation of the department submission.	September 30
2.	Submissions to be submitted to and reviewed with the department leader for acceptability and ranking.	October 31

3. Complete departmental submission to be reviewed by
    department leader with all department personnel for   November 30
    consolidation, further ranking and forwarding to the
    Superintendent of Business.

4. Superintendent of Business to collate and summarize in   December 31
    proper form all departmental submissions.

5. Analysis of consolidated submissions including
    recommendations of Executive Council for the purpose   January 31
    of ranking from the perspective of system needs and
    priorities.

6. Review of consolidated submissions including
    recommendations of Executive Council by the Board   March 1
    of Trustees including trustee input and
    recommendation.

7. Finalization of budget and tax requisitions when grant   April 30
    regulations received.

Figure 4-5 shows a sample Ontario school board's financial statistics for
1991.

1991 Expenditures

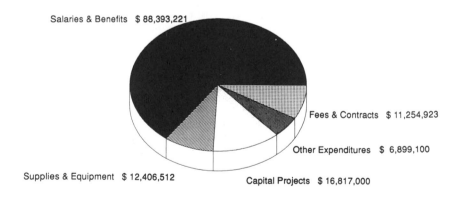

Salaries & Benefits $ 88,393,221

Fees & Contracts $ 11,254,923

Other Expenditures $ 6,899,100

Supplies & Equipment $ 12,406,512

Capital Projects $ 16,817,000

1991 Revenues

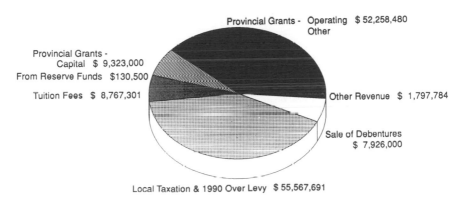

Provincial Grants - Operating $ 52,258,480
Other

Provincial Grants -
Capital $ 9,323,000
From Reserve Funds $130,500

Tuition Fees $ 8,767,301

Other Revenue $ 1,797,784

Sale of Debentures
$ 7,926,000

Local Taxation & 1990 Over Levy $ 55,567,691

Figure 4-5
A Sample School Board's Financial Statistics
From *Director's Annual Report 1991* by Lakehead Board of Education,
Thunder Bay, ON, 1991.

Recent Considerations

Many changes in education funding are being contemplated as Ontario society develops. Lawton (1989) states the following:

> What we are seeing is the introduction of restructuring – *perestroika* – into the public sector. This means, among other things, (1) opening school systems to market forces, (2) using tight-loose management strategies developed in the private sector (central control over goals and evaluation, but local control over operational decisions), (3) deregulation, (4) entrepreneurialism, (5) privatization, and (6) an emphasis on the benefit theory of taxation; that is, the user pays. (p. 4)

He elaborates with a discussion of the five key concerns that affect ability to pay for education – enrolment, property assessment (residential and corporate), personal income, debt, and competing demands, and how these concerns effect provincial and local contributions to education. From 1975 there has been a steady decline in the province's contribution. The provincial share recently has been around 40% of all elementary and secondary spending. (Refer to Figure 4-2)

Research Questions

From the foregoing funding framework, thirteen research questions were formulated under five headings A to E (following Lawton, 1987).

A. *Governance of Education*

1. Is the sharing of power supported by the sharing of costs?

    2. Should there be more federal funds coming into education?

B. *Revenue*

a) Taxation

    1. Is property the ideal basis for tax?

    2. What are the implications of pooled industrial and commercial assessment?

b) Provincial Grants

    1. How adequate are the current ceilings?

    2. Are the funding formulas too complex?

C. *Budgeting*

    1. Are decisions to spend politically or need driven?

D. *Expenditures*

    1. Does more money translate to better education?

    2. Are there ways of cutting costs through the sharing of services?

    3. What are the implications of a regular audit of school board expenditures?

E. *Issues for the Future*

    1. What effects will the aging population have on the costs of education?

    2. How will the funding model evolve to accommodate the increasing demands on the school system?

    3. What attitudinal changes are necessary?

Method

A sample of twenty individuals experienced in the practice and study of educational finance was drawn from Ontario. These people were involved in graduate courses in finance or were working for the Ministry of Education or a school board.

Using a modified Delphi technique, these persons were asked to consider trends in society and education, and then reach consensus on an ideal scheme for financing elementary and secondary education in the future through addressing the above research questions.

The Delphi Technique

The Delphi technique is a method for forecasting future events. It was originally developed at the Rand Corporation by Dalkey and Helmer in 1953 (Berghofer, 1971).

The technique involves soliciting opinions on a particular issue of the future from a group of individuals who are very knowledgeable about the issue. First, individual opinions are collected. Then, all these opinions are shared with the group. Discussion proceeds prior to a second round of obtaining individual opinions on the same issue (the hope is for convergence of opinion). In three iterations (at least) of collecting the individual opinions and discussion, and collecting opinions again, the respondents revise their earlier views, until convergence of opinion on the future event is reached. The end product is a consensus of experts. There are variations as to the application of the Delphi method, the number of sessions and the use of paper or verbal communication are points requiring a decision.

In this study the twenty respondents performed three iterations of the technique in a four-hour session. Consensus on the answers to the research questions was reached after this time.

Results and Discussion

Generally, the respondents agreed that the current education funding model needs revision, particularly in that there needs to be increased input in decision-making from local municipalities.

There was consensus on the following points:

– there is need for some simplification of the present funding system;

– there is too much centralization of control;

– there should be a reassessment of the relative proportions of provincial and local funding with a view to raising ceilings.

Following are specific responses to the research questions presented under Lawton's five headings (Table 4-1 indicates degree of consensus):

A. *Governance of Education*

1. Is the sharing of power supported by the sharing of costs?

Response:

The current trend of provincial grants with escalating local share from taxation will continue if measures are not put in place to halt it. If the provincial share continues to decline, the centralized control of education may become more of an issue.

Discussion:

Taylor (1985) describes a certain degree of mutual mistrust that exists between the school boards and the provincial government. He says:

> The province is fearful of letting the school boards have too much autonomy because they feel that, left alone, the various school boards will increase,

rather than bridge, disparities and therefore jeopardize their policy of equal education throughout Ontario. (p. 31)

A goal has been to have the province and the local boards share education costs in a 60%/40% split, respectively. However, in recent years the provincial government has been practising devolution, whereby there is a greater delegation of fiscal decisions on distributed funds to local boards. This distances the government from politically unpopular choices concerning the use of scarce resources for education but it creates more politics and costs for individual communities. (Jefferson, 1989, p. 253)

Table 4-1

Degree of Respondent Consensus re Finance Research Questions (n = 20)

Question	Iteration 1	Iteration 2	Iteration 3 (final)
A. *Governance of Education*			
1. Is the sharing of power supported by the sharing of costs?	70%	85%	100%
2. Should there be more federal funds coming into education?	80%	95%	100%
B. *Revenue*			
(a) Taxation			
1. Is property the ideal basis for tax?	55%	90%	100%
2. What are the implications of pooled industrial and commercial assessment?	90%	100%	100%
(b) Provincial Grants			
1. How adequate are the current ceilings?	100%	—	100%
2. Are the funding formulas too complex?	90%	95%	100%
C. Budgeting			
1. Are decisions to spend politically or need driven?	90%	100%	100%
D. *Expenditures*			
1. Does more money translate to better education?	50%	80%	100%
2. Are there ways of cutting costs through the sharing of services?	80%	90%	100%
3. What are the implications of a regular audit of school board expenditures?	60%	90%	100%
E. *Issues for the Future*			
1. What effects will the aging population have on the costs of education?	55%	80%	100%
2. How will the funding model evolve to accommodate the increwasing demands on the school system?	60%	75%	100%
3. What attitudinal changes are necessary?	85%	95%	100%

The province's contribution has continued to increase – even in real terms. The provincial **share** has decreased because the provincial contribution has not increased as rapidly as total spending. However, more and more Ministry program mandates to boards suggest a trend toward regaining of program power rather than further devolution.

What is required is a balance between preserving local autonomy and exercising centralized control such that the principles of equal educational opportunity and equal tax burden are followed as much as possible. (Concerning the assumption that equal educational opportunity underlies financing, there is a the view that this opportunity is largely tied to classroom organization and activities and that there is no direct relationship between spending and student outcomes). A suggestion was made that partnerships among various government Ministries be formed. For example, the Ministries of Education, Health, and Community and Social Services together could serve students – there is talk of forming a Ministry of Youth too.

2. Should there be more federal funds coming into education?

Response:

There should be no further influx of federal funds, in the interest of maintaining provincial control.

Discussion:

Even though education is a provincial responsibility, the federal government does share in the financing of education in two major ways:

> First, it is directly responsible for providing educational services to the following groups: native students residing in both the provinces and the territories; children resident in the non-provincial parts of Canada, that is, the territories and Arctic islands; children of armed forces personnel both at home and abroad; and inmates of penitentiaries.
>
> . . . The federal government is also involved in financing education because of the nature of Canadian federalism. Since Confederation, federal governments have made various fiscal arrangements or have entered into various agreements to make transfer payments to the provinces out of the general federal revenues. (Dibski, 1991, p. 61)

Both Dibski and Brown (1985a) express concern about the growth in interprovincial inequalities with respect to educational funding, and see revised federal-provincial fiscal arrangements as important.

The respondents felt that, at this time, particularly with Canada's constitution being reexamined and with federal Government Sales Tax (GST), the current situation of federal input should be maintained but not upscaled, in the interests of provincial autonomy. However, there was the suggestion that special education be considered under a federal framework sometime in the future.

B. *Revenue*

a) Taxation

1. Is property the ideal basis for tax?

Response:

In addition to property taxes, a wealth tax, increased rental of facilities, year- round travel surcharges, and increased personal income taxes should be explored. With respect to the last item, Lawton (1989) states that increases in personal income, like increases in assessment, are not equally spread across the province (p.6). Other suggestions were an educational voucher scheme, educational bonds, special lotteries to provide funds (or a tax on lottery tickets to support education), and a levy on industry in return for the education of the skilled workers it employs. Despite considerable opposition in recent years, government has attempted to collect education tax from cottage and mobile home owners. There was the suggestion that there be a growing shift to a commercial base for education funding. On the other hand, it was suggested that all commercial and industrial assessment be pooled provincially to be more equitable (because only residential taxpayers would share the burden).

In the response to this research question a number of other ideas pertaining to new sources of revenue generally were presented. These included using retirement gratuity monies and directing into education money from wealthy immigrants to Canada (e.g., from Hong Kong).

2. What are the implications of pooled assessment?

Response:

The current effort to introduce a new system of industrial assessments should be continued. This may help to more equitably distribute the funds across the public and separate school systems.

Discussion:

In 1989, Bill 64 was introduced into the Ontario Legislature. This legislation provides that separate school boards will receive a fairer share of the education taxes paid by the businesses and factories in each community. The plan will be phased in over a six-year period. Basically, it provides for revenues from businesses, industries, and telephone and telegraph payments to be shared between the public and separate systems on the basis of their respective residential and farm assessments. This will increase taxation revenue for the separate systems and create a loss of revenue for the public systems. When revenues from taxes decrease, provincial grants increase; when revenue from taxes increase, provincial grants decrease. Therefore, in part at least, losses and gains tend to balance themselves out. The government has pledged to indemnify public boards against losses. Before this new legislation, 90% of the commercial and industrial assessment was going to the public school boards. Despite the claim by some public school ratepayers that they are being forced to pay for the extension of funding to separate schools, the new pooling scheme does aim for fairness and balance. Morris (1989) provides background to the plan.

b) Provincial Grants

1. How adequate are the current ceilings?

Response:

The ceilings are too low. Data shows that almost all boards in the province spend above the provincially determined ceilings.

Discussion:

Several authors (e.g., Brumer, 1990; Dibski, 1991; Lawton, 1989) confirm this. Most Ontario boards exceed provincial grant ceilings in both panels, and have done so for several years. Ignoring assessment inequities, provincial grant ceilings (or "floors") should be established to more closely relate to actual costs. This upward adjustment should allow boards of lesser wealth (and perhaps some inferior standards of education) an opportunity to improve their standard of educational delivery, knowing the Province is sharing in the additional cost. Also, a suggestion was made that capital expenditure be provincially supported to the higher percentage of 85%.

2. Are the funding formulas too complex?

Response:

The funding formulas are too complex. They should be simplified without making them insensitive to the relevant, diverse equity issues and explained better.

Discussion:

As mentioned earlier in this chapter, the current formulas in the GLG documents are very complex. Ontario should strive towards a more simplified structure in the interest of greater understanding and support. It was suggested that *Recognized Ordinary Expenditure (R.O.E.)* be based on a simple classroom/school approach, e.g., for 25 pupils in a 16-room school, costs to cover teacher, support personnel, utilities, supplies, and so on. Also, there was the suggestion that boards that "produce" well under program-specific grants be rewarded in some way. No doubt in the future there will be a period of instability in which the government changes grant characteristics – removing some, starting some new ones, and shifting others, in whole or in part, to different classifications.

C. *Budgeting*

1. Are decisions to spend politically or need driven?

Response:

The decisions to spend are more politically driven than they should be, thereby not meeting the educational needs of the community adequately.

Discussion:

Andrew-Cotter and Thom (1987) describe the influence of politicians:

> Declining enrolments have created other stresses on the educational system; it is much easier to grow than to shrink. In times of growth, problems are solved by throwing money at the problem. This does not always provide a good solution but it is easier for the clients to understand than the reverse which is so often true in the declining phase. Taking away things that parents, students and teachers have grown to accept as normal is not a popular political move. One must never forget that the predominant factor in educational finance is the politician acting primarily at the provincial and school board levels. They are motivated as heavily by the vote as by what is educationally and administratively sound. (p. 39)

It is somewhat naive to think that educational policy cannot be political. Trust can be lacking, whether it be with respect to local, provincial, or federal-level decision-makers. In the future, local plebescite voting on educational issues (as in the U.S.) may assist with the concerns.

D. *Expenditures*

Does more money translate to better education?

Response:

More money does not necessarily mean better education. It is only through a careful application to accurately assessed needs that quality education can be achieved.

Discussion:

Seemingly, increased payments to local municipalities by either the federal or provincial governments increases the community's fiscal capacity. But, as Hanushek (1986) states, there appears to be no strong relationship between school expenditures and student performance (p. 1162). Decision-making must be sharpened and province-wide testing of students could provide a guage as to expenditure effectiveness.

2. Are there ways of cutting costs through the sharing of services?

Response:

Yes, there are ways. Some suggestions are the formation of unified school boards, the sharing of transportation costs by separate and public systems, and providing joint school and community centre services.

Discussion:

Andrew-Cotter and Thom (1987) and Lawton (1989) discuss these approaches. The former suggest that unified boards could reduce costs by the creation of one support service, one administration, and one board; and, within a board, schools could be instituted with parent advisory councils to develop their own unique programs (p. 43). One caution is that sharing services might seem to be a way to reduce costs, but it may result in an increase in problems because of several jurisdictions being involved.

Several other ideas on cost-saving emerged. These included instituting provincial collective bargaining and one salary grid, freezing salaries, cutting back on special education (this is becoming a reality), reducing the number of administrators, consultants, and custodial staff, reducing travel costs, altering the months for the school year (to save money on heating costs for instance), charging student materials' fees to parents, actively seeking from communities and individuals funds to assist in building schools, and raising the provincial share of funding to 80%. (It is worth noting that in Quebec provincial bargaining has generally resulted in higher salaries compared to other provinces.) Many respondents felt that just one public school system, with choice within, would be most efficient.

Finally, there is a feeling that the timing for transfer of general legislative grants from the Province and the transfer of local property taxes from municipalities does not suitably relate to the financing needs of school boards (Macdonald Commission, 1985). Since school boards incur significant expenditures in the months of January, February, and March before any significant transfers from the two major revenue sources commence in March, there are significant borrowing costs. A suggestion is that provincial transfers be adjusted to more accurately reflect the incurrence of school boards' expenditures.

3. What are the implications of a regular audit of school board expenditures?

Response.

All but two of the respondents supported regular audits. All agreed that cost was a significant factor, but not all agreed that the benefits of the audits would justify that cost.

Discussion:

In October, 1989, two Ontario school boards became the first-ever to be given an audit by the provincial auditor's office. School boards are a transfer payment program of considerable dollars and the audit was to reveal whether the boards have done what they promised to do with the provincial funding received. These audits take several months and are costly. The majority of the respondents supported them as a regular occurrence.

E. *Issues for the Future*

1. What effects will the aging population have on the costs of education?

Response:

There will be several effects. The political decisions made by this older, median population will reflect their attitudes and philosophies. It will become increasingly difficult for this group to accept paying school costs when their own offspring have completed their formal education. The vote will be to direct more government funds into health care and welfare schemes to cater to this older majority.

Discussion:

Brown (1985b) mentions that elementary and secondary education is the most age-related of all public services. Further, he states that changes in real educational need, real educational burden, and political attitudes toward spending for education are greatly influenced by the age structure of the population. Table 4-2 displays important population and enrolment trends for Ontario, 1961 to 2001.

Table 4-2
The Changing Age Structure of the Population, Ontario, 1961 to 2001

Age Groups	1961	1971	1981	1984	1991	2001
Ontario						
Population						
0-19	2 444 700	2 921 900	2 695 700	2 600 400	2 787 600	2 820 900
20-44	2 136 000	2 662 200	3 318 900	3 579 900	4 092 800	4 128 200
45-64	1 147 400	1 474 500	1 742 100	1 819 900	1 909 200	2 511 700
65 and over	508 000	644 500	868 000	937 200	1 108 600	1 292 500
Total	**6 236 100**	**7 703 100**	**8 624 700**	**8 937 400**	**9 908 200**	**10 753 300**
Percentage Distribution						
0-19	39.30	37.93	31.26	29.10	28.13	26.23
20-64	52.55	53.70	56.68	60.42	60.68	61.75
65 and over	8.15	8.37	10.06	10.48	11.19	12.02
Total %	**100**	**100**	**100**	**100**	**100**	**100**
Dependency						
Ratio*	89.93	86.21	70.41	65.51	64.81	61.95

From "Problems and Issues in Education Finance Across Canada" by Wilfred J. Brown, Thunder Bay, ON. July, 1985.

These trends, together with the fact that there continues to be deteriorating health of provincial economies, signals the possibility of much less money for education in the future.

2. How will the funding model evolve to accommodate the increasing demands on the school system?

Response:

The respondents agreed that the model must be simplified and that more input into decisions must be given to local ratepayers. We may see a significant reduction in provincial funding and increased local taxation. Just what specific form the future model will take is uncertain, but hopefully planners will be assisted by the ideas from the research which underlies this article.

Discussion:

For this question many additional ideas emerged. Among them were the development of healthy public attitudes toward schools and education; a fair system of provincial and local responsibility; continuing exploration of new tax bases and sources of revenue generally; provision of education to French students; and the development of an independent schools system.

Many of the above issues are highlighted in the literature, e.g., Dibski (1991). Discussions from the Select Committee on Education (1987) are relevant. Bezeau (1987) debates public financial support for private schools and the effects of an aging population ("dependency in the Canadian population"). He emphasizes that the former can be obtained without an increase in public control (p. 562). Further, he advocates the school of the future as a community resource available to the citizens of all ages who provide support. It was suggested that the Catholic church fund the Catholic schools more than is the case now.

Brumer (1990) describes some coming changes under four categories – transportation, continuing education, average daily enrolment, and goods and services (p. 19). The bigger school boards will lose provincial revenue because many of these changes are designed to bring service in line with actual need, and Northern boards specifically will be affected by the goods and services revisions.

Conclusions

There is a growing feeling that the reach of the education system is beyond its grasp. Regardless, services must carry on. The financing of elementary and secondary education in Ontario has been undergoing rigorous review. Such principles as equal yield for equal effort will be retained but others could be modified. For instance, direction is toward opening education systems to market forces and placing more onus on municipalities to pay the costs of education. Thus, alternative taxation schemes are being explored. Perhaps school boards will disappear and personal income become a tax base. Further, the debates surrounding support for independent schools has led to a rethinking of what constitutes "public" education. The Macdonald Commission and the Select Committee on Education represent the beginning of new, creative ideas. No doubt the younger generation will be left with paying for schemes created by those before them.

The complex society is creating a situation in which it is difficult to predict the exact form that the future funding model will take. In recent years there have been some significant developments within the province – full funding of separate (Catholic) schools, communities declaring themselves "English only," and the introduction of multi-faith religious programs in public schools. At the federal level there have been the Meech Lake Accord (re Quebec being afforded a distinct identity), Free Trade agreements, and a federal Government Sales Tax (GST) plan. These things, in the broader context of an aging population, have contributed to new religious, language, ethnic, and economic influences which ultimately will impact on schools. Just how and when is open to question. It is known that there is a disturbingly large payout in social welfare monies.

The revision of the funding model by the Ontario Ministry of Education is an effort to increase clarity, to simplify, and to increase allocation fairness. However, more needs to be done. New governments bring new ideas. It would appear that the Ontario NDP government has overspent. Priorities must be rethought. In early 1992 it was announced that, over the next years, money to education would increase just a few percent. Hopefully the 1990s will see slow and steady recession recovery.

For future research a model of cultural consequence would be useful, e.g., Hofstede, 1980. Dr. Lawton, in conversation with the author, has suggested the use of the framework from Marshall et al.'s *Culture and Education Policy* (1989). The Delphi technique could be contrived with some of the ideas on state/regional culture to provide an explanatory framework. Several divisions of regional culture could be made – North, West, Central, and East in Ontario; separate, public, and French system affiliation; and British Columbia, Alberta, Quebec, and a Maritime province interprovincially. Further, in future research more attention could be focused on effective usage of revenues. Stronger focus could be on the governance of resources, local decision-making, priority-setting, and research utilization, further adding to the contribution of the MacDonald Commission and the third report of the Select Committee. As well, the focus on northern boards could be lessened and a predominent focus on boards from other areas could be adopted, so as to reflect a broad enough cross-section of attitudes, expenditures, and need to provide a base for province-wide policies. Finally, following Sale and Levin (1991), in studying reform, attention should be given to adoption and implementation factors such as limits of decision-makers' time, attention, and understanding, the difficulty of integrating all relevant reform considerations, political limitations, and problems of implementation. Coase (1988) is noteworthy in all of this. His work suggests that reform must occur at a deeper level of society's belief system (e.g., law), as this determines the economic market and, in turn, its impact on institutions such as schools. Contracts, laws, and property rights are Coase's main focus.

Several things are clear and these were confirmed in this research: there is a desire by local municipalities for more input on decisions; there is a wish for higher "ceilings"; and the growing multicultural, just society means that there will be increasing pressures to develop other school systems. Native languages are in place in many systems and in November, 1991, the Ontario Jewish community began its push for government funding of its language teaching. Actual educational needs and new sources of revenue to meet these needs must be explored. Future research should address these themes in detail. The Delphi technique is one of several methodologies which could be useful.

At the practical level there are many issues to be decided. Can systems handle the pushing down of decision-making responsibility and accountability to the community/school level? How much school-based management should there be? Will such things as a shift to program-based funding and privatization of schools save money? How much of a priority should educating disadvantaged students be? In actuality, does an *increase* in spending in recession times lead to long-term gains? (a Keynesian idea). Wastage must be addressed, and it should be appreciated that, overall, our country is fortunate to have the school system which it has - one which is envied by other countries. The temptation to meet short-term wants at the expense of long-term needs should be addressed carefully.

The 1992 work of the Education Finance Reform Project, the Fair Tax Commission, and the commission on disentanglement is important. At least what will be required for future effectiveness and efficiency are healthy public attitudes toward schools, patience with the continuing turbulence (e.g., as older, higher paid teachers retire, many school systems will see better times), increased cooperation between the Ministry of Education (called Ministry of Education and Training as of 1993) and school boards, excellent systems of long range planning (with the use of such things as unreserved fund balance), and acceptance of the fact that, initially, expectations with respect to firm solutions must be modest and fair.

Questions for further research

1. Does the source of educational funding determine how it is spent, and if so, how?

2. To what extent are "needs" in education political?

3. Will less money for education in the future eventually come to bear on the principle of universal provision and accessibility?

4. Can the theory of "transaction costs" of Nobel economics prize winner, American Ronald Coase, be fruitfully applied to the educational finance scheme?

References

Andrew-Cotter, P., & Thom, D.J. (1987, September). Financing education: Some models for the 1980's. *Comment on Education, 18*(1), 12-16.

Awender, M.A., & Nease, A.S. (1987). Government control of education. In L.L. Stewin & S. McCann (Eds.), *Contemporary educational issues: The Canadian mosaic* (pp. 540-557). Toronto, ON: Copp Clark Pitman.

Berghofer, D.E. (1971). An application of the delphi technique to educational planning. *The Canadian Administrator, 10*(6), 25-28.

Bezeau, L.M. (1987). The financing of Canadian education. In L.L. Stewin & S. McCann (Eds.), *Contemporary educational issues: The Canadian mosaic* (pp. 558-568). Toronto, ON: Copp Clark Pitman.

British North America Act, 1867 (amended to *Constitution Act, 1867* in 1982).

Brown, W.J. (1985a, April 13th). Reemergence of inequalities in education finance among the provinces of Canada. Summary of a talk by Wilfred J. Brown at the American Education Finance Association Annual Conference, Phoenix, AZ.

Brown, W.J. (1985b, July 23rd). Problems and issues in education finance across Canada. Notes prepared for guest lecture, Educational Finance class (D.J.Thom), Thunder Bay, ON.

Brumer, L. (1990, January/February). Financing education in Ontario – New directions. *Education Today*, 2(1), 17-19.

Coase, R.H. (1988). *The firm, the market, and the law.* Chicago, IL: University of Chicago Press.

Dibski, D. (1991). Financing education. In R. Ghosh & D. Ray (Eds.), *Social change and education in Canada* (2nd ed.) (pp. 59-72). Toronto, ON: Harcourt Brace Jovanovich.

Hanushek, E.A. (1986, September). The economics of schooling: Production and efficiency in public schools. *Journal of Economic Literature*, 1141-1177.

Hofstede, G. (1980). *Culture's consequences: International differences in work-related values.* Beverley Hills, CA: SAGE.

Jefferson, A.L. (1989). Financing public education: The Canadian way. *Economics of Education Review*, 8(3), 247-253.

Lakehead Board of Education (1991). *Director's annual report 1991.* Thunder Bay, ON.

Lawton, S.B. (1987). *The price of quality: The public finance of elementary and secondary education in Canada.* Toronto, ON: Canadian Education Association.

Lawton, S.B. (1989, October). Who's running the shop? The revolution in Ontario school finances. *Orbit*, 20(3), 4-7.

Marshall, C., Mitchell, D., & Wirt, F. (1989). *Culture and education policy in the American states.* New York, NY: The Falmer Press.

Morris, J.H. (1989, September/October). Pooling of commercial and industrial assessment. *Education Today*, 14-15.

Ontario (1989). *Legislative select committee on education* (report). Toronto, ON.

Ontario Ministry of Education (1985). *Report of the commission on the Ffnancing of elementary and secondary education in Ontario* (Macdonald Commission). Toronto, ON: Queen's Printer.

Ontario Ministry of Education. (1989 and 1991). *Education funding in Ontario* (The General Legislative Grants Regulations, including The Funding Model). Toronto, ON: Ontario Ministry of Education.

Ontario Ministry of Education. (1992). *Toward education finance reform* (GLGs, etc.). Toronto, ON: Ontario Ministry of Education.

Sale, T., & Levin, B. (1991, Winter). Problems in the reform of educational finance: A case study. *Canadian Journal of Education*, 16(1), 32-46.

Taylor, M. (1985, April). An assessment of the educational property tax. *Comment on Education*, 15(4), 24-31.

Further Readings:

Allen, I.J. (1991, October). Unreserved fund balance and public school system finance. *School Business Affairs*, 10-15.

Brown, D.J. (1993). The initial inquiry into enterprise in public education. Paper presented at the American Education Finance Association annual conference, Albuquerque, NM, March 19th.

Davies, B., & Ellison, L. (1992). Delegated school finance in the English education system: An era of radical change. *Journal of Educational Administration, 30*(1), 70-80.

Jefferson, A.L. (1991, March). Provincial school finance plans: Their recognition of the equity principle. Paper presented at the American Education Finance Association Conference, Williamsburg, VA.

Jefferson, A.L. (1992). Financing education and the retention of students. Discussion Notes. *Canadian Journal of Education, 17*(1), 95-99.

Lawton, S.B. (1990, February). Taxation of corporate assessment. The revolution in Ontario school finances. *Orbit, 21*(1), 20-22.

Lawton, S.B. (1990, October). Funding private schools. The revolution in Ontario school finances. *Orbit, 21*(3), 16-17.

Lawton, S.B. (1992). Equity and accountability in Ontario school finance. Department of Educational Administration, The Ontario Institute for Studies in Education, Toronto, ON.

Livingstone, D.W., Davie, L.E., & Hart, D. (1991, April). Educational funding (in special issue on public attitudes towards education in Ontario – 1990). *Orbit, 22*(2), 1–8.

McCormick, C. (1990). The persistence of provincial and regional inequities in education finance in Canada. *Education Canada, 30*(4), 23-26.

Michaud, P. (1992). Equity in the funding of elementary and secondary education in Ontario. Education Finance Reform Project, Ministry of Education, Toronto, ON.

Odden, A.R. (Ed.). (1992). *Rethinking school finance: An agenda for the 1990s.* San Francisco, CA: Jossey-Bass.

Ontario Ministry of Education (1992). Materials from the presentation by S. Lawton, D. Corson, & P. Haskell on "School-based management and its implications for school finance reform." Education Finance Reform Project, Toronto, ON.

Ontario Secondary School Teachers' Federation (1992, September). Fair taxation for responsible education: Report of the funding initiatives and new directions committee. Submission to the Ontario Fair Tax Commission. Toronto, ON: OSSTF.

Ontario Secondary School Teachers' Federation (1993, January). Adequacy, equity and democracy: A proposal for education funding in Ontario. Toronto, ON: OSSTF.

Ornstein, A.C. (1990). School finance in the '90s. *The American School Board Journal, 177*(1), 36-39.

Paquette, J. (1991, March). Fiscal policy for a changing social contract in Ontario education. University of Western Ontario, London, ON.

Paquette, J. (1992). Fiscal equity in Ontario: Toward a new millennium. University of Western Ontario, London, ON.

Paquette, J. (1993). Educational spending and fiscal capacity trends across Canada: 1970 to 1992. Paper presented at the American Education Finance Association annual conference, Albuquerque, NM, March 20th.

5

Values

Historical Overview

There exist many ideas on the essences of educational management and leadership. Educational law and educational finance were overviewed in Chapters 3 and 4, respectively. In this chapter more ideas are summarized, and the seeds are planted for a leadership model which is relevant to these times and beyond. The model itself is presented later in the book.

Historically, the development of organization and administrative thought and practice has followed certain patterns. (Thom, 1978, 1979, 1982, and McCuaig & Thom, 1988, together trace in detail this development with respect to educational administration) In the early years the hope was that one day a general theory would be developed – one which would integrate theories of organization, leadership, decision-making, communication, ethics, policy analysis, and so on. Initially the trait approach, which is an attempt to determine forces within a leader him/herself which contribute to his/her effectiveness, was popular. Next came the context approach, an attempt to explain administrative effectiveness by looking at variables within the situation. Then, the trait and contextual approaches were combined. In fact, the literature describes the concept of "emergent leadership" whereby different personalities take charge in different settings (Gibb, 1970). Other approaches were to consider the maturity of the leader and the maturity of the group being led (Hersey & Blanchard, 1977). Fiedler and Chemers (1984) present a follow-up to Fiedler's Least Preferred Cohert approach. (See Appendix D.) Perrow (1973) indicates that leadership is "contingent" upon a large variety of important variables such as nature of task, size of the group, length of time the group existed, type of personnel within the group and their relationships with each other, and the amount of pressure the group is under. These developments in understanding things through the person, the context, and the job have accompanied the more broadly based developments of changing views of organization. Progression was from the Classical (Scientific Management) view and the reductive Theory X managing style, to Human Relations and the developmental Theory Y, to Structuralism, through to the open systems, Phenomenological, Contingency, Organization Development, Marxist and Critical Theory viewpoints (Campbell, 1977-78; Griffith, 1979; and Thom, 1984b). Viewing organizations as organisms (e.g., Haire, 1975) has recurred over the years, as have somewhat liberal approaches to running them (e.g., Lindblom, 1959). Figure 5-1 summarizes. Scientific management is linked to Taylor (1923). Belief in the human relations managerial style, which is often associated with Mayo (1933), is now widespread. Theory Z (Ouchi, 1981) was highlighted for a period, and interest in organization development has been renewed, but within a context which recognizes the contemporary, often-harsh political realities of organizations (Greiner & Schein, 1988). One innovative general management approach is that of "nine dots" Mega-departmental decentralization described by Thom (1990).

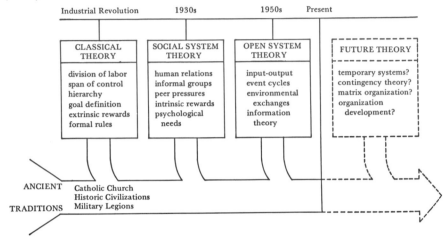

Figure 5-1
Historical Development of Organization and Administration

Adapted from *Educational Administration and Organizational Behavior* by E. Mark Hanson, 1979, p. 8. Copyright 1979 by Allyn & Bacon, Inc., Boston, MA. Reprinted by permission.

More recent years have brought literature that reflects uncertainty and reform in the educational management and leadership arena (e.g., McPherson et al.'s *Managing Uncertainty: Administrative Theory and Practice in Education*, 1986; Walker's "Tight Ship to Tight Flotilla: The First Century of Scholarship in Educational Administration," 1991; and Dolmage's "The Quest for Understanding in Educational Administration . . .," 1992). Perhaps not surprisingly then, in the past decade several education authors (Beck, 1986; Begley, 1990; Corson, 1985; Enns, 1981; Farquhar, 1981, 1989; Foster, 1986; Greenfield, et al., 1985; Hodgkinson, 1978, 1983; Holmes, 1989; Holmes & Wynne, 1989; Lakomski, 1987a, 1987b; Schön, 1983, 1987, 1989; Sharples, 1984; Smith & Blase, 1991; Sola, 1984; Starratt, 1991, 1992; and Thom, 1982, 1984a, 1986, 1990, 1992) have been focusing on the values/ethical and reflective aspects of administration. In large part this represents a renewed focus on leader traits – his/her values, beliefs, and conscience. Further, it signals a return to an emphasis found in earlier general literature such as by Barnard (1938) and, with respect to educational administration specifically, Althouse (1953), Flower (1958), Broudy (1965), Miller (1965), and Farquhar (1970). Ryan

(1991) is developing the humanities focus. Koestenbaum's *Leadership: The Inner Side of Greatness* (1991) is a superb, newer general book.

Figure 5-2 indicates key contributors to the educational administration literature over the years. Each contributor tends to be known for a specialty area, e.g., Daniel G. Griffiths (systems), Andrew Halpin (leadership), Christopher Hodgkinson (philosophy), etc.

1. Chester I. Barnard	21. James M. Lipham	41. T.B. Greenfield
2. Daniel E. Griffiths	22. Talcott Parsons	42. Richard Bates
3. Jacob W. Getzels	23. James D. Thompson	43. Vernon Gilbert
4. Egon G. Guba	24. Edwin Bridges	44. Stephen Lawton
5. Herbert A. Simon	25. Jack Culbertson	45. Kenneth Leithwood
6. Max Weber	26. Robert K. Merton	46. Robin H. Farquhar
7. Andrew W. Halpin	27. R.J. Hills	47. T.E. Giles
8. Amitai Etzioni	28. James G. Anderson	48. Chris Hodgkinson
9. Douglas McGregor	29. Richard H. Hall	49. W.L. Boyd
10. Warren G. Bennis	30. Roald Campbell	50. Thomas Sergiovanni
11. Rensis Likert	31. Cecil Miskel	51. Donald Schön
12. L. von Bertalanffy	32. Thomas S. Kuhn	52. Frank W. Lutz
13. Robert Presthus	33. Charles Perrow	53. Michael LaMorte
14. Jerald Hage	34. Donald Layton	54. George Baron
15. George C. Homans	35. Keith Goldhammer	55. Michael Fullan
16. Robert Dubin	36. Donald J. Willower	56. A. Ross Thomas
17. Alvin W. Gouldner	37. Meredydd Hughes	57. Spencer Maxcy
18. Henri Fayol	38. Max G. Abbott	58. Wayne Hoy
19. Hubert M. Blalock, Jr.	39. W.G. Walker	59. Eric Hoyle
20. John K. Hemphill	40. Kenneth E. McIntyre	60. Gabrielle Lakomski

Figure 5-2

Key Contributors in Educational Administration

Adapted from "Theory in Educational Administration: An Instructional Module Teaching Approach" by Eddy J. Van Meter, Autumn 1973, *Educational Administration Quarterly, 9*(3), p. 8.

General

In these times the knowledge and skills which are required to administrate effectively and efficiently in all sectors, including education, are beyond what the literature usually presents. Though expertise in major interest areas such as structures and roles, law, finance, politics, and planning is readily acknowledged, in specifics there is much more involved than meets the eye. Generally the literature depicts an administrative process (as in Figure 5-3) and educational leaders as possessing good task (initiating structure) and maintenance (consideration) skills, the former related to "getting the job done" and the latter related to "looking after the needs of the people being led." [Figure 5-3 follows a typical Easton (1957) input, process, output scheme.] Newer education books such as Beare et al.'s *Creating an Excellent School* (1990), Evers and Lakomski's *Knowing Educational Administration* (1991), Popper's *Pathways to the Humanities in School Administration* (1990), Walker, Farquhar, and Hughes' *Advancing Education: School Leadership in Action* (1991), Jacobson and Conway's *Educational Leadership in an Age of Reform* (1990), Smyth's *Critical Perspectives on Educational Leadership* (1989), Wendel's *Enhancing the Knowledge Base in Educational Administration* (1991) and *Applications of Reflective Practice* (1992), Keith and Girling's *Education, Management, and Participation* (1991), Hodgkinson's *Educational Leadership: The Moral Art* (1991), Maxcy's *Educational Leadership: A Critical Pragmatic Perspective* (1991), Sergiovanni's *Moral Leadership* (1992), Clark's *Educational Leadership and the Crisis of Democratic Culture* (1992), Miklos and Ratsoy's *Educational Leadership: Challenge and Change* (1992), Greenfield and Ribbins' *Greenfield on Educational Administration: Towards a Humane Science* (1992), and Nanus' *Visionary Leadership* (1992) have sophistication, but they still do not go far enough. Particularly Greenfield (1992) and Hodgkinson (1991) with their view of the discipline as "humane science" and "moral art," respectively, are on a promising track.

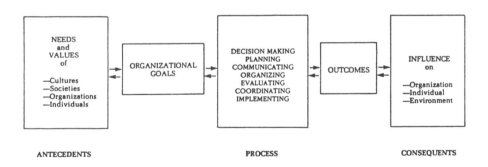

Figure 5–3
The Administrative Process in Its Context

From *An Introduction to Educational Administration in Canada* (2nd ed.) by Leslie R. Gue, 1985, p. 23. Copyright 1985 by McGraw-Hill Ryerson Ltd., Toronto, ON. Reprinted by permission.

It is no longer sufficient just to have good personal task and maintenance skills within a given familiar education/society culture. Society has become a quite legalistic and economic-concerned entity in which the people who are being led insist on their rights and freedom in a context of fairness and justice. Further, politics is always present. The administrator/leader who succeeds has a great sensitivity to these things and is not adverse to being challenged on issues in the area of human rights and justice. In "the big picture" these issues are critical. There are many "hats to wear" and this is no easy task. More of a hardline approach to happenings is required than is often thought. The educational administrator is an instructional and an administrative leader. In these roles a general knowledge of the traditional theories and techniques of organization and administration is valuable. Good task and maintenance skills are necessary; so is a basic grounding in law and educational finance. These skills and background are needed to manage and lead well on an initial, basic, routine level where it may be assumed that those being managed are cooperative and have institutional loyalty. However, contemporary workers wax and wane with respect to cooperation and loyalty. In collective action they can present some extremely challenging situations for executives. As a result, an administrator sometimes operates on an advanced level where he/she must "play hardball." More is required then. To survive and to be effective, the executive needs an added ingredient – a values/spiritual/moral core informed by sound knowledge of what is right and wrong. He/she must have a conscience.

The Role of Values

> The field of executive action and the administrative endeavour which embraces it make philosophical demands. It is the highest function of the executive to develop a deep understanding of himself and his fellows, a knowledge of human nature which includes motivation but reaches beyond it into the domain of value possibilities.

> Hodgkinson, 1983, p. 53.

Values play a significant role in education and its leadership. For example, in the decisions concerning educational finance this is the case – What does the public deem to be of value in education? What does the finance administrator personally believe? What is the range of value possibilities? Walker (1991) highlights that "values" as theory bases in educational administration, generally, have rightly regained the prominence that they held many years ago (p. 14).

In order for people to feel comfortable about what is happening in society, education, and educational administration, they must personally hold sound values and beliefs and use them to interpret what is happening. But just what do these values and beliefs appear to be? Ricker et al. (1982) state:

> Most Canadians believe in, and value, democracy, individual freedom and the rule of law. But there are other values and beliefs about which we differ. Some Canadians are conservative in outlook. They tend to believe that changes in society and government should be made gradually. And they should be made only when there is clear proof that change is really necessary. Other Canadians

are more radical in outlook and tend to welcome change. Some Canadians believe that the country's wealth should be shared among its citizens. Others believe that everyone should look after his or her own interests. Some favour religious instruction in schools; others oppose it. (p. 28)

Townsend (1988) delves into politicians' beliefs and education activity. Our values and beliefs are determined in part by our upbringing and the ideas of our parents and relatives. They are shaped as well by our formal education, our religion, our reading, and our observations of the world around us. The attempt is to pass noble ideals down from generation to generation, but there is no certain way to predict what values or beliefs anyone will hold. Two people may come from the same kind of home. They may attend the same school, work in the same factory and make the same amount of money. Yet, they are almost certain to have different opinions on many questions. When these differences are expressed in words, actions and votes, they have an effect on government.

Thus, one infers that individuals can believe whatever they want to believe. Correct. But this is not sufficient. What is needed is a concrete, useful definition of values and beliefs. In recent years Christopher Hodgkinson has been considered in the forefront of elucidating such for educational leaders. His three types of personal values (1978) appears in Figure 5-4.

Begley (1990) summarizes:

Type III values, personal preferences, are based on individuals' feelings about what is "good"; they are self-justifying and primitive. Type IIB values are based on consensus or the will of the majority in a given group. Type IIA values derive from projecting a desirable future state of affairs or analysing of the consequences entailed by the value judgement. Whereas Type II values are rational, the Type I values at the highest level of hierarchy are transrational: they are based on principles, ethical codes, injunctions, or commandments. Like any value, they are not scientifically verifiable and cannot be justified by logical argument. Type I values are based on will rather than on reason. According to Hodgkinson, the adoption of Type I values implies some act of faith, belief, or commitment. (1978, pp. 112-113)

Hodgkinson's work confirms the importance of humanism and values (as well, he delves into the more foundational "metavalues" of organizations). His comments concerning "not scientifically verifiable" and "implies some act of faith, belief, or commitment" are intriguing. They are suggestive of a religious doctrine. Faith is crucial. What or which faith? What specific belief?

Value Type	Grounding	Correspondences
Type I Transrational	Principle	– Ethical Codes – Based on will – Metaphysical – What is rightest
Type IIA Rational	Consequences	– Analysis of consequences – Desirable state of affairs – Right outcomes
Type IIB Rational	Consensus	– Influence of peers, experts, etc. – Will of majority – What is right
Type III Subrational	Personal Preference	– Individual preference – Self-justifying – Affective – Good

Figure 5-4
Hodgkinson's Administrative Values

Adapted from "How Administrators' Values Influence Theirr Decisions" by P.T. Begley, Oct. 1990, *The Canadian School Executive,* 10(4), p. 5.

The author began his own research and publication on values in the 1970s. In this book Hodgkinson's ideas are extended to define the appropriate value base, for at least developed societies, as one tied to the laws of the land and its inherent moral values (which ultimately have their origin in theology). The model, as presented, will not be popular in many sectors when considered in terms of multiculturalism. However, when talking faith, ultimately one comes to accept. It is not the purpose of this book to argue religion. However, the author feels that the literature has failed to promote sufficiently that Judaeo-Christian doctrine is an important foundation underlying effective educational systems and society, and that this doctrine determines a sound conscience. To present such takes courage such as that shown by Wynne (1989). Thom's "The Spiritual Factor in Educational Administration" (1984) forms a basis for idea development.

The contemporary educational culture exists in changing value contexts. The author's work on values, beliefs, and ethics is expanded in the following report. Some input from D. Klassen is gratefully acknowledged (Thom & Klassen, 1988).

Educational Administration and Changing Value Contexts

Background

Currently our society is witnessing a changing social order largely because of a multicultural emphasis. So too, values surrounding education, family, and institutions such as the church are changing. This is the context in which educational administration is performed.

More recent literature on educational administration extends a value focus to consider concomitantly the values of the leader and the values in the particular cultural context. For instance, Codd (1989) argues that "professional administrators should be distinguished by their overall commitment to a set of educational values and principles for practice" and "educational leadership is a form of moral action which can be meaningful only within a given cultural context."

Rallis in Mitchell and Cunningham's *Educational Leadership and Changing Contexts of Families, Communities, and Schools* (1990) exclaims that:

> Leadership is a process of bringing people together, helping them to belong, so they may do the work of the organization. They belong by accepting and sharing the norms, values, and beliefs of the organizational culture, however large or small it may be. (p. 204)

Further, Sungaila (1990), in her discussion of the "new naturalism" in understanding organization and society, explains how individuals make choices – "Choosing is not easy, because every living system exists in a world of possibilities – the grand total of all the possibilities in the system and in its environment".

Several theorists have clearly specified that religious values must be considered. For instance, in discussing decadence in society and organization Torbert (1990) states:

> The only specific that wards off decadence is a moral, religious, and educational vision that locates each participant – whether person, family, faction, profession, or organization – as serving, and as responsible to, some higher calling than one's own comfort, pleasure, or self-interest. (p.252)

The following relates to a study in which educational administrators were asked about the nature of their job and what is required to be effective. The results extend knowledge in the values, beliefs, and ethics area.

Framework

A Premise

An observation of our present culture is that there is an obsessive preoccupation with self. This self-serving, "me-first" mind set has crept into the circles of educational leadership. Certainly the increase in litigation is sufficient cause for administrators in education to be wary of their decisions and actions. Yet, too often it appears that they are so preoccupied with "getting it documented" and "case-tight," that little time or energy is left for doing the job with which they were entrusted. Some become so efficient at covering their tracks that they leave little evidence for ever having been there, and leave nothing for members of their organization to follow. They fear that "losing a case" could curtail their chances of promotion up the ladder of leadership. This kind of administration represents a love for self and can lead to a meaningless existence. A premise in this discussion is that meaning comes from a love that transcends the self and reaches to others. For leaders to find meaning in leadership, service must extend beyond self to others.

A New Model: Meaning Through Doing

One of the principles of Logotherapy (Frankl, 1963, 1967) contends that meaning comes from doing a deed. One of the responsibilities of effective leadership is to give followers meaning in their work.

A young dean who had taken leadership of a small college noticed that many of his faculty members seemed discouraged and lacked clear direction in their work. The dean was convinced of their talents and worth and devoted a great deal of time and energy to encouraging the faculty members by telling them how he valued them as persons. He also broadcast the accomplishments of his faculty members in the community. As the dean continued this practice over a period of years, new life, vitality and purpose came to that group of academics. He thereby demonstrated two essential principles of Logotherapy. Not only did he find meaning for himself, as he valued his colleagues, but also he gave meaning to his followers.

In an address delivered to a Toronto audience, Frankl (1971) affirmed that one of the causes of meaninglessness in our culture is the incredible erosion of values. Some people would suggest that, not only have values eroded, but there has been a dramatic change in the process of arriving at values, and a substitution in shifting from the collective group to the individual.

Educational organizations are dynamic and therefore are constantly in the state of change. At no time is an organization subjected to as much stress as when change is occurring (Klassen, 1991; Levin, 1991). It is during these periods of transition that organizations are stressed to the maximum. When more change is demanded than organizations can tolerate, they become inflexible and finally break, akin to the metaphor that old wine skins will not tolerate the fermentation of the new wine. Because organizational changes introduce a great deal of uncertainty and frequently are very threatening to individuals, there must be a high level of order and a high degree of commitment and predictability for the members of the organization, to allow smooth transition and change to occur. When an organization changes order, confidence and trust can be built around the ongoing values and *principles* of that organization. Predictability can be structured around people or principles.

A young administrator found himself in the position of director of a school board, and from his initial days in that position he mentored potential leaders in that organization for his departure. He trained them well. When his five-year term expired and he was leaving, the organization functioned smoothly in spite of the Director's absence. The acting director was chosen from within the ranks. Despite the potential for stress and dissension, the organization had functioned smoothly throughout the eighteen-month search period. Even though people in leadership changed, the established principles continued to give stability and predictability to the organization. In this case, stable values and doing by the administrator (as discussed by Frankl) gave meaning to the organization in a time of tension. It is particularly important to have stable values within the organization when the values in the broader societal context surrounding it are changing.

A New Language

A generation ago values were measured on a continuum. In the model, positive and negative were the antithesis of each other; right and wrong were not only different but opposites. Today it would appear that another model is being used to assess values. Instead of a model based on antitheses or opposites we assess on the assumption of synthesis from a premise that values are not opposing each other, but rather, are merely different. Differences can most often be reconciled. Therefore, the question of right and wrong does not arise; the issue is simply which preference one has. All choices appear to be amoral.

The traditional model assumed an objective right and wrong response to moral dilemmas. Not that every deed could be neatly placed in one of those two categories, but it was believed that even where it was not clear in a given set of circumstances, there was an objective right and wrong response, although not fully known to the person at the moment. Just as microscopic inspection of filings over a magnetic field reveal each minute particle of metal taking an orientation to either north or south pole, so all events were valued as right or wrong. There was only one scale with two absolute directions and these directions were perceived to be the antithesis of each other. Consequently, the mind must be open to all possibilities. Nothing is to be missed or "devalued."

Our evolving language we speak is now reflecting this change in our valuing system. The focus is now on individualization with possibilities across a broad spectrum. Here, opposing distinctions of up/down, right/left, good/bad are being abandoned so individuals are free to make unbiased, unprejudiced decisions without any hint of external or previous value judgments in any way coloring or impinging on the decision-making process. In this system, generally, the judgments of our fathers are discounted, the wisdom of the ages is ignored, the voice of the church is silenced, the lessons of history are forgotten, and conscience is muzzled.

The trend is that every decision is based on its own merits; precedents are of no influence. A new age has dawned. The old is discarded. This calls for a continuous scanning and searching of the premises and assumptions which are held. Going back to "square one" is a perpetual exercise. This happens when the value base is no particular value base. There is unlimited freedom to make essential and foundational alterations in one's values. Although this pervasive freedom is at the heart of current existential philosophy, many writers lament its reality and seriously doubt the possibility of an individual's ability to effectively handle freedom of this magnitude (Fromm, 1941; Gairdner, 1990; May, 1983).

The change in the valuing system has had a profound effect on educational administration decision-making (Enns, 1981; Farquhar, 1981; Thom, 1984a; Thom & Klassen, 1986). The administrator is placed in a position where he must lead an organization whose members are not in fundamental agreement on the issue of values. Some argue that the present difficulties are nothing more than communication difficulties. Certainly, there are communication problems. But at the root of many conflicts in educational organizations is a more fundamental issue: there is a conflict of values and widely varying views on how to arrive at values. Writings of such individuals as Culbertson (1983), Renihan (1985), and Sharples (1984) pertain to this conflict.

Not all have adopted the new approach for deciding moral issues. Therefore, there are those who claim that right and wrong are opposing moral polarities, as well as those who claim that right and wrong are purely individual preferences with no need to be moral about it. This results in not only a conflict of communication, but a conflict of constructs. The former claim there are real issues that are worth dying for, and the latter claim that all issues can be reduced to the level of whether one prefers green or brown socks. This is not merely a question of a generation gap, of old school versus new school. It is a fundamental question of whether there are such constructs as correct and incorrect.

At times the search for limits is expressed by submission to a person, and at other times the need for limits is expressed by submission to a rule or principle. Millions in Germany were as eager to surrender their freedom as their fathers were dedicated to fight for it. Instead of wanting freedom, they tried to find ways to escape from it by submitting themselves to someone who could lead them.

The Bonds of Freedom

Paradoxically, while this generation cries for freedom to cast away the bonds of history, conscience, and church, it also begs for limited parameters and a locus of evaluation. It is generally assumed that two year olds and adolescents act out their aggression because they are rebelling against the limits that are imposed on them. However, it is likely that the motivation is a need to discern and discover the real limits. They have an intuitive need to know where the line is. Life itself can be accurately described as a search for limits (Fromm). There is a need to operate from a place that is firm and safe. However, it is only a well-defined, structured place, a place which can be clearly discerned from its environment that allows an individual to move to another place. Change to something is possible only when there is something definite to change to.

Dr. Reuven Feuerstein (1979, 1980) has dedicated the major part of his life to working with children, adolescents, and adults from the world over as they attempt to take up residence in Israel. Dr. Feuerstein initially used the traditional psychometric means of assessment in determining the level of learning ability for placement in the schools. To his surprise, he noted that there were some people groups which, as a culture, appeared to have an advanced ability to learn. Given the nature of these psychometric instruments Dr. Feuerstein knew that this was clearly impossible. Genes are not doled out in that way. He was curious as to how some people as a group had a learning ability which was superior/inferior to other groups. It was his experience that those groups which were superior would acculturate much more quickly. They could learn new ways of living more quickly; they fit into the new culture more quickly, with much less tension, and with greater comfort. Feuerstein, therefore, was interested in finding the nature of the culture which allowed people the ease of changing to another culture, and also the nature of the culture which made it difficult to change from one to another.

He discovered that in those cultures/contexts, no matter how primary or how advanced, which had *clearly defined thinking and behaving patterns*, were the people who could quickly find their way in a new culture. However, those cultures in which the thinking and behaving patterns were not well delineated or were ambiguously defined comprised the majority of individuals who found a new culture to be most confusing and the level of resistance to acculturation very high. The Feuerstein example illustrates the importance of structure.

A Safe Place

Common sense might suggest that those who are comfortable in a well-defined culture would resist the new, but this is not the case. In Feuerstein's work those who had a safe, well-defined, comfortable culture were the ones who could best learn and best accommodate to the new.

The key seems to be having a safe, comfortable place from which to start. It is as a launching pad is to a rocket. If the launching pad is solid and firm and immovable, the rocket will have a proper initial boost and will be accurate in its direction. If the launching pad is unstable, the lift-off will be in a random direction.

Feuerstein claims that those with a well-defined culture have "learned how to learn," while those with an ill-defined culture have been prevented from "learning how to learn." The main difference between the two seems to be the accuracy with which individuals are able to define the structures of their culture. In one culture the parents take ownership and go to great lengths to invest themselves in their children, carefully teaching them through formal and informal means the moral distinctions – what should and what should not be done where values ought to be placed, and how to arrive at values. Bold lines are drawn between right and wrong, preserving the wisdom of the forefathers. In that system, values are not judged by how old they are. The other culture takes little ownership in teaching their young. The parents understand little of the distinctions between values, so they just choose randomly or allow their feelings to guide them. Here, reason and logic have little place. Random chance becomes the order of the day. Here, neither parent nor child recognizes the moral distinctions.

Changing Cultures and Value Issues

Feuerstein is not alone in a belief he has that the basic building block of learning is the ability to distinguish, discriminate, and value positive from negative behaviors, good from bad beliefs, and right from wrong. To be able to discriminate fine differences is the secret to learning how to learn. We have many other examples of cultures (e.g., Native American Indian, Inuit, Innu) who for economic and other reasons have chosen to leave the traditional way and adopt the wider North American life style. But the change is a difficult one. Frequently they lose a generation or two in the transition period. The generation is lost because it neither clings to the traditional ways, nor has it fully embraced the new ways. So there it vacillates, between something which was and something which is not yet accepted.

The children in the transition generation have not learned to learn. There is little for them to hold on to, little they are sure about, no clear hierarchy of values, nothing really more important or less important than anything else. And children are the main "raison d'être" for schools and education, and this is the business of educational administrators.

Perhaps the most harmful blurring of our vision occurring today is in our language (Krauthammer, 1985). Where great value seems to be placed on "understanding" and being "empathetic," the language can become the vehicle of cognitive confusion. In our fear of being biased, being judgmental, and letting our prejudices show, we tend toward the use of words which are bleached of moral distinctions, neutral, value-free, and non-judgmental. When that happens, distinctions and debate surrounding values become impossible. It would appear that our language and culture presently favors the person who need not know distinctions, who lives in a sort of limbo – in a land where up and down, left and right, good and bad, right and wrong, and light and dark are synonymous, hopelessly blended, mingled and confused. Such lives can become a cloudy, murky haze, a twilight zone where shades of grey predominate, where distinctions are discouraged.

Dag Hammarskjöld, a former president of the United Nations, reminds us that the first commandment of mankind is that we respect the word. Through confusion of meanings and words we lose our ability to think clearly, to reason, and to communicate. Again, "learning how to learn" is dependent on the ability of individuals to make distinctions, having a language which allows individuals the ability to make distinctions between constructs, ideas, values, and behaviors. This is an important insight for educators to have.

There are some individuals who feel that those who claim to have some sort of a monopoly on the "truth" in educational administration are closed-minded and discourage open discussion on the subject. Yet, a mind set that gives equal weight and priority to all values, that is equally open to all, makes discussion most impossible. This position takes the very tools for arguing away.

When words for connoting differences are neutralized, we have chaos. Regardless, in all of this apparent conceptual confusion, educational leaders must make decisions.

The remainder of this discussion investigates how educational administrators manage and lead in changing value contexts.

Method and Findings

Over a five-year period educational administrators were questioned by the author in contact through various aspects of his work as a professor of educational administration – teaching, researching, consulting, and developing. There were particular contacts through being editor of the Canadian Society for the Study of Education (C.S.S.E.) *News*. The sample members were asked to comment on the nature of their job and what is required to be effective.

Following are some relevant highlights from the research:

– First, educational administrators are finding that the changing social order requires them to take great care in decision-making. Particularly, the Canadian Charter of Rights and Freedoms must be understood and carefully acknowledged.

– Second, administrators recognize that our mainstream society is Judaeo-Christian-based, a fact which influences them especially in considering how their decisions will be received by individuals and groups.

– Third, respondents did not totally agree on one set of profound, necessary, scientific conditions which produce excellence in educational administration. It would appear that the "scientific" model, alone, falls short of providing a complete explanation.

– Fourth, respondents did say, in general, that effective educational leaders are confident, optimistic about the worth of those being led, and take steps to provide conditions whereby the followers will release their potentials.

Discussion

General

This study was kept general considering the ongoing turbulence within society and education. The goal was to get an indication as to how educational administrators perceive the current milieu and to point some future directions.

The highlights above need consideration.

It should not surprise that educational administrators are feeling the effects of the Charter of Rights and Freedoms and the Judaeo-Christian cultural base. The Charter itself is prefaced with "Whereas Canada is founded upon principles that recognize the supremacy of God and the rule of law . . . " (Ricker et al., 1982), and Neuhaus (1984) comments:

The American experiment, which more than any other has been normative for the world's thinking about democracy, is not only derived from religiously grounded belief, it continues to depend upon such belief. (p. 27)

Further, Neuhaus states that democratic constitutions were made for a moral and a religious people. Historically, our first schools were established by Christian missionaries.

The Ontario *Education Act* cites as a duty of the teacher the following:

to inculcate by precept and example respect for religion and the principles of Judaeo-Christian morality and the highest regard for truth, justice, loyalty, love of county, humanity, benevolence, sobriety, industry, frugality, purity, temperance, and all other virtues; [Sec. 235.-(1)(c), p. 528] [revised to Sec. 264. in 1992].

Finally, Wynne (1989) believes that "effective school management is fostered by the application of relatively traditional moral values" (p. 128) where the Judaeo-Christian ethic is the base. "The Great Debate," University of Western Ontario, 1990, resulted in Christianity being decided a most rational world-view. These things should not surprise when one considers that Biblical values originally shaped and still shape many societies. These values are the source of many of the civilizing tendencies we take for granted. To construct a world-view or *Weltanschauung*, as it is called, is to systematize all human experience and knowledge (including the supernatural) into a unitary philosophy.

The literature on educational administration increasingly is giving attention to the importance of the spiritual or ethical/moral dimensions. The moral approach with conscience allows administrators to enjoy their position, leaving them with a sense of integrity and wholeness. Ultimately people are interested in ethics and goodness and justice and our common life does have a moral and religious character. Meaning and purpose, as Frankl reminds us, come through meeting the needs of someone other than ourself.

The challenge for administrators of our educational institutions today would appear to be a commitment to the beliefs upon which our society, our families, and our schools are based and to enhance one's capacity to resolve conflicts in competing belief systems. One does not have to be uncomfortable with the idea of principles, unless they are the hard, rigid principles defined by the pietistic. Principles such as respect, trust, kindness, and integrity make sense.

There are danger signals in our educational systems. There is a leadership crisis (Kerr, 1984). There are too few "great" administrators and too much administration without soul. Meaning, in the Frankl sense, must be found. Education is an extremely important activity in a society. It needs to have **absolutely excellent** individuals in charge of it. It is said that traditionally educational administration has not been able to attract the brightest talents, that the talented become the doctors and the lawyers. There is some validity in this. But this does not mean that our discipline should stop trying. Educators need to make every effort to recruit very capable individuals, provide them with superb training, and then give them continuing support for the sake of the students and the next generation. Administrators with a fundamental belief in values and conscience are desired.

Our cultural heritage and our written laws and constitution support that moral judgment and conscience be given attention among educational administrators. Only more recently have publications firmly addressed this. The study of educational administration for decades has been perceived predominantly as of a "scientific" flavor. But as Walker (1984) says, "surely, the whole organizational animal can be understood only when the 'scientific' and 'unscientific' are taken together". Management scholars of years ago, such as Barnard (1938), wrote of this. Walker strikes our moral sensitivities when he refers to the teacher as "ambassador of the society to the Kingdom of the child", and in the following:

> Contemporary practice in administering a kindergarten or system of kindergartens further exemplified the use of "soft" theory. Froebel, in developing the concept of the Kindergarten, justified his "children's garden" through transcendentalism, the unity of all living things with God. Thus, the flowers, trees, open air, and handling of the symbolic gifts all had mystical significance. Today, in most parts of the world, administrators of kindergartens are still guided in large part by Froebel's ideas. True, the "gifts" have gone, but the color, the movement, the activity have not. No principal, no teacher, no architect involved in this area of schooling can avoid the stubborn realities of that tradition. Moreover, in the elementary school and to some extent in the secondary school, these ideas linger on. Dewey, whose influence on the education of young children of the world is widely and gratefully acknowledge, did not hesitate to acknowledge his debt to Froebel. (p. 16)

The ambiguity and irrationality which abound within modern-day organizations creates an impression of many irreconcilable truths. Yet, in the end we are practical, rational people who value sincerity and caring, and the dignity of children and the family. Too often we let the idea that we have a secular society lead to the notion that a leader should not have a firm set of personal beliefs and values. It should be possible for administrators of our schools to be spiritual – leaders with a conscience – without apologizing.

Let us now summarize various beliefs which effective leaders hold.

Milton Rokeach (1969, 1973) has contributed a great deal to our understanding of the place of beliefs in human personality. Further, Arthur W. Combs has for many years continued research on the relationship between the belief system of professionals and their level of effectiveness. Also, Keirsey and Myers-Briggs personality scales and the values and goals instruments of Ervin Staub (1989) are of interest. Overall, what has been found is that certain beliefs lead to more effective leadership and the opposite beliefs lead to less effective leadership. It is therefore suggested that belief systems give each person a unity and harmony within and influence behavior. Logically then, there is a relationship between one's beliefs and one's effectiveness. Beliefs about the self, beliefs about others, and beliefs about the leader's purposes can be delineated.

Leader Beliefs About Self

It appears now that the leaders who have a strong sense of identification with others and who see themselves as a part of others are more effective. The less effective leaders see themselves apart from others. The leaders who have a sense of belonging with others, those who include a large circle and variety of individuals as part of themselves are effective. Leaders who are prone to making arbitrary distinctions leading to the exclusion of others are less effective. The more effective leader is comfortable in making the transition from "me" to "we." The less effective leader makes the transition from "me" to "we" with greater difficulty and with less frequency. (Refer to Figure 5-5)

The leaders who are more effective see themselves as adequate; they believe they can do it. They have a sense of identity with their task and profession and feel they can get the job done. Less effective leaders have serious doubts about their repertoire of skills to handle the situation and at times doubt their more stable characteristics (for example, intelligence).

More Effective Leader	Less Effective Leader
Identified:	Alienated:
A–Part–Of	A–Part–From
Capable	Incapable
Adequate	Inadequate
Wanted	Unwanted
Worthy	Unworthy
Trustworthy	Untrustworthy

Figure 5-5
Leader Beliefs About Self

More effective leaders perceive themselves as trustworthy. They believe that their decisions reflect commitment which leads them to do what they say they will do. They mean what they say, say what they mean, and do what they say they will do. Less effective leaders are not as certain that their own decisions will actually lead to what they promised. This is not to say that effective leaders do not fail. However, they realize that their response to failure is more important than failure itself. Leaders who see themselves as trustworthy take the necessary step to correct their failures in judgment and behavior. The less effective leaders use their mistakes as a reinforcement of their self-doubts. C.R. Swindoll (1985) supports an idea of the late President Eisenhower:

> . . . the supreme quality for a leader is unquestionably integrity. Without it, no real success is possible, no matter whether it is a section gang, on a football

field, in an army, or in an office. If his associates find him guilty of phoniness, if they find that he lacks forthright integrity, he will fail. His teachings and actions must square with each other. The first great need, therefore, is integrity and high purpose. (p. 37)

Effective leaders see themselves as worthy. They perceive that what they think, believe, and do makes a difference. They have a strong sense of self-worth and self-respect and a high regard for self. The effective leader has a high regard for self-balance, with an equally high regard and respect for others. The regard the effective leader has for self is not conditional upon a constant unending line of successes. Failures are taken in stride and interpreted as growth experiences. The less effective leaders lack this deep sense of respect for themselves and others. They have difficulty believing that their decisions matter and sense that what they believe, think, or do does not matter. They discount themselves and their failures simply reinforce their lack of significance.

Swindoll comments on leaders as being real people:

The popular yet mistaken mental image of a successful leader is the tough-minded executive who is always in control, who holds himself aloof, who operates in a world of untouchable, sophisticated secrecy. If he or she has needs, feels alone, wrestles with very human problems, lacks the ability to cope with some particular pressure . . . no one should ever know about it. And certainly there is no place for tears! That would be a sign of weakness, and real leaders don't cry . . . nor do they evidence any other emotion than a self-assured air of confidence. (p. 60)

Leader Beliefs About People

Leaders believe that people are able. They believe that people make the best decisions when given the freedom and responsibility. Part of the effective leader's task is to raise the autonomy level of the followers. There is a deep sense of trust in others and their capabilities.

Less effective leaders believe others are unable. They believe that others need constant surveillance and scrutiny. They do not delegate because the autonomy of their followers may be a threat to them. Furthermore, ineffective leaders need their followers to be dependent on them for personal reasons. They fear that their purpose and place will be taken away or diminished if the followers gain too much autonomy. Therefore, the less effective leader continues to hover over and make decisions for followers in a centralized authority.

The more effective leaders believe people are friendly and that generally people are well-intentioned. This belief is not held naively, as though people are not capable of negative or selfish intentions. However, the effective leader believes that people do the best they can. Sometimes this leader is mistaken, sometimes deceived, but when given the choice he/she would choose to be friendly rather than unfriendly. In contrast, less effective leaders see others as unfriendly and as a present or potential threat. They tend toward a "they-are-out-to-get-me" mentality.

The more effective leader believes others have worth, dignity, and respect which is not to be violated. They believe that the dignity of the individual is such that there is no end and no purpose so great that the devaluation of another's dignity is justified. Further, they view others as continually developing. The less effective leader, however, believes that there are purposes greater than some person's dignity. At times, when feeling personally threatened, less effective leaders will attack the dignity of the person rather than differ with an opponent on the issue of discussion.

More Effective Leader	Less Effective Leader
Able	Unable
Friendly	Unfriendly
Internall ymotivated	Externally motivated
Worthy	Unworthy
Helpful	Hindering
Dependable	Undependable

Figure 5-6
Leader Beliefs About People

More effective leaders believe that others are intrinsically motivated, that the prime source of motivation is within the person. The belief is that the most effective and the most lasting rewards are the ones which the individual senses inside himself/herself. Intrinsically motivated individuals respond best to encouragement. Effective leaders realize that the greatest benefit comes when they allow the creative energies of their followers to flow. Followers need time to think, reflect, decide, and act and, consequently, be responsible for their choices.

Less successful leaders believe people are most highly motivated by external sources. These leaders generally believe people need to be told, pushed, coerced, manipulated and cajoled. Their belief is that people are reflexive rather than reflective; react rather than act; are passive rather than creative and dynamic; and that the Stimulus-Response model describes people best rather than a model that incorporates insightful, reflective, and dynamic decision-making processes. Furthermore, less successful leaders believe that people are undependable – you cannot count on them – and that human behavior is so complicated and complex that you cannot really make sense out of it. Less effective leaders believe that human behavior is generally chaotic and best described as being controlled by chance of fate.

More effective leaders believe that people are helpful, less effective leaders believe people are hindering. The more effective leaders find their work with others fulfilling and a source of a great personal satisfaction. Less effective leaders find their work with others frustrating and more a source of irritation. They find their suspicions about the hindering nature of others to be more often than not fulfilled. Most important, effective leaders use conscience. (Figure 5-6 summarizes)

Leader Beliefs About Purposes

More effective leaders believe that their purpose is to free individuals and liberate them. Less effective leaders believe their purposes are to control people. The more effective leaders want to leave the individual with more options and more choices and therefore more freedom and more personal power. Less effective leaders lean in the direction of limiting the choices of their followers by reducing their power and control. More effective leaders aim to share power and control with their followers. They believe that competition with their followers results in loss of energy, whereas cooperation between leaders and followers regenerates the energy. Less effective leaders believe that competition between leader and follower are natural and that power struggles are reduced by pitting power against power. More effective leaders believe that their purpose is fulfilled when their followers are nurtured (mentored) to assume the role of leadership. The more prepared the followers are, the better the leaders feel they have completed their purpose. More effective leaders believe their purposes surround the larger issues of life, whereas less effective leaders believe their purposes are about particular and present tasks. The more effective leaders are able to focus on the principles and laws of life which regulate not only the present task but which rule the universe. Less effective leaders become quickly confused with present variations and changes and alterations because they fail to see "the big picture." Because their view is so limited in space and time, the less effective leader lacks historic perspective and depth and lacks vision about the present and the future. Every change to the less effective leader is more a source of irritation. The more effective leader places the present change of events within the larger framework of world events from the past, acknowledging the guidelines of life which have served mankind for all time. In this light, the present has purpose and direction and is comfortably challenging.

More effective leaders are self-revealing whereas less effective leaders are self-concealing. The more effective leaders are comfortable in disclosing their own private selves in appropriate ways. This does not mean that they constantly refer to themselves, but it does mean that their whole life is represented in their work. More effective leaders are involved in the lives of their followers whereas the less effective leaders keep alienated. The less effective leaders have a need to be secretive about their private selves which creates alienation and disinterest.

More Effective Leader	Less Effective Leader
Freeing	Controlling
Larger Issues-Oriented	Smaller Issues-Oriented
Principles-Oriented	Rules-Oriented
Long Term-Oriented	Short Term-Oriented
Whole- Oriented	Part- Oriented
Self- Revealing	Self-Concealing
Involved	Alienated
Altruistic	Narcissistic

Figure 5-7
Leader Beliefs About Purposes

Generally, the purposes of the more effective leader are altruistic whereas the less effective leader's purposes are self-serving. (Figure 5-7 summarizes)

It would appear from the above that there are only two kinds of leaders: those more effective and those less effective. However, we know that, in reality, leaders are found at different times and in differing circumstances somewhere along a continuum between effective and ineffective. It is not a simple question of either/or.

Beliefs of effective leaders are not recent discoveries of the social sciences. They have been represented continually and are a prominent part of our heritage. Our consciences are well versed in them. They are positive and important ideals stemming from sound values. This overview suggests that when leaders consciously incorporate these beliefs into their leadership roles they will be effective; they will excel both personally and professionally.

Conclusion

Values underlie all human activity. Contemporary society is in a values turbulence. This chapter has considered values as an essence of educational management and leadership and how administrators can operate effectively in changing value contexts. First, the progression of the influence of values in organizations and administration was explained, starting with a historical overview and culminating in discussion on the current role of values. Then, material from a research study of a group of contemporary educational administrators was presented.

It appears that society is opening up wide to accept all values – sound or unsound. This has caused educational administrators to take great care in decision-making, particularly in situations in which the Charter of Rights and Freedoms comes to bear. Interestingly, traditional Judaeo-Christian roots seem to be attaining new strength, perhaps due to the yuppie generation's maturing, and administrators sense a revival of clear notions of right and wrong with respect to decisions about education. Solid beliefs about self, about others, and about purposes give the educational administrator/leader a basis for integrity, justice, and conscience in leading in changing situations.

References

Althouse, J.G. (1953, September). The challenge of leadership. *Canadian Education, 3*(4).

Barnard, C.I. (1938). *The functions of the executive.* Cambridge, MA: Harvard University Press.

Beare, H., Caldwell, B., & Millikan, R. (1990). *Creating an excellent school: Some new management techniques.* New York, NY: Routledge.

Beck, C. (1986, Summer). Education for spirituality. *Interchange, 17*(2), 148-156.

Begley, P.T. (1990, October). How administrators' values influence their decisions. *The Canadian School Executive, 10*(4), 3-8.

Broudy, H.S. (1965). Conflicts in values. In H. Broudy, R. Ohm, & W. Monohan (Eds.), *Educational administration philosophy in action* (pp. 42-58). Norman, OK: College of Education, University of Oklahoma.

Campbell, R.F. (1978). A history of administrative thought. *Administrator's Notebook, 26*(4), 1-4.

Clark, D.L. (Ed.). (1992). *Educational leadership and the crisis of democratic culture.* University Park, PA: University Council for Educational Administration.

Codd, J. (1989). Educational leadership as reflective action. In John Smyth (Ed.), *Critical perspectives on educational leadership* (pp. 157-178). Philadelphia, PA: The Falmer Press.

Combs, A.W. (1979). *Myths in education: Beliefs that hinder progress and their alternatives.* Boston, MA: Allyn and Bacon.

Combs, A.W., Avila, D.L., & Purkey, W.W. (1978). *Helping relationships: Basic concepts for the helping professions* (2nd ed.). Boston, MA: Allyn and Bacon.

Corson, D. (1985, Summer). Quality of judgment and deciding rightness: Ethics and educational administration. *Journal of Educational Administration, 23*(2), 122-130.

Culbertson, J. (1983, December). Theory in educational administration: Echoes from critical thinkers. *Educational Researcher, 12*(10), 15-22.

Dolmage, W.R. (1992, August). The quest for understanding in educational administration: A Habermasian perspective on the "Griffiths-Greenfield debate." *The Journal of Educational Thought, 26*(2), 89-113.

Easton, D. (1957, April). An approach to the analysis of political systems. *World Politics, 9*, 383-400.

Enns, F. (1981, May). Some ethical – moral concerns in administration. *The Canadian Administrator, 20*(8), 1-8.

Evers, W., & Lakomski, G. (1991). *Knowing educational administration: Contemporary methodological controversies in educational administration research.* Oxford, England: Pergamon.

Farquhar, R.H. (1970). *The humanities in preparing educational administrators.* Eugene, OR: ERIC Clearinghouse on Educational Administration.

Farquhar, R.H. (1981, June). Preparing educational administrators for ethical practice. *Alberta Journal of Educational Research, 27*(2), 192-204.

Farquhar, R.H. (1989). Competence, confidence, and Carleton. An address presented on the occasion of his installation as President and Vice-Chancellor of Carleton University, Ottawa, ON, November 19th.

Feuerstein, R. (1979). *The dynamic assessment of retarded performers.* Baltimore, MD: University Park Press.

Feuerstein, R. (1980). *Instrumental enrichment.* Baltimore, MD: University Park Press.

Fiedler, F.E., & Chemers, M.M. (1984). *Improving leadership effectiveness: The leader match concept* (2nd ed.). New York, NY: Wiley.

Flower, G.E. (1958). Ideas and ideals of leadership in action. In G.E. Flower & F.K. Stewart (Eds.), *Leadership in action: The superintendent of schools in Canada.* Toronto, ON: W.J. Gage.

Foster, W. (1986). *Paradigms and promises: New approaches to educational administration.* Buffalo, NY: Prometheus Books.

Frankl, V.E. (1963). *Man's search for meaning: An introduction to logotherapy.* New York, NY: Washington Square Press.

Frankl, V.E. (1967). *Psychotherapy and existentialism.* New York, NY: Simon and Schuster.

Frankl, V.E. (1971). Youth in search of meaning. CGCA address delivered in Toronto, ON.

Fromm, E. (1941). *Escape from freedom.* New York, NY: Farrar and Rinehart.

Gairdner, W.D. (1990). *The trouble with Canada: A citizen speaks out.* Toronto, ON: Stoddart.

Gibb, J.R. (1970). Dynamics of leadership – Defensive and emergent. In J.E. Heald, L.G. Romero, & N.P. Georgiady (Eds.), *Selected readings on general supervision.* Toronto, ON. Collier-Macmillan.

The great debate: Christianity versus secular humanism (Professor William Craig and Dr. Henry Morgentaler). (1990). Held at the University of Western Ontario, London, ON, January 24th (on videocassette produced by Paragon Production Services, Vancouver, BC).

Greenfield, T.B., with Ribbins, P. (1992). *Greenfield on educational administration: Towards a humane science.* London, England: Routledge.

Greenfield, T.B., et al. (1985). The re-emergence of values and the transformation of organization and administrative theory. CASEA Symposium at the Canadian Society for the Study of Education Annual Conference, University of Montreal, Montreal, PQ, May 28th-31st. T.B. Greenfield (Putting meaning back into theory: The search for lost values and the disappeared individual); C. Hodgkinson (The value bases of administration and leadership: New directions in research); M. Holmes (The effects of the revival in traditional thought on educational administration as a profession); D. Allison (A critical response); E. Miklos (A critical reponse).

Greiner, L.E., & Schein, V.E. (1988). *Power and organization development: Mobilizing power to implement change.* Reading, MA: Addison-Wesley.

Griffith, F. (1979). Changing views of organizations and their administration. In F. Griffith (Ed.), Overview; *Administrative theory in education: Text and readings.* Midland, MI: Pendell.

Gue, L.R. (1985). *An introduction to educational administration in Canada* (2nd ed.). Toronto, ON: McGraw-Hill Ryerson.

Haire, M. (Ed.). (1975). *Modern organization theory.* Huntington, NY: R.E. Kreiger.

Hanson, E.M. (1979). *Educational administration and organizational behavior.* Boston, MA: Allyn and Bacon.

Hersey, P., & Blanchard, K.H. (1977). *Management of organizational behavior: Utilizing human resources* (3rd ed.). Englewood Cliffs, NJ: Prentice-Hall.

Hodgkinson, C. (1978). *Towards a philosophy of administration.* Oxford, England: Basil Blackwell.

Hodgkinson, C. (1983). *The philosophy of leadership.* Oxford, England: Basil Blackwell.

Hodgkinson, C. (1991). *Educational leadership: The moral art.* Albany, NY: State University of New York Press.

Holmes, M. (1989). On being correct without being right: Philosophical ultra-rationality and educational administration. *Interchange, 20*(3), 74-49.

Holmes, M., & Wynne, E.A. (1989). *Making the school an effective community.* New York, NY: The Falmer Press.

Jacobson, S.L., & Conway, J.A. (Eds.). (1990). *Educational leadership in an age of reform.* White Plains, NY: Longman.

Keith, S., & Girling, R.H. (1991). *Education, management and participation: New directions in educational administration.* Boston, MA: Allyn and Bacon.

Kerr, C. (1984). *Presidents make a difference: Strengthening leadership in colleges and universities.* Washington, DC: Association of Governing Boards of Universities and Colleges.

Klassen, D. (1991). A model for successful change in organizations. Paper, School of Education, Lakehead University, Thunder Bay, ON.

Koestenbaum, P. (1991). *Leadership: The inner side of greatness.* San Franciso, CA: Jossey-Bass.

Krauthammer, C. (1985). *Cutting edges: Making sense of the eighties.* New York, NY: Random House.

Lakomski, G. (1987a). Critical theory and educational administration. *Journal of Educational Administration, 25*(1), 85-100.

Lakomski, G. (1987b). Values and decision making in educational administration. *Educational Administration Quarterly, 23*(3), 70-82.

Levin, B. (1991, June). Understanding changing environment. Paper presented to CASEA at the Canadian Society for the Study of Education conference, Kingston, ON.

Lindblom, C.E. (1959). The science of "muddling through." *Public Administration Review, 19,* 79-88.

Maxcy, S.J. (1991). *Educational leadership: A critical pragmatic perspective.* Toronto, ON: OISE Press.

May, R. (1983). *The discovery of being.* New York, NY: W.W. Norton.

Mayo, E. (1933). *The human problems of an industrial civilization.* New York, NY: Macmillan.

McCuaig, M., & Thom, D.J. (1988, Fall). [Review of *World yearbook of education 1986: The management of schools* (edited by E. Hoyle & A. McMahon)]. *Canadian Journal of Education, 13*(4), 526-527.

McPherson, R.B., Crowson, R.L., & Pitner, N.J. (1986). *Managing uncertainty: Administrative theory and practice in education.* Columbus, OH: Charles E. Merrill.

Miklos, E., & Ratsoy, E. (Eds.). (1992). *Educational leadership: Challenge and change.* Edmonton, AB: Department of Educational Administration, University of Alberta.

Miller, V. (1965). Inner direction and the decision maker. In W.H. Hack, et al. (Eds.), *Educational administration: Selected readings.* Boston, MA: Allyn and Bacon.

Myers, I.B., & Briggs, K. (1962). *The Myers-Briggs type indicator.* Princeton, NJ: Educational Testing Service.

Nanus, B. (1992). *Visionary leadership: Creating a compelling sense of direction for your organization.* San Francisco, CA: Jossey-Bass.

Neuhaus, R.J. (1984, October). The naked public square. *Christianity Today,* 26-32.

Ontario Ministry of Education. and Training. *Education act.* Toronto, ON: Queen's Printer.

Ouchi, W.G. (1981). *Theory Z: How American business can meet the Japanese challenge.* Reading, MA: Addison-Wesley.

Perrow, C. (1973, Summer). The short and glorious history of organizational theory. *Organizational Dynamics, 2*(1), 2-15.

Popper, S.H. (1990). *Pathways to the humanities in school administration.* Tempe, AZ: University Council for Educational Administration.

Rallis, S.F. (1990). Professional teachers and restructured schools: Leadership challenges. In Brad Mitchell & Luvern L. Cunningham (Eds.), *Educational leadership and changing contexts of families, communities, and schools* (pp. 184-209). Chicago, IL: University of Chicago Press.

Renihan, P. (1985, Fall). Organizational theory and the logic of the dichotomy. *Educational Administration Quarterly, 21*(4), 121-134.

Ricker, J., Saywell, J., with Skeoch, A. (1982). *How are we governed in the '80s?.* Toronto, ON: Clarke, Irwin.

Rokeach, M. (1969). *Beliefs, attitudes and values.* San Francisco, CA: Jossey-Bass.

Rokeach, M. (1973). *The nature of human values.* New York, NY: Free Press.

Ryan, J. (1991). Transcending the limitations of social science: Insight, understanding and the humanities in educational administration. Paper, Department of Educational Administration, OISE, Toronto, ON.

Schön, D.A. (1983). *The reflective practitioner: How professionals think in action.* New York, NY: Basic Books.

Schön, D.A. (1987). *Educating the reflective practitioner.* San Francisco, CA: Jossey-Bass.

Schön, D.A. (1989). Professional knowledge and reflective practice. In Thomas J. Sergiovanni & John H. Moore (Eds.), *Schooling for tomorrow: Directing reforms to issues that count* (pp. 188-206). Boston, MA: Allyn and Bacon.

Sergiovanni, T.J. (1992). *Moral leadership: Getting to the heart of school improvement.* San Francisco, CA: Jossey-Bass.

Sharples, B. (1984, Fall). Values: The forgotten dimension in administration. *Education Canada, 24*(3), 32-37.

Smith, J.K., & Blase, J. (1991). From empiricism to hermeneutics: Educational leadership as a practical and moral activity. *Journal of Educational Administration, 29*(1), 6-21.

Smyth, J. (Ed.). (1989). *Critical perspectives on educational leadership.* Philadelphia, PA: The Falmer Press.

Sola, P.A. (1984). *Ethics, education and administrative decisions: A book of readings.* New York, NY: Peter Lang.

Starratt, R.J. (1991, May). Building an ethical school: A theory for practice in educational leadership. *Educational Administration Quarterly, 27*(2), 185-202.

Starratt, R.J. (forthcoming). *Building an ethical school.*

Staub, E. (1989, May). What are your values and goals? *Psychology Today,* 46-48.

Sungaila, H. (1990, May). Organizations alive! *Studies in Educational Administration, 52,* 1-26.

Swindoll, C.R. (1985). *Three steps forward, two steps back.* New York, NY: Bantam Books.

Taylor, F.W. (1923). *The principles of scientific management.* New York, NY: Harper and Bros.

Thom, B.E. (1990, December). Organization and management of the new municipal mega-department. *Municipal World, 100*(12), 3-6.

Thom, D.J. (1972). *The selection of new graduate students for an educational administration program.* Unpublished M.A. thesis, Ontario Institute for Studies in Education, University of Toronto, Toronto.

Thom, D.J. (1978, October). [Review of *Educational administration: The developing decades* (edited by L. Cunningham, W. Hack, & R. Nystrand, 1977)]. *Journal of Educational Administration, 16*(2), 229-231.

Thom, D.J. (1979, June). Educational administration in Canada: A tentative look at the academic culture. *The Saskatchewan Educational Administrator, 11*(4), 36-61.

Thom, D.J. (1982, May). Educational administration in Canada: Critical analysis and recommendations. *The Canadian Administrator, 21*(8), 11-15.

Thom, D.J. (1984a, Winter). The spiritual factor in educational administration (To make great gains in our schooling systems). *McGill Journal of Education, 19*(1), 79-93.

Thom, D.J. (1984b, November). Educational administration theory development in the 1980s: A practical academic's assessment. *New Horizons, 25,* 161-176.

Thom, D.J. (1986). On improving society and schools. *Comment on Education, 17*(1), 7-12.

Thom, D.J. (1990, Spring/Summer). Bureaucracy, informal systems, and school leadership. *The Saskatchewan Educational Administrator, 22*(2), 25-33.

Thom, D.J. (1992). The Hong Kong council for educational administration (HKCEA): Conscience and leadership. Invited address to the Seventh Regional Conference of the Commonwealth Council for Educational Administration, "Educational Administrators - Facing the Challenges of the Future," Hong Kong, August 21st.

Thom, D.J., & Klassen, D. (1986, Spring). Educational administration with conscience: Seeking the 'truth'. *McGill Journal of Education, 21*(2), 125-139.

Thom, D.J., & Klassen, D. (1988). Educational administration in search of meaning: Serving with conscience. In D.J. Thom with D. Klassen, *Education and its management: Science, art, and spirit* (pp. 299-318). Needham Heights, MA: Ginn Press of Simon & Schuster.

Thom, D.J., with Klassen, D. (1988). *Education and its management: Science, art, and spirit.* Needham Heights, MA: Ginn Press of Simon & Schuster.

Torbert, W.R. (1990). Reform from the center. In Brad Mitchell & Luvern L. Cunningham (Eds.), *Educational leadership and changing contexts of families, communities, and schools* (pp. 252-264). Chicago, IL: University of Chicago Press.

Townsend, R.G. (1988). *They politick for schools.* Toronto, ON: OISE Press.

Van Meter, E.J. (1973, Autumn). Theory in educational administration: An instructional module teaching approach. *Educational Administration Quarterly, 9*(3), 81-95.

Walker, W.G. (1991). Tight ship to tight flotilla: The first century of scholarship in educational administration. Invited address, Committee on International Relations, American Educational Research Association, Chicago, IL, April 4th.

Walker, W.G. (1984, Fall). Administrative narcissim and the tyranny of isolation: Its decline and fall, 1954-1984. *Educational Administration Quarterly, 20*(4), 7-23.

Walker, W.G.,Farquhar, R.H., & Hughes, M., (Eds.). (1991). *Advancing education: School leadership in action*. Basingstoke, Hamps: The Falmer Press.

Wendel, F.C. (Ed.) (1991). *Enhancing the knowledge base in educational administration*. University Park, PA: University Council for Educational Administration.

Wendel, F.C. (Ed.). (1992). *Applications of reflective practice*. University Park, PA: University Council for Educational Administration.

Wynne, E.A. (1989). Managing effective schools: The moral element. In Mark Holmes, Kenneth A. Leithwood, & Donald F. Musella (Eds.), *Educational policy for effective schools* (pp. 128-142). Toronto, ON: OISE Press.

6

Organizational Framework

During a century's quest for knowledge, leading scholars of educational administration have constantly worn cloaks of science. However, the fabric from which the cloaks were cut, the patterns that shaped them, the distinctive styles they reflected, and the societal climate in which they were worn have changed as one era gave way to another.

Culbertson, 1988, pp. 20-21

Introduction

The discussion in the previous chapter highlights the importance of values, beliefs, and sound morals and ethics for leadership in education. In the quest for a general theory, scholars have become more courageous in asserting that ethics and morals provide the paradigm solution; Hodgkinson goes so far as to mention "faith." But they still lack the courage to extend the concept of leadership as a moral science or art to religion, and to clearly say that a person's foundation belief in a divine being is logical and true.

It is suggested that the Judaeo-Christian doctrine with God, its core "do unto others," and the ten commandments is a good base from which to understand and to operate. Again, without belaboring religious arguments, there is ample support for this base. Our society and culture and its educational systems traditionally are rooted in Judaeo-Christianity. And it could be said that it is a tolerance inherent in the doctrine which has permitted the development of multiculturalism (many countries would not allow such). The Bible, with all its imperfections, is the best-selling book in the world; Christianity is a popular, rational world-view. Moreover, it is intriguing how so many people turn to religion in troubled times. People have always sought self-discipline, and theology provides needed standards for this control, external to human beings themselves. The "yuppie" generation are coming around to Judaeo-Christian values (those with which many of them were raised and then abandoned for awhile). Christian advocates are "fighting back," as people do, as they feel threatened by critics, a depersonalizing technological society, and complex outcomes from multiculturalism. Ellul (1986) refers to "the subversion of Christianity" whereby a Christian-based society has developed to look opposite to what it should according to the Bible. As maturing individuals grow away from "me first" thinking to concerns of actions and consequences, death and decay, and caring and forgiveness, they gain understanding and wisdom. Conscience becomes Christian-shaped.

Educational leadership definitely is moving away from science interpretations and now has an emphasis of moral entity and the spirit (Bates, 1989). And moral values tie to customs, law, and, ultimately, theology, things which hold the society together. Perhaps what makes people hesitant to accept Judaeo-Christian doctrine as an important base is that the Bible is from long ago, is quite academic, and, without careful and intense study, it is not easily comprehensible. Not everyone wants to put out the effort. No doubt, Christians have been given "a bad name" in recent years because of such things as morality scandals among media evangelists and feminist interpretation that the Scriptures record women as subservient to men. Further, secular humanism, with its denial of evil, is a tempting competitor. And oftentimes oppression of the poor and wars are blamed on religion when politics and economics are largely the basis. Or when innocent people are killed in a crash, it is asked, "How can there be a God to let this happen?" Here, physics and God are confused. People are sometimes mistaken as to what *is* and *is not* "of Christianity." Emotional reactions to religion can get in the way of intellectual ones (see "The Great Debate," 1990).

Jacques Ellul's ideas provide some illumination:

> Jacques Ellul in *The Technological Society* calls for a re-examination of what he describes as the essential tragedy of a civilization increasingly dominated by technique. He puts forceful emphasis upon the erosion of moral values brought about by technicism (referring not only to machine technology but to any complex of standardized means for attaining often carelessly examined ends). The society becomes, not the expression of the will of the people nor a divine creation, but an enterprise providing services that must be made to function efficiently. Politics revolves around what is useful rather than what is good. Ellul sees every part of a technical civilization responding to the social needs generated by technique itself, and progress then consisting in progressive dehumanization. Men suffer from a spiritual privation.
>
> Jacques Ellul's therapy for the technical disease which he sees as pervading society, including the activity of management, is Christian therapy – whereby one affirms one's freedom through the revolutionary nature of one's religion. . . . Ellul actively encourages recognition of "the extraordinary power of spiritual resistance to technical invasion of which human beings are capable," and exclaims, "it does not seem that those sources of vital energy which might be summarized as sexuality, spirituality, and capacity for feeling have been impaired." (Thom, 1984a, p. 85)

As well, Ellul (1986) presents sound arguments against the claim of chauvinism in the Scriptures.

Chester Barnard (1938) in his writings gave ample support to the "spiritual factor" in management/leadership and a philosophy generally consistent with

Christianity. He held a general "organization as a religion" type of view. He says:

> . . . organization is a new entity. You cannot get organization by adding up the parts. They are only one aspect of it. To understand the society you live in, you *feel* organization – which is exactly what you do with your non-logical minds – about your nation, the state, your university, your church, your community, your family. (p. 317)

Further:

> Such a story (the story of man in society) calls finally for a declaration of faith . . . I believe that the expansion of cooperation and the development of the individual are mutually dependent realities, and that a due proportion or balance between them is a necessary condition of human welfare. Because it is subjective with respect both to a society as a whole and to the individual, what this proportion is I believe science cannot say. It is a question for philosophy and religion. (p. 296)

At several points Barnard suggests he believes the best leaders to be religious, in the true sense of the word:

> Executive responsibility, then, is that capacity of leaders by which, reflecting attitudes, ideals, hopes, derived largely from without themselves, they are compelled to bind the wills of man to the accomplishment of purposes beyond their immediate ends, beyond their times . . . when these purposes are high and the wills of many men of many generations are bound together they live boundlessly. (pp. 283-284)

Both Ellul and Barnard see a need for very optimistic Christian people.

Moreover, world-famous surgeon and scientist Wilder Penfield concluded that the scientific study of the brain would not explain the mind and spirit:

> Wilder Penfield had come a long way from the basic scientific conclusions that had made him famous. In the years after his career as an active scientist and surgeon ended, he had watched science contributing to an increasingly materialistic world. He felt that scientists had allowed people to believe that science would ultimately provide all the answers, and in doing so had undermined their faith in God. If humans were no more than sophisticated animals then talk of the soul and God must be rubbish; love was no more than an excess of hormones, a sense of destiny no more than self-delusion. He refused to believe it was so. Perhaps the time had come for him to speak as a scientist, to go back to his basic data and at least reiterate his point about the limits of scientific understanding. (Lewis, 1981, p. 295)

Ellul, Barnard, and Penfield thus support the theological base. The prevalence of Judaeo-Christian doctrine worldwide and its basis in education and educational leadership is notable.

Truth in the world is "hidden," and both spirit and science need to be included in persons' making choices, else the search for what is there is limited. From study of the universe, Hawkings (1988, 1992) acknowledges this view.

More and more, science and religion are coming to agreement on how the universe came to be. As a final reference, consider Campbell (1988):

> – the edge, the interface between what can be known and what is never to be discovered because it is a mystery that transcends all human research. The source of life – what is it? No one knows. We don't even know what an atom is, whether it is a wave or a particle – it is both. We don't have any idea of what these things are.

> That's the reason we speak of the divine. These's a transcendent energy source. When the physicist observes subatomic particles, he's seeing a trace on a screen. These traces come and go, come and go, and we come and go, and all of life comes and goes. That energy is the informing energy of all things. (p. 132)

An appreciation of committing oneself to the "unknown" part of experience – nurturing faith – is gained.

Educational leadership as a moral entity is developed and extended throughout the remainder of this book. It is done so in a realistic fashion, always acknowledging the need to balance human relations/spiritual concepts with the realities of organizational politics and power. Before focusing on the latter realities, the Organization Development (teambuilding) technology is now presented.

Organization Development (Teambuilding)

As Bennis (1989) indicates, there have emerged in society important social forces – "such as the sense of alienation from the powers that shape our lives and the increasing tension between individual rights and the common good" which are making it difficult for administrators to be effective. How can leaders develop the vision and authority required?

We live in a society in which we cannot control everything and those who deserve credit for things do not always get it. Further, both good and evil *do* exist; Perrow refers to the "forces of light" and "forces of darkness." This is the broader context in which the educational administrator must work.

Earlier, various research-based sociological and administrative perspectives were presented. These included the main structures and groups involved in the education culture. Two key points to be recalled and kept in mind are that students and the teaching/learning process are ultimately what educational administrators' work is all about and (2) it is crucial for the administrator/leader to have a philosophy which is based in sound values ("believe in something or you will fall for anything").

Within the structures and surrounding the groups earlier presented, the educational administrator must employ a style. The question is what is an effective style in the contemporary educational context?

What is of interest here is "what works." Earlier it was mentioned that in these times a values/law-justice approach to being an effective educational administrator/leader is required. Following are some preliminary elements of this approach:

• Certain skills are required in the following areas – listening/feedback; leadership; communication patterns, and decision-making;

• A sound character is required, supplemented by political astuteness;

• Overall the effective administrator must be prepared, be organized, be optimistic, stay healthy, and have good relationships with others who are influential in accomplishing goals. (Sometimes it is "not what you know but who you know");

• The administrator needs to be a politician in several areas. He/she needs to respect various groups, such as women, natives, the handicapped etc., to have concern for their rights and freedoms, and to listen and be responsive to their concerns. Yet, a balance is required so as to not have the non-minority groups feeling overlooked. The administrator needs to have the ability to "wear different hats" in different situations and often to stay uninvolved emotionally. This relates to being able to sometimes disagree with superordinates, to make unpopular decisions, and to sometimes place issues on hold. It also means, when required, staying out of some situations and emphasizing others. The bottom line is that the administrator needs to practice *democratic administration*;

• The effective educational administrator needs to understand the importance of the family in society. The family is societal "glue" which is necessary to yield good students and citizens. It needs to be supported especially in these times when many educational institutions increasingly are excluding values and religion ideas from their programs; and

• The effective educational administrator needs to be concerned about money, but he/she must be extremely careful to not overemphasize personal economics.

Some individuals believe that there are no clear, valid guidelines for being an effective educational administrator. This is unfortunate. Although contexts may be different and may change over time, many years of research and development have revealed effective common elements for success.

Considering all that has just been said, the technology of Organization Development (O.D.) is an appropriate preliminary framework on which to build an upgraded educational leadership approach.

In these times of uncertainty and reform, one thing which is certain is change. Many writers have predicted the future, but events happen so fast that it is difficult to be accurate. George Orwell, in his book *1984*, was amazingly uncanny with respect to what eventually did develop, in predicting such concepts as "big brother"-directed bureaucracies and individuals pursuing personal interests often to the extreme. Further, Fullan (1982), Sarason (1982), and Toffler (1990) each present unique views.

Accepting the inevitability of change, the concept of "teambuilding" is a very workable approach in educational organizations. This is an approach that combines sociology and administrative ideas, both past and developing, and is rooted in sound values which are appropriate for education of today and tomorrow. It includes the need at times for toughmindedness, courage, and the application of law, politics, and justice particularly.

Teambuilding is now presented with a focus on skill development under the categories: Listening/Feedback; Leadership; Communication Patterns; and Decision-Making. This material provides a foundation for Thom's "Educational Leadership with CONSCIENCE" (TELC) Model which is introduced later.

Teambuilding is a core of the general organizational management technology called "Organization Development" (O.D.). It does not occur in a vacuum but, to be effective, must take a realistic account of the relevant organizational culture.

Every organization has a structure. It has at least a set of goals, policies, an administrative hierarchy, a program or curriculum, a physical facility, equipment, finances, a group of workers, decision-making processes, and a clientele to serve. This structure may or may not be effective depending on the quality of human relations within.

Elton Mayo's ideas apply well to the management of educational institutions. N.K. Henderson summarizes Mayo's contribution to the "art of management":

(a) Work is a group activity.

(b) The social world of the adult is primarily patterned about work activity.

(c) The need for recognition, security, and sense of belonging is more important in determining workers' morale and productivity than the physical conditions under which he/she works.

(d) A complaint is not necessarily an objective recital of facts; it is commonly a symptom manifesting disturbance of an individual's status position.

(e) The worker is a person whose attitudes and effectiveness are conditioned by social demands from both inside and outside the work plant.

(f) Informal groups within the work plant exercise strong social controls over the work habits and attitudes of the individual worker.

(g) The change from an established to an adaptive society (i.e., from the older type of community life to the atomistic society of isolated individuals, from eotechnic to paleotechnic society) tends continually to disrupt the social organization of a work plant and industry generally.

(h) Group collaboration does not occur by accident; it must be planned for and developed. If group collaboration is achieved, the work relations within a work plant may reach a cohesion which resists the disrupting effects of adaptive society.

These ideas support teambuilding.

Further, from Henderson's research on what employees like and expect in their leaders he has found the following:

(a) *He must inspire confidence* – e.g., be authoritative, consistent, clear-headed, "know what he himself wants".

(b) *He must be humane, and approachable* – not too far "above the crowd." People like to know their leader is fair-minded and just, kind and reasonable.

(c) *He must not be so familiar and common* that his followers do not respect him ("familiarity breeds contempt"). A certain distance, a respectable status is expected.

(d) *He must be predictable* – People like leaders they understand and "know how to take." Bad temper, unreliability and inconsistency, and favoritism are all *bad* qualities in leaders and undermine people's good regard.

(e) *The leader must understand people* – He must be a good judge of human nature. He can allow for human weaknesses yet optimize the efforts of his employees or followers.

The leader must be dominant without being too dominating and have the ability to make decisions but involve the group in the process.

Democracy in educational administration is very important. Democratic administration does not necessarily mean majority rule, for a majority's opposition to an administrator's sound proposed solution may be based on such things as ignorance of total information or fear of change. However, it is characterized by a professional attitude, a spirit of mutual concern, respect for every individual, and a willingness to work together toward valued goals (Griffith, 1966). It is amazing how long a time some leaders require to appreciate that democracy implies a *sharing* by leader and followers.

Most of these contextual ideas point to a teambuilding approach as most effective for managing and leading contemporary organizations, particularly in handling change in educational institutions.

Again, "teambuilding" is the core of the technology called Organization Development (O.D.). As the term itself implies, it involves the building of effective work teams within organizations. O.D. is a planned, system-wide, and sustained change effort designed to accomplish a satisfactory integration of the needs and goals of the organization and its members. It focuses on the work culture and diagnosis, and it aims for renewal and improvement.

This is a powerful technology which changes individuals' lives because of its strong emphasis on human relations and on communication particularly. It is an attractive approach because it involves all members of the organization, and it accepts the reality of change and promotes practical ways of dealing with it. Through O.D./teambuilding training, people develop their listening, leadership, and caring skills. The organization development technology involves the *application* of behavioral science theories *to practice* which, in itself, is very powerful.

There are purported weaknesses of the O.D. approach. To a large extent they can be overcome. For instance, the human relations emphasis is thought by some to be "soft," with not enough authoritative clout behind it. Some administrators feel that they need to maintain more distance between themselves and workers than this approach allows. Further, when organizational members all input into decisions, it is sometimes difficult to determine who is accountable for outcomes. Another concern is that once the O.D. technology is in place, long-term commitment and in-house training agents are required for it to realize its full potential. Finally, some argue that O.D. involves manipulating participants' behavior too much. Despite these arguments, O.D. is generally more meaningful and leads to more involvement than many other management approaches, and it can produce lasting gains in organizations. The seasoned leader appreciates that a group is not necessarily a team, and O.D. contributes to attaining teams of high function in this age of collaboration and collectivism. It is interesting how the approach was popular up until the 1970s, then fell out of favor for awhile, and is now again popular. This is no doubt a reflection of changing attitudes within society. Figure 6-1 compares traditional and O.D. values.

	Traditional Values	O.D. Values
1.	People cannot be trusted.	People can be trusted.
2.	People are productive resources: they are almost like office equipment; when they don't work, they can be replaced.	People are human beings: we have a commitment to provide an opportunity for each member, as well as the organization as a whole, to live up to their potential. This may mean reworking the office structure so that it fits the unique capabilities and weaknesses of the staff.
3.	People are primarily motivated by material rewards: pay them enough and you'll keep them happy.	People are motivated primarily by planning and influencing how they relate to their work. This does not mean that salary is unimportant, but alone it does not motivate people to achieve in any unusual way.
4.	Time spent in getting and keeping clients is the most important thing for a partner.	Time spent in people management within the firm is as important as client contact.
5.	People can't or won't change.	People are our largest untapped resource. One of the most important aspects of a key executive's job is to help his people find how they want to change for their own and the firm's benefit, then help them to alter their style and performance.
6.	Partners should go along with the wishes of their other partners so that they all get along together; rocking the boat should be avoided.	Conflict between partners, when it is well managed, is the lifeblood of the partnership.

7.	It is up to the individual to motivate himself.	It is my responsibility as a partner and manager to create an environment where it is possible for my subordinates to find exciting and creative work.
8.	One of the important skills of a manager is to convince people to accept what you want by making them think it is what they want.	It is important to be open and authentic in expressing your thoughts and feelings to your staff. This may cause conflict, and unhappiness temporarily, but in the long run the atmosphere is much more conducive to growth and productivity.
9.	The measure of a meeting's effectiveness is how many decisions per hour have been made. The measure of my success in a meeting is whether my suggestions were accepted.	The quality, not quantity, of decisions is most important – and quality is related to the quality of the process for making decisions; it requires openness, frank conflict, and a spirit of trying to find the best solution, rather than win-lose atmosphere where individuals and coalitions root for their own ideas.

Figure 6-1
Traditional vs. O.D. Values
From *The Financial Post* (Canada), June 17, 19⁷⁶.

O.D. is broadly based. It is associated with all of the following concepts: listening/feedback; leadership; communication; decision-making; process; perception; consensus; ownership, delegation; confrontation; conflict; synergy; competition/cooperation; help/hinder/intervention; collaboration; trust; openness; renewal; dyads; triads; and fishbowl (inner/outer circles). Further, many excellent training films on conflict, group decision-making, time management, and so on, exist for use in O.D. work. (Some major oil companies, such as Shell, are producers.)

The hierarchy of human needs by Abraham Maslow and Douglas McGregor's Theory X and Theory Y relate nicely. The essence of these appear in Figures 6-2 and 6-3.

Maslow's hierarchy is of special importance because it gives insight into what motivates the individual, recognizing that an unsatisfied need is a strong motivator. It is said that, in his later years, Maslow added above self-actualization the two need areas of "wonder" and "order" as shown, and generally regretted that he had not emphasized more the spiritual in his life's work.

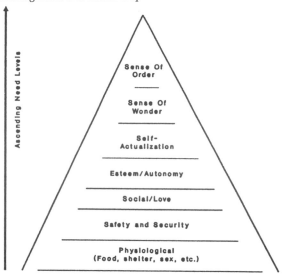

Figure 6-2
Maslow's Hierarchy of Human Needs

	THEORY X (reductive)		THEORY Y (developmental)
1.	The average human being has an inherent dislike of work and will avoid it if he can.	1.	Work is as natural as play if the conditions are favorable.
2.	Most people are not ambitious, have little desire for responsibility, and want security above all.	2.	The average human being learns, under proper conditions, not only to accept but to seek responsibility.
3.	Most people must be closely controlled, and often coerced to achieve organizational objectives.	3.	Man will exercise self-direction and self-control in the service of objectives to which he is committed.
4.	Most people have little capacity for creativity in solving organizational problems.	4.	The capacity for creativity in solving organization problems is widely, not narrowly, distributed in the population.
5.	Motivation occurs only at the physiological and security levels.	5.	Motivation occurs at the affiliation, esteem, and self-actualization levels as well as the physiological and safety levels.
	The Central Principle of Organization: Direction and Control through the exercise of authority.		The Central Principle which derives from Theory Y is integration: Individual and Organizational goals.

Figure 6-3
D. McGregor's Assumptions About People

The McGregor theory is of importance largely because it gives insight into how individuals interact. A basic premise of the Theory Y approach is that individuals by nature wish to do well, and if the conditions in which they work are favorable they will be responsible and perform well.

A multitude of theories on human behavior and organization, including those of Maslow and McGregor, can be interconnected. From all of this, the author has come to view the maintenance of rigor in the education system in terms of basic human needs, institutional needs, home and church, and a sound values system. These entities interact at a point in time and the sound values system should control all.

Skill Development

An essence of O.D. training is skill development in the areas of listening/feedback, leadership, communication patterns, and decision-making. Texts such as Daresh (1991) provide a nice summary of theories in these areas.

Listening/Feedback

It is interesting how poorly we listen, particularly as we age and become more set in our ways. Often O.D. trainees have a difficult time because they arrive from a job in which there is a fast pace and time pressure and they are used to making quick decisions and giving orders. In the training it is difficult for many of these individuals to slow down. Often the first phase is to re-educate participants on how to listen (and to feed back) to others; many have difficulty.

Figure 6-4 indicates effective listening skills. Some of the most important guidelines are the following: judge content, rather than delivery (e.g., voice quality); hold your reaction until you are certain that you thoroughly understand the speaker's point; look at the other person; control any anger; avoid jumping to conclusions; and avoid stereotyping.

"Feedback" skills involve some of the same listening skills. It is best when feedback is descriptive rather than evaluative, specific rather than general, well-timed, and when it involves perception checks or rephrasing for understanding.

Granted, to keep one's emotions out of listening/feedback as the above suggests is a tall order for any mature person.

There are many exercises for teaching listening/feedback skills. One is to set up three people in a triad – one the speaker, one the listener, and one the observer. The speaker first reads some provided, brief story to the listener, the listener then feeds back the essence of the story to the speaker and the observer describes to the other two how well the listening and feedback went. Another exercise is to give a shape on a piece of paper to one person, then, without letting the second person see, have the first describe the shape to the second and have the second person draw the shape from their listening. Then, see how congruent the drawn shape is with the original. A first round might involve the speaker with his/her back to the listener and then the two facing each other as a second round. Further, the complexity of the shapes can be increased through various rounds. There are many variations on this exercise. Again, it is useful to have an observer to give objective feedback to the speaker and listener.

INEFFECTIVE	EFFECTIVE
Non-Verbal Behavior	
Listener looks bored, uninterested or judgmental; avoids eye contact; displays distracting mannerisms (doodles, plays with a paper clip and so forth).	Listener maintains positive posture; avoids distracting mannerisms; keeps attention focused on speaker; maintains eye contact; nods and smiles when appropriate.
Focus of Attention	
Listener shifts focus of attention to himself; "When something like that happened to me, I . . . ,"	Listener keeps focus of his/her comments on the speaker; "When that happened, what did you do?"
Acceptance	
Listener fails to accept speaker's ideas and feelings; "I think it would have been better to . . ."	Listener accepts ideas and feelings; "That's an interesting idea; can you say more about it?"
Empathy	
Listener fails to empathize; "I don't see why you felt that . . . "	Listener empathizes; "So when that happened, you felt angry."
Probing	
Listener fails to probe into an area, to follow up on an idea or feeling.	Listener probes in a helpful way (but does not cross examine); "Could you tell me more about that? Why did you feel that way?"; listener follows-up; "A few minutes ago you said that . . .."
Paraphrasing	
Listener fails to check the accuracy of communication by restating in his own words important statements made by the speaker.	Listener paraphrases at the appropriate time.
Summarizing	
Listener fails to summarize.	Listener summarizes the progress of the conversation from time to time.
Advise	
Listener narrows the range of alternatives by suggesting a "correct" course of action.	Listener broadens the range of ideas by suggesting (or asking the speaker for) a number of alternatives.

Figure 6-4
Listening Skills

Leadership

Development of leadership skills is a second important step in O.D. training. Earlier there was mention of effective leadership styles. Many individuals do not know their style and there are tools which can measure this. (See Appendix D.) Effective leaders have skills in *task* (goal-oriented) and *maintenance* (people-oriented) realms and tend to fall into one of three styles: authoritarian; laissez-faire; or democratic. The most effective leader in these times generally is democratic but, in the interest of accountability, will reserve the right to the final decision on issues ("executive privilege").

A useful exercise for leadership skills development is to give a group an issue to discuss, have them choose their leader(s), and then have the group evaluate the quality of leadership displayed during the exercise. Leadership involves good listening and feedback.

The specific leadership frameworks of Appendix D have the task/maintenance core.

Communication Patterns

Group members often are not aware of important communication problems. Perhaps a few people do most of the talking. An individual might talk too long on a point. The discussion might be one-way, not two-way. It is detrimental to have some members "left out." Figure 6-5 summarizes some key communication detractors.

1.	Overtalk	13.	Topic avoidance
2.	Undertalk	14.	Topic shifting
3.	Fast talk	15.	Topic persistence
4.	Slow talk	16.	Remote statements
5.	Loud talk	17.	Overresponsiveness
6.	Quiet talk	18.	Underresponsiveness
7.	Emotional talk	19.	Excessive question-asking
8.	Verbal obtrusions	20.	Dogmatic assertion
9.	Abusive talk	21.	Presumptive attribution
10.	Acknowledgement deficit	22.	Double-level messages
11.	Positive talk deficit	23.	No eye contact
12.	Countercomplaining		

Figure 6–5
Communication Detractors

Body language/gestures and nonverbal cues generally can be important – facial expression, comfort of the setting, posture, touching, eye contact, hand gestures, spatial distance, and so on. Caplow (1983) even suggests that the shape of the meeting table, e.g., round, oval, rectangular, etc. and the position and color of chairs can make a difference. Figure 6-6 indicates preferred places to sit.

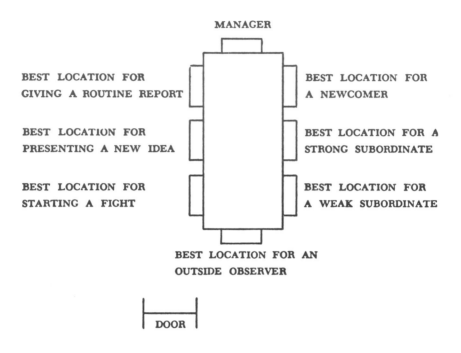

Figure 6–6
Preferred Seating in a Meeting

From *Managing an Organization* (2nd ed.) by Theodore Caplow, 1983, p. 76. Copyright 1983 by Holt, Rinehart & Winston, Toronto, ON. Reprinted by permission.

A useful training exercise for developing skills with respect to communication patterns is to set up a "fishbowl," or inner/outer circle structure, and have the inner-circle people discuss an issue while the outer-circle people use the scheme in Figure 6-7.

You are asked to *observe*: 1) Who talks to whom? 2) How often? 3) How long? You record observable overt behavior without making an analysis of it.

A simple way to chart this pattern is illustrated.

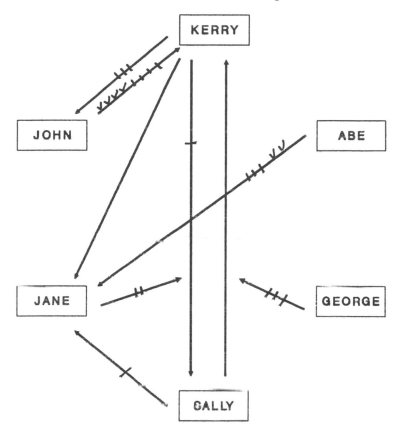

In this chart you will observe that:

1. John spoke to Kerry 4 times and not to anyone else. "1" across an arrow indicates one time).

2. Kerry spoke to John 3 times and once to Sally.

3. Jane received communication from 2 of the participants, but spoke to the group generally 2 times.

4. Abe spoke to Jane 3 times and not to anyone else.

5. George did not speak to anyone directly but spoke to the group 3 times. Similarly, George was not the recipient of any communication.

6. Length of the time is measured by putting down a check mark (v) along the upper side of interaction lines every few seconds, as long as the speaker continues.

e.g., John's statements were fairly lengthy; Abe's were very brief.

Figure 6-7
Group Communication Patterns

The O.D. trainees will come to appreciate the patterns of communication and then can proceed to analyze why it is that way and how to improve on it. For instance, Jane, in the example above, should be encouraged to participate more. Who is showing leadership? What are the effective and ineffective styles?

Decision-making

In O.D. skill development there is a skills "building effect" as the areas of listening/feedback, leadership, communication patterns, and decision-making are covered. In other words, the skills learned under the prior areas are developed through practice in exercises used in skill development under following areas.

Effective decision-making involves several steps: understanding the situation; identifying the problem; identifying and comparing alternatives; deciding; and implementing the decision. Figure 6-8 (read each line across fully and move down line-by-line) elaborates the process.

Identify the Problem	The problem must be separated from its symptoms and properly identified (a critical step). Then you should be able to
State the Goal of Your Work	The goal defines the specific result you expect to accomplish through your decision-making work. The next step should be to
Gather Information	This step may also occur at other places in the process. The questions Who?, What?, When?, Where?, How?, and Why? should be useful. The answers are separated into columns of What is? and What is not? The next step is a
Component Analysis	which is used to identify the major components of the problem/situation or system. They key question here is, "What major factors can be changed?" Then you should
Generate Possible Solutions	which will achieve the goal. The question here is "How can each component be changed?" Then you should consider
Constraints & Assumptions	Constraints limit what can be done. Assumptions help simplify the problem. The next step is to make a
Choice	A choice is made by applying the constraints and any other criteria which are relevant to the possible solutions and carefully examining the positive and negative consequences of different options. A table is sometimes used to help organize this work and the solutions may be ranked from best to poorest. The best solution is selected for further work. This is also a critical step in the decision-making process because a great deal of detailed work will follow. This work begins with an
Analysis	of the chosen solution. An excellent way to perform this step is to identify all the components that must be considered and ask as many questions as you can about the choice using the words Who, What, When, Where, How, and Why. After all the components have been identified, it is time to begin the
Synthesis	In step 1 the analysis questions are answered; in step 2 a detailed solution is devised. When this work is completed, an

Evaluation	is performed to see if the plan satisfied the goal and meets any criteria that are appropriate. Here again the positive and negative consequences should be examined. If the evaluation shows that the solution is not acceptable, it may be necessary to return to the possible solution step, make another choice, and proceed again through the analysis, synthesis, and evaluation steps. If the work is acceptable, a plan to evaluate the implemented solution should be devised. Then
Recommendations	may be made and a
Report	prepared. If the work is approved you will
Implement	the plan and prepare to
Check the Results	

Figure 6 8
The Decision-making Process

Decision-making takes place within several broader contexts with which it is useful to be familiar. First, in any situation there are forces which help or facilitate and forces which hinder or debilitate. Kurt Lewin (1947) suggests that a force field analysis be conducted. He delineates driving and resisting forces and explains how over time an unfreezing, changing, and refreezing of factors is performed. The framework is depicted in Figure 6-9 and it has been very useful in organizational change research.

There is a school of thought that change is more easily effected by reducing the forces against change than by strengthening the forces for it.

Another important, broader framework pertains to procedures for getting effective results. Some of the best consultants (e.g., those who resolve staff conflicts in organizations) suggest the following guidelines for becoming involved in projects:

1. Meet with the top decision-maker in the organization, e.g., president, director, etc., completely inform him/her of what you plan to do with respect to decision-making within the organization, and get their full support. If you cannot get that support, drop the project. Some heads play the game of sending an assistant to the meeting and then later, when a decision which the head does not like has been made, he/she will use the excuse that he/she was not informed directly of what was going on. Avoid this.

2. Involve in group decision-making all parties who will be affected by the decision which will be made. This creates a healthy feeling of "ownership" of the decision. If numbers are too unwieldly, a *representative(s)* of the parties to be affected will suffice.

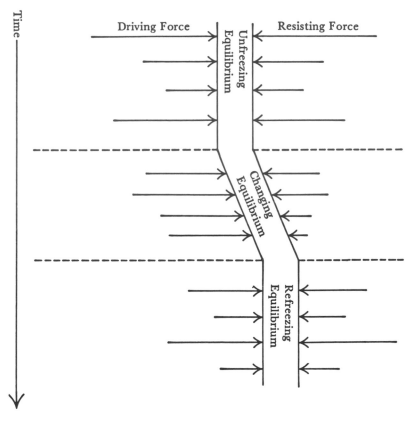

Figure 6-9
Lewin's Force Field Analysis

From *Educational Administration and Organizational Behavior* by E. Mark
Hanson, 1979, p. 314. Copyright 1979 by Allyn and Bacon, Inc., Boston,
MA. Reprinted by permission.

3. The group decision should be a consensus decision. What this means is
that every group member leaves the situation feeling that his/her opinions were
given a fair hearing and that he/she can "live with the decision" which was
made. It does not mean that every member agrees with the decision but each
will support it.

4. Before disbanding, the group should clearly identify members who will
be responsible for implementing the various aspects of the decision which has
been made. Who will inform various constituencies? Who will be responsible
for acting first, and so on. This is very important, for if people are not identified
the decision might go nowhere. Along the same lines, once an external trainer
has completed his/her work in-house, an internal organization member should

be appointed to continue the training. Otherwise, the impact of O.D. will be lessened.

Several ideas are important in the context of actually making the decision itself. "Synergy" is the notion that a decision made by a number of people will be of higher quality than the sum of the decisions of the individual members. In other words, "the sum of the whole is greater than the sum of its parts." "Groupthink" is a term which pertains to the same idea as does the notion of "quality circles." Further, every decision can be viewed in terms of quality and acceptance. Figure 6-10 indicates the possibilities.

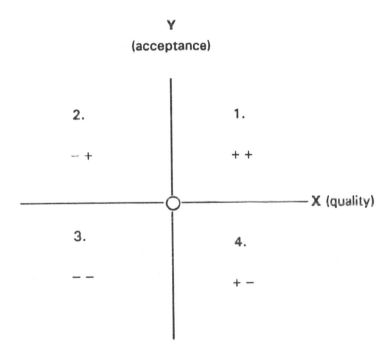

Figure 6–10
Quality and Acceptance of Decisions

Quadrant 1 indicates a decision of both high quality and high acceptance; quadrant 2 indicates one of low quality and high acceptance; quadrants 3 and 4 indicate decisions of low quality/low acceptance and high quality/low acceptance, respectively. A group leader and the group can assess the desired mix of quality and acceptance. How important are these things? Are there big risks in making a poor decision? For instance, a decision on how to spend a three million dollar budget involves considerations different from a decision on the color of waste baskets for the staff room. Edwin Bridges (1967) refers to the "zone of indifference" with which school principals should be familiar; this is the collection of issues to which teachers are indifferent with respect to their being involved in decisions. If the administrator is aware of such issues, he/she does not need to involve so many persons in the decision, and quality and acceptance will be left in the hands of a few. Of course, in all decision-making the top administrator realizes that ultimately he/she is accountable and responsible despite who inputs. Bolton (1971) provides an excellent overview of decision-making guidelines.

In O.D. training, decision-making skills are taught through exercises with the group. The typical scenario is to give an inner group (perhaps six people) an issue on which to make a decision. At this point the group will practice all the O.D. skills of listening/feedback, leadership, communication patterns, and decision-making. Individuals on an outer circle are singled out to observe in one of the skill areas. A time limit is placed on the inner group; they begin by choosing leaders for the discussion. When the decision is reached, the outer group members give a report on the quality of skills observed.

Summary

The technology of Organization Development (O.D.) has been overviewed. It is suggested as an important component of leadership in education for now and the future. It is particularly powerful in that it accepts the inevitability of change and leads to renewal in both organizations and its members. It emphasizes the team approach. (Johnson & Johnson, 1991, is an excellent book on teams.) O.D. promotes the "collegiality," "congeniality," and "learning community" factors which Sergiovanni (1992) values.

In the implementation of this technology, the following guidelines (from Dyer, 1987) might well be kept in mind:

– team building takes time

– people in power must support changes

– involvement, trust, acceptance and open communication enhance commitment and morals and increase possibilities for change

– team building may need to be repeated considering the great deal of personnel turnover in contemporary organizations

– team building involves a great deal of energy and time; thus, those involved must be rewarded – they must see that the system recognizes their efforts (p. 167).

Organizational Realities of Politics and Power

Management indeed needs executives who are willing to risk being unloved, who can choose among unpleasant alternatives, and who "bite the bullet." Too many executives put social acceptance and risk avoidance ahead of organizational welfare and misunderstand power. In seeking a decisive, tough-minded leader, organizations risk being taken in by the pathologically hostile. These people may look good and sound wonderful; they're great at manipulating superiors (including boards of directors who see them as saviors). But they can destroy the very business they claim to be saving.

L.R. Sayles in *Leadership*, 1979, pp. 237-238.

We need to understand the existential realities of leading and following in organizations. We need to understand the wielding of power and the making of decisions when much is on the line. And we need to appreciate what it is to suffer the decisions of such power.

T.B. Greenfield, 1986, p. 76.

The discussion of effective educational management and leadership approaches might end with the human relations-based Organization Development (O.D.) technology. In fact, when it appeared in the 1960s it was thought by some to be the complete model. However, the contemporary theory and practice of O.D. acknowledge the political and power realities of organizations to a much greater extent than used to be the case. This is important to the development of ideas in this book.

Greiner and Schein (1988) provide an insightful overview. They explain that traditional O.D. has held simplistic notions about power, e.g., Theory X is bad and Theory Y is good, but that the contemporary organization reality of a proliferation of technologies, scattered and limited resources, and intense competition dictates more realistic views. Both downward and upward politics and power in organizations must be accommodated (pp. 18-19). An effective leader utilizes any knowledge gained from working at the various levels of his/her organization. Warren Bennis supports the Greiner/Schein view:

> The organization development consultant tends to use the truth-love model when it may not be appropriate and has no alternative model to guide his practice under conditions of distrust . . . and conflict.. . . This means that in pluralistic power situations . . . organization development may not reach its desired goal . . . This may explain why O.D. has been reasonably successful where power is relatively centralized . . . organization development has not met with success in diffuse power structures. (Bennis, 1969)

From this comment, the one in charge appreciates how he/she may become viewed as a puppet or as "one of them" (higher-ups) versus "one of us."

Greiner and Schein present three models with which to understand organizational reality – the Rational/Bureaucratic Model; the Collegial/Consensus Model; and the Pluralistic/Political Model:

> The Pluralistic/Political model is, in our opinion, a less idealized model than the other two models. These other models may be worth striving for in certain situations, because research evidence suggests that the Rational/Bureaucratic model may be more effective in dealing with simple technologies and stable environments, while the Collegial/Consensus model fits better with more complex and uncertain environments. (p. 19)

Thus, all three models are useful but the Pluralistic/Political Model is advanced as a more accurate representation of how organizations and those in charge really function. Later in their book, the authors report findings from research with respect to the influence strategies used by individuals in the political/power games. Figure 6-11 is an example.

Thus are listed some behaviors of more political-type administrators.

Overall, the point is that within contemporary organizations, including educational ones, it is not just all "love and trust" and fair play and justice. If some individuals are given power they can be dangerous. In practice, human relations and the humanism movement generally have their limits. A good deal of separation of person and position (or the personal and the professional) goes on. Thus, Organization Development must be viewed as just a part of a more comprehensive realistic approach to effective leadership – a total model which blends truth-love with politics and power. But, before developing such a comprehensive model in Part Three of this book, the stage should be fully set.

Present a persuasive viewpoint	Be persistent
Deal directly with key decision makers	Offer favors/monetary rewards
Use data to convince others	Use threats
Focus on needs of the target group	Commit the uncommitted
Work around roadblocks	Use organizational rules
Exaggerate information	Give guarantees
Use personal attributes	Discredit the opposition
Use contacts for information	Deal with others socially
Surround self with competent others	

Figure 6–11
Power Strategies Used by Managers

From *Power and Organization Development: Mobilizing Power to Implement Change* by L.E. Greiner and V.E. Schein, 1988, p. 43. Copyright 1988 by Addison-Wesley Pub. Co., Reading, MA. Reprinted by permission.

Following, some personal philosophy of eleven excellent administrators (acquired through research) is presented to illustrate how persons of integrity and sound character in educational leadership appreciate that within organization there is a complex mix of good and bad:

administrator number 1 – "If your educational administrator is bad, you as a teacher should focus on satisfying your students and do what you can to have the administrator replaced; bow down to no man."

administrator number 2 – "I find that I lose 60% of the time. My approach however is to assume workers want to do well and I create an environment where they can. It is helpful to adopt the long-term patience of an Eastern philosophy. Also, conflict and competition among departmental units is healthy."

administrator number 3 – "Sometimes one must break ranks with a superordinate; a good fight once in a while is good; do not trust anyone; confidentiality and intuition are tools for me."

administrator number 4 – "Do not get mad; get your focus off of the politics and people; if there is a problem, grieve, and then work for change; always work at 'being up,' lighthearted, and optimistic; put some issues on hold for long periods of time."

administrator number 5 – "Education involves politics with a capital 'P.'"

administrator number 6 – "Apply the best knowledge you have and try not to step on too many peoples' toes; 'when a hammer strike – when an anvil bear.' The reason why 'how to' management books sell so well is that few people know how to do management properly."

administrator number 7 – "Fall down 7 times, get up 8."

administrator number 8 – "Be good to your people on the way up, because you meet them coming down."

administrator number 9 – "An administrator should step down after 10 years to let 'new blood' take over."

administrator number 10 – "We all have vengeance in us; one can get satisfaction in different ways; rise above it all; time heals; believe in yourself."

administrator number 11 – "It is important to learn that many things that one worries about never happen."

These administrators are intelligent, sensitive, tough-minded (not easily intimidated), experienced individuals. They are "family-first" oriented. Some of their comments indicate that they know that people (including themselves) are not perfect, that they recognize that both good and evil exist and that sometimes they, as leaders, must act with force and cunning. These administrators who have stayed for a long time in their organization and have maintained their integrity. Generally, they are highly thought of. As with all effective leaders (Goodwin, 1981, p. 27), they embody the principles of the organization they lead, they relate positively to people, they communicate the purposes of the organization, they plan and promote programs, they develop procedures for executing and evaluating the programs, and they recruit and develop personnel.

From the author's observation of these administrators, he found them to carry out their duties with a sustained sensitivity to what is right and wrong. People, loyalty, and the law are very important to them. They show the signs of being good persons, integrated in word, spirit, and deed. Among other things, they model justice and fairness.

These successful educational leaders first are "people persons," but they recognize the more seedy side of life too. Myths surrounding organizational cultures and leadership are not foreign to them. They are extremely patient and have the ability to see "the big picture." They inspire the model of Conscience-based Educational Leadership coming in Part Three.

Conclusion

In this Part Two, Essences of Educational Management and Leadership, the following have been discussed:

- educational law
- educational finance
- values, with a historical overview and a survey, and an
- organizational framework.

Throughout, bureaucratic theory is prevalent, with a recognition that thought now has been shifted into a more postpositivistic arena whereby leadership is viewed in terms of moral entity. Moreover, the political and power realities of contemporary education and the altering bureaucratic dynamic of collectivism and individualism must continually be considered. In a preliminary fashion, Hodgkinson's ideas on values were extended to a legal/theological base suited to both developed and developing societies; more elaboration is coming. Then, skills of the Organization Development (O.D.) technology were presented as a necessary foundation for the practical application of the values and base. The stage is set for the presentation of a timely, original leadership model in Part Three.

References

Barnard, C.I. (1938). *The functions of the executive*. Cambridge, MA: Harvard University Press.

Bates, R.J. (1989). Is there a new paradigm in educational administration? Paper presented at the annual conference of the American Educational Research Association, San Francisco, CA.

Bennis, W. (1969). *Organization development*. Reading, MA: Addison-Wesley.

Bennis, W. (1989). *Why leaders can't lead: The unconscious conspiracy continues*. Don Mills, ON: Maxwell Macmillan.

Bolton, D.L. (Ed.). (1971). *The use of simulation in educational administration*. Columbus, OH: Charles E. Merrill.

Bridges, E.M. (1967, Winter). A model for shared decision-making in the school principalship. *Educational Administration Quarterly, 3*(1), 49-61.

Campbell, J., with Moyers, B. (1988). *The power of myth*. New York, NY: Doubleday.

Caplow, T. (1983). *Managing an organization* (2nd ed.). Toronto, ON: Holt, Rinehart & Winston.

Culbertson, J. (1988). A century's quest for a knowledge base. In N. Boyan (Ed.), *Handbook of research on educational administration* (pp. 3-26). New York, NY: Longman.

Daresh, J.C. (1991). *Supervision as a proactive process.* Prospect Heights, IL: Waveland Press.

Dyer, W.G. (1987). *Team building: Issues and alternatives* (2nd ed.). Reading, MA: Addison-Wesley.

Ellul, J. (1965). *The technological society* (Translated from the French, 1954, by John Wilkinson). London, England: Jonathan Cape.

Ellul, J. (1986). *The subversion of Christianity* (G.W. Bromiley, Trans.). Grand Rapids, MI: Wm. B. Eerdmans.

The Financial Post (Canada). (1976, June 17).

Fullan, M. (1982). *The meaning of educational change.* Toronto, ON: OISE.

The great debate: Christianity versus secular humanism (Professor William Craig and Dr. Henry Morgentaler). (1990). Held at the University of Western Ontario, London, ON, January 24th (on videocassette produced by Paragon Production services, Vancouver, BC).

Greenfield, T.B. (1986, Summer). The decline and fall of science in educational administration. *Interchange, 17*(2), 57-80.

Greiner, L.E., & Schein, V.E. (1988). *Power and organization development: Mobilizing power to implement change.* Reading, MA: Addison-Wesley.

Griffith, F. (1966). Six mistaken meanings of democratic administration. *Phi Delta Kappan.*

Hanson, E.M. (1979). *Educational administration and organizational behavior.* Boston, MA: Allyn and Bacon.

Hawkings, S.W. (1988). *A brief history of time: From the big bang to black holes.* New York, NY: Bantam Books.

Hawkings, S.W. (Ed.) (1992). *A brief history of time: A reader's companion.* Prepared by Gene Stone. New York, NY: Bantam Books.

Henderson, N.K. (Circa 1975). Lecture notes on education administration and organization – Towards better school management. School of Education, University of Hong Kong.

Hodgkinson, C. (1983). *The philosophy of leadership.* Oxford, England: Basil Blackwell.

Johnson, D.W., & Johnson, F.P. (1991). *Joining together: Group theory and group skills* (4th ed.). Englewood Cliffs, NJ: Prentice- Hall.

Lewin, K. (1947). Frontiers in group dynamics. *Human Relations I.*

Lewis, J. (1981). *Something hidden: A biography of Wilder Penfield.* Toronto, ON: Doubleday.

Maslow, A. (1954). *Motivation and personality.* New York, NY: Harper and Row.

Mayo, E. (1933). *The human problems of an industrial civilization.* New York, NY: Macmillan.

McGregor, D. (1960). *The human side of enterprise.* New York, NY: McGraw-Hill.

Orwell, G. (1949). *1984.* New York, NY: Harcourt.

Perrow, C. (1973, Summer). The short and glorious history of organizational theory. *Organizational Dynamics, 2*(1), 2-15.

Sarason, S.B. (1982). *The culture of the school and the problem of change* (2nd ed.). Newton, MA: Allyn and Bacon.

Sayles, L.R. (1979). *Leadership: What effective managers really do...and how they do it*. New York, NY: McGraw-Hill.

Sergiovanni, T.J. (1992). *Moral leadership: Getting to the heart of school improvement.* San Francisco, CA: Jossey-Bass.

Thom, D.J. (1984a, Winter). The spiritual factor in educational administration (To make great gains in our schooling systems). *McGill Journal of Education, 19*(1), 79-93.

Toffler, A. (1990). *Powershift: Knowledge, wealth, and violence at the edge of the 21st century*. New York, NY: Bantam Books.

Part Three

Educational Leadership with CONSCIENCE

People can be logical, consistent, and convincing . . . but wrong.

—

No one knows who will live in this cage in the future, or whether at the end of this tremendous development entirely new prophets will arise, or there will be great rebirth of old ideas and ideals, or, if neither, mechanized petrification, embellished with a sort of convulsive self-importance. For of the last stage of this culture development, it might truly be said: "Specialists without spirit, sensualists without heart; this nullity imagines that it has attained a level of civilization never before achieved."

Weber, 1958, p. 182.

Part Three includes two Chapters, the first on advancing leadership in education and, the second, a conclusion. A conscience-based leadership model is introduced with the hope that its application will offset the potential problems of which Weber warns.

7

Advancing Leadership in Education

Challenges

When one considers the current state of society, one might conclude that David Cohen's observation of years ago applies:

> Beginning in the second quarter of the nineteenth century there developed an acute sense that society was coming unstrung, that common values and cohesive institutions were eroding. This sense of loss powerfully influenced social policy. It evoked the belief that families were failing and produced efforts to shore them up to replace them with new institutions . . . . It evoked the belief that primary institutions – families, churches, and communities – had lost their ability to pass a common culture along and this became a powerful inspiration for the development of public education.

The concerns of lost community, poor family cohesiveness, and troubled youths are very much prevalent. From Cohen's comment, the omen is for renewal in society and education. Correspondingly, there will come development in educational administration/leadership.

For Society

General society would seem to have major challenges in weathering the growing pains of global village objectives. Foremost, our culture is increasingly dominated by *technology*, particularly machine technology such as computers. Writers such as Ripple (1986), Roszak (1986), and Toffler (1990) explain how this is harming humanity with respect to the quality of human interrelationships. Ripple analyzes and suggests:

> Most introductions of automated technology into the workplace in the past were made by engineers and technical experts without consideration or understanding of the human dimension or their effects on employees. If any historical lessons are to be learned from this earlier experience, they are that the human dimension is critical . . . when problems develop with hi-tech automation they most often are some combination of human, social, and organizational factors that were not anticipated during development and implementation. The lesson is that humans who have to live with the change process and make it work should have a substantial role in planning for and implementing every aspect of the process. This includes management, unions, and workers as well as technical engineers making joint planning decisions.

He is suggesting that an O.D.-type philosophy is required. This is a good beginning. Society's challenge is to make an appropriate use of technology – to strike a balance with humanism by harnessing the computer and by regularly checking its purposes and gains. People can become too dependent on machines which can lead to a stressful and frustrating existence.

A second major challenge is in the area of *multiculturalism* per se. Society perhaps underestimates the impact of cultural diversity. The ideal of a country as a multitude of groups of different ethnic and religious persuasions living together in harmony is a tall order. The commitment to inclusivity values and legitimizes all traditions (e.g., language, religion, etc.). Historically the ideal has had difficulty being realized. In competing for limited resources, the diverse groups experience breakdowns in communication because of their different backgrounds and beliefs. For instance, we underestimate the fanaticism which exists within some minorities. Society's challenge is to move slowly and surely with respect to effecting the new society, especially in applying the Charter of Rights and Freedoms. (John Gardner's book *Excellence: Can We Be Equal and Excellent Too?* suggests some problems if we do not.) A key issue is whether a country can exist as a *multivalue* society.

A third major challenge is in the area of *thinking about money*. This is associated with redefining clear societal goals and making value choices. A danger exists in societies with too much diversity. With many choices and lack of clear direction, dollars and cents can generally become the ultimate goal and religion. The Hong Kong society is an example. Greenewalt comments on the factor of money in human motivation:

> Of all the motivations to which the human mechanism responds . . . none has proved so powerful as that of financial gain. . . . self enrichment is a dream which must rank with the most compelling forces in shaping the destinies of the human race. It has always been so, and when we are disturbed over being members of a "materialistic generation," we can look back over history and note that we are simply expressing a basic human trait . . .

> The importance of a financial lure is not that the accumulation of wealth is in itself significant, but because money is the only form of incentive which is wholly negotiable, appealing to the widest possible range of seekers. As people differ so markedly, it is difficult if not impossible to apply any other common denominator of inducement fully acceptable to all. Money was invented for the precise purpose of meeting widely dissimilar desires. (p. 14)

There are ample signs in our society that money is becoming an all-important factor (the GST and Free Trade are a few examples). This situation leads to many phenomena including both parents working, daycare, and lessening of family cohesion. When students are asked about their goals in life, many answer, "To make a lot of money." Public organizations such as universities increasingly emphasize a financial as well as a scholarly basis. Early retirement at 55 years of age plans save money as senior people leave and often are not replaced. There is a need for a return to some "money isn't everything" mentality – as balance.

Following the point above, *family* is another major challenge for society. Basically, family is the cornerstone of society, it is being weakened by the circumstances surrounding divorce and separation – particularly the ease of mobility, and repairs are needed. Holding family together (preventing the "dysfunctional" family) is work which takes great effort, but it needs to be done. Haines and Neeley (1987) and Thom (1986) provide insight into the challenge. Koestenbaum (1991) makes specific reference to the importance of family. Family keeps one in touch with reality.

Later, all of these challenges and ones still to be discussed can be contemplated in terms of Thom's "Educational Leadership with CONSCIENCE" (TELC) Model.

For Education

The education system reflects the society. Also, changes in the system tend to lag changes in the society. Thus, one would expect schools and post-secondary institutions to be responding to the multicultural and just society which is evolving. In this context two major challenges confront the education system: (a) to *define goals*, and (b) to *establish credibility*.

The stated goals of education generally fall into the four broad categories of development in basic skills (the 3 Rs), vocational skills (re joining the workforce), socialization/citizenship skills (including fitness/recreation), and skills in aesthetic appreciation (including critical thinking). As society has diversified and become more complex, the educational institutions have taken on new, specific objectives within these categories. For example, curricula in law, women's studies, drug education, and media literacy have been introduced and, with the current concern for the environment, the goals of reduce, reuse, and recycle are in place. Further, the public system has been moving toward replacement of the specific Judaeo-Christian base with a base which caters to all religious persuasions. On the other hand, there has been expansion of the Catholic separate system. A question is, "How much church influence should there be?" Also, "How much should transmission of culture be a goal?"

Many individuals argue that education and educators are expected to do too much, that the system is viewed as a panacea for all of society's problems. Certainly the proliferation of goals would indicate this. A major challenge is to define clear, appropriate goals from this point. The seriousness of this task is reflected in Roszak's comment that in our institutions we may soon be graduating students who believe that thinking is indeed a matter of information processing, and, therefore, without a computer no thinking can be done at all; and Ripple's haunting thought that unless technology is checked, without doubt human notions like self, work, goodness, truth, beauty, love, ambition, motivation, aesthetics, free will . . . may all need re-definition (p. 51). Further, in goal setting, educators need to be realistic. For example, a proposed goal is to ultimately produce graduates who can make our country competitive in global markets. Yet, the reality is that this will be difficult so long as salaries are so high and our country's work ethic and the number of hours of school instruction are inferior to Japan and European countries. (On the other side, Japan has a high rate of student suicides.)

Evident are two, different, main educational philosophies – child-centered and traditional/subject oriented. The former assumes that students arrive in schools with an eagerness to learn – whole language proponents are supportive of this. The latter philosophy assumes that there is specific knowledge that should be taught and views the teaching of responsibility and self-discipline as crucial. In many ways the two core approaches are opposed and this confounds goal setting. Confounded are ideas on education as "formation" versus education as "information," or as an emphasis on process as opposed to content. A related point is that educators must not make education jargon (e.g., "whole language," "holistic curriculum") too baffling to lay people.

Some approach the goal-setting issue by considering the question, "What is Worth Knowing?" (Postman & Weingartner, 1969). It is oversimplifying to answer that no specific subjects and attitudes are required – just critical thinking skills which permit learners to make viable meanings of the future. The critical thinking skills are part of it. They represent the rightful importance of empowering learners as opposed to educators "doing things" to learners. (See Bereiter, 1972.)

However, there are facts about our world that should be taught also. For instance, one who has studied science appreciates that there are strong physical forces surrounding the universe – forces such as wind, fire, gravity, and so on – of which a great deal is known. This is the type of information that should be taught in subject concentrations to produce capable future scientists. Perhaps a problem is that there are so many branches of knowledge and the average educator cannot be familiar with all branches. Dupuis indicates the complexity (Figure 7-1), a complexity that is increased when the *humanities* are considered as well.

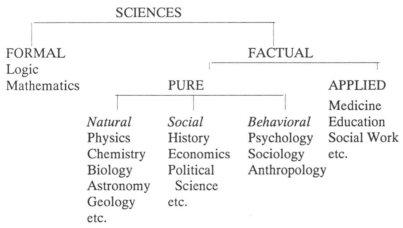

Figure 7-1: Relationship Among the Various Sciences

From *Philosophy of Education in Historical Perspective* by Adrian M. Dupuis, 1985, p. 254. Copyright 1985 by University Press of America, Lanham, MD. Reprinted by permission.

The following ideas are important in setting the educational goals:

• the tremendous power of a learner's brain must be acknowledged; the person consists of mind, body, and spirit; the subconscious mind is important too; imagination allows a person to understand both reality and fiction;

• basic skills are necessary to get along in life;

• beliefs, morals, self-discipline, and responsible self-actualization all are important;

　• thinking and writing abilities are separate and should be joint-nurtured;

　• history is an important subject; so is the promotion of patriotism;

　• the home has a tremendous influence on what a learner learns; and

　• young, impressionable learners should be a key focus.

The education system should overall teach an Organization Development (O.D.) technology. There should be skill development in the areas of listening/feedback, leadership, communication patterns, and decision-making. These skills, along with skills in learning how to relax, will help learners cope with a world characterized by continual change, good and evil, many choices, and occasional insanity (Adler). Klassen (1991a) presents sound insights into effecting successful change; also see Baldridge (1972).

Congruent with the suggestion of bringing the O.D. (teambuilding) emphasis into education is another valid idea which some might criticize as being too nostalgic. In the society of years ago, when technological pace was not so rapid and mobility not so easy, schools had quite a sense of community. There was a "neighborhood" flavor which is not prevalent in many schools of today. Students went to the same school where their parents had gone, and teachers and administrators tended to serve the school for their entire career. This created a familiarity, a unique caring, and a sharing of responsibility which had many positive benefits. Many factors have led to an "impersonality" within today's society and schools. A philosophy that evaluation of individuals must be strongly rooted in objectivity has gained prominence. Good feelings about the one being evaluated are not to enter in, lest the "purity" of things will suffer. Educators should consider organizing education in the future using some of the community features of old, for, particularly with respect to the development of young pupils, sense of "neighborhood" is important.

With respect to the challenge of establishing credibility, educators should properly define the goals, work toward them within favorable organizational structure, and, then, publicize their successes. Among other things, this will bring continuing support for the system.

All in all, the challenge for education is to address the multi-dimensions of the learner – cognitive, affective, physical, etc. – not to be too narrow in delivering in the teaching/learning process. A suggestion is that all learners would do well to have some liberal arts education. The world needs well-rounded products from education.

For Educational Leadership

There is a multitude of perspectives from which to view administration/leadership in education. A crucial perspective is that of whether one views what is happening in society and education as a pessimist or an optimist. Also, is one liberal or conservative in perspective? The attitude one adopts is a choice. In this section challenges to educational leaders are highlighted. Edwin Bridges' comment that training programs for educational administrators are dysfunctional, emphasizing the disparity between the slow rhythm and reinforcing of subordinate behaviors in academic activity and the hectic pace and need to take charge in day-to-day school administration (in Hart, 1975) supports the notion that the opinions of both academics and practitioners are important. Further, as Schlechty (1990) suggests, there is a need both to understand the past *and* look to the future.

At a broad (systems) level the following thrusts are developing: increasing cross-cultural work; power and political processes becoming the major explanatory variables in organizational behavior; a rising interest in inter-organizational behavior; and a resurgence of subjectivism. At a more specific level, two issues that unnerve contemporary administrators are *external regulation* and *intense public scrutiny and pressure*, particularly resistance to schools' funding needs and demands for influence over curricula (Campbell et al., 1987). T. Parson (1958) originally presented these types of organizational concepts. "Disentanglement" among organizations has become a popular term. All of this has implications for theory, practice, and training. The notion of external regulation is elaborated later, in the discussion on "Educational Leadership with CONSCIENCE" and its law, moral values, and theology underpinnings.

An example of a pessimistic view is the following:

> Educational Administration is a turbulent field in a hostile environment . . .
> We must explore more deeply and more rigorously how administrators and administrative action influence real life in real schools. (Mitchell & Cunningham, 1990, p. 16)

Yet, as will be highlighted later, to adopt an optimistic view is much more beneficial.

Some key issues facing education are depicted in Figure 7-2. These were expounded by a Director of a larger, Canadian public school system.

- Separate funding
- possible funding of private schools
- declining support for education by the Province
- competition from public and private sources
- need to clarify *What business are we really in?*

- back to basics/learning how to learn
- growth of French Immersion
- accountability
  - Long-Range Plan
  - Priority Budgeting
- evaluation
  - student
  - teacher
  - program
- perceptions/politics
- research
- aging teaching force
  - short term (five years) implications
  - morale
  - retraining
  - little 'new blood'
  - longer term (ten years) implications
  - young teaching force
  - tremendous opportunities
  - new leaders ready?
  - teacher shortage

- declining enrolment/school closure

- commitment to ongoing people development
  - P.D. days
  - inservice
  - upgrading
  - recertification
- how best to utilize new technology?
  - the potential of computer technology
  - use in non-traditional areas
  - types of technical programs for the future - *General*
- need to encourage public involvement/support
  - those *with and without* students in the system
  - more active public relations/marketing programs
  - we are a *Service Industry* and need to understand that "the customer is always right" and that the customer has options
  - focus on the school as basis of improvement
  - key role of teacher and principal
  - theory to practice

Figure 7-2
Contemporary Issues Facing Education

Of note are the fifth and thirteenth entries pertaining to goal setting and technology, respectively. Figure 1-2, presented in Part One of this book, elaborates many of the issues.

Educational leadership faces a multitude of challenges. Society and education are extremely complex and educational administrators are expected *to take charge* in this context. Especially with respect to large educational systems, it is impossible for the leader to personally be on top of all that is happening. It definitely helps if he/she is a broadly educated individual, has ample experience in life and education, and keeps up his/her reading. (Many administrators read little, if at all.)

Plato once described his ideal of the head of his Republic's schools:

> Let the person who is to rule over these be, according to the laws, not less than fifty years old, and the father of children lawfully begotten, males and females especially, but if not, of either sex. And let both him who selects, and him who is selected, consider that this office is by far the greatest of the chief offices of the state. (from James, 1965, p. 21)

What is suggested as a starting point is a mature person of qualifications, experience, and good family and moral fibre. This is still appropriate today.

However, there is much more that is required. Society has become very sophisticated. People are more formally educated than they used to be. They question more and they want democratic practices from leaders. Yet, the leader is responsible and accountable for what happens in his/her organization. So, a blend of democratic and directive leadership is required. The general administrative style required is one of empowering others (Bennis & Nanus, 1985) while reserving final ratification of decisions based on vested authority of the role. It requires a delicate balance and, as is a message of this book, a continual regard for justice and fairness at every level. Sergiovanni (1990) suggests that all of this be done with "gambare" [meaning "to persevere; to do one's best; to be persistent; to stick to one's purposes; to never give up until the job is done and done well" (p. 1)] In *Moral Leadership* (1992) he promotes a "stewardship" style.

To survive, the administrator needs to distance himself/herself somewhat from the system and society. One must be a good politician, but in fairness to one's followers one should not force the politics on them. A large part of the administrator's job is to handle the politics – that multifaceted system created by human beings. The administrator must learn to "rise above" wrongdoings in the political system, and not to react with anger but to work for change. This shows leadership ability. One needs to stay optimistic. Margaret Thatcher comments on this "rare quality:"

The quality of being able to say what you believe whether it is popular or not
. . . the quality of taking all the positive aspects of life and making them
triumph over the difficulties.

- March, 1991, in Canadian Newspa-

pers

A summary view of the educational administrator/leader's position is in
Figure 7-3.

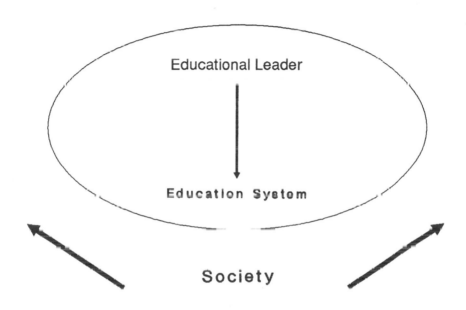

Figure 7-3
The Educational Leader, Education, and Society

Firstly, a leader in education should be *a spiritual, moral person.* In
contemporary society this is a real challenge, as Mann (1986) purports. Beck
(1986) describes the characteristics of a spiritual person, appropriate for both
religious and nonreligious people. To him, such is characterized by all or most
of the following: awareness, breadth of outlook, a holistic outlook, integration,
wonder, gratitude, hope, courage, energy, a balance between attachment and
detachment, acceptance, love, and gentleness (pp. 151-153). This person needs
to have a good value system and must recognize that both good and evil exist.
(Hermann Hesse, 1989, p. 9, describes these entities as "Two Worlds"; the
Bible, Genesis iii, refers to "the Fall" – the transition of Adam from primal
innocence to a knowledge of evil.) Many administrators have made the mistake
of believing that they can act immorally and then control the consequences of

their choices. However, according to moral codes there are expected consequences of particular chosen acts. A particularly important and sensitive
challenge is the respectful treatment of females by males. As Ellul once
remarked, there is a politics of people and a politics of God. The former involves
balanced right and wrong while the latter involves absolute right and wrong.

Another major challenge is to have *balance* in one's life (Thom, 1986).
This is a balance of work, family, and hobbies, as well as a balance within
oneself – of parts of personality and emotions. Greiff and Munter (1981) and
Tubesing and Tubesing (1991) provide insight on the former; Beck's attach-
ment/ detachment characteristic ties to the latter. Further, *physical fitness* is
very important – the administrator *must* pay attention to diet and exercise. For
example, these days low-cholesterol diets are worthwhile; for most, weight
reduction is life insurance. One needs to appreciate that mind, body, and spirit
all are important. Earle, Imrie, and Archbold (1989) teach the following:
values/goals clarification, nutrition, exercise, communication, and relaxation.
Visualizing is suggested; add to this the power of positive thinking. These all
contribute to vitality and vigor, with balance in one's life.

A final, major challenge is to apply *conscience* continually. This is the core
theme of this book and the next section reviews and elaborates.

Thom's "Educational Leadership with CONSCIENCE"

Extending Hodgkinson and Postpositivism

A general point of this book is that there is an approach based in moral
values, law, and theology which is necessary for effective educational leadership in these and the coming times. This approach goes beyond the literature
to date.

In their book *Knowing Educational Administration: Contemporary Methodological Controversies in Educational Administration Research* (1991),
Evers and Lakomski trace the intellectual change in the field of educational
administration over the years. Their discussion includes the theory movement
(past and present), ethical theory, policy analysis, and the contributions of
Greenfield and Hodgkinson. They highlight the humanism emphasis of
Hodgkinson and then, using a particular coherentist view of knowledge, they
critique existing administrative theories and develop an alternative. "The
alternative is a new postpositivist science of administration which is able to
include ethics and subjectivity within the scope of sound administrative knowledge."

Educational administration/leadership for years was thought of in terms of
logical positivism – the philosophical movement that holds characteristically
that all meaningful statements are either analytic or conclusively verifiable or
at least confirmable by observation and experiment (science). Now, as the "new
postpositivist science of administration" of above suggests, the thinking includes both the empirical/practical and the metaphysical. The latter includes

the ethics, values, and beliefs of the administrator and the former represents the applied side of things.

Current thought and spirit is characterized by caring and justice. The leader makes "personality investments" (Douglas, 1930) in superordinates, peers, and subordinates so as to successfully meet challenges. Hodgkinson (1983) indicates the interplay of complexity and simplicity and of the abstruse and the applied:

> Of course, different kinds of men will come to the role of administrator, men with different characters and characteristics; men, that is to say, with different patterns of values. And their roles will be embedded in different types of organizational context, again with different patterns of values. But whatever the variations of context and role, the philosophical theme will persist and certain philosophical skills will be desirable and appropriate even for rudimentary survival. At its lowest level, organizational life is a sort of daily combat. Even here, however, the deadliest weapons in the administrative armoury are philosophical: the skills of logical and critical analysis, conceptual synthesis, value analysis and commitment, the powers of expression in language and communication, rhetoric and most fundamentally, the depth understanding of human nature. So in the end philosophy becomes intrinsically practical. (p. 53)

Mann (1986) provides an insightful summary of undercurrents in modern society – the context in which educational leadership will be exercised in the future. Like Ripple, he discusses technological advances with concern for people's welfare. He sees all leaders as needing an excellent belief system when he states:

> A leader leads by virtue of his beliefs. That is what will motivate him. And the first ingredient will be a self-interest. At its best, self-interest will mean being true to oneself. Polonius' advice to Laertes has never been bettered: 'This above all: to thine own self be true, and it must follow, as the night the day, thou canst not then be false to any man.' As a Christian, I am commanded to love God, and to love my neighbour *as myself*. To want to do one's best is an entirely noble value. Self-interest which is motivated by a strong belief in integrity, duty, humour, and responsibility will be enlightened. But if it is inspired by greed, envy, selfishness and conceit it will lead in a different direction. What matters are the values that activate our natural self-interest – what it is in which we really believe. (p. 401)

Currently, leadership is more characterized by philosophy than science. Both the scientific and spiritual dimensions have independent lives and credibility of their own in the seeking of truth, but for years the former dimension has been emphasized over the latter (Klassen, 1991b). In 1986, Greenfield discussed "The Decline and Fall of Science in Educational Administration." The discipline has now arrived at a point where an enlightened, comprehensive model characterized by applied ethics is required. Initially, the area of law provides this model. (The awarding of the 1991 Nobel prize in

Economics to Ronald Coase for law research with respect to rights and effective use of resources in organizations indicates that other disciplines are recognizing law's importance.)

The bottom line in today's society is that leaders need to be fair. People are very sophisticated, and there is no better indicator of the successful use of understanding, wisdom, and righteousness, and proper utilization of knowledge by a leader than the application of justice and fairness. Further, by administrative law, administrators are no longer simply responsible to a board of directors and those being led, but now are accountable to the courts and other tribunals as well. In this section the author's "Educational Leadership with CONSCIENCE" model is introduced.

Some Starting Tenets

Six basic tenets underlie "Educational Leadership with CONSCIENCE":

• being an effective educational leader is a demanding challenge;

• one cannot control everything;

• one does not always get credit for one's achievements; one is rarely liked by everyone;

• the moral character of the leader is crucial; times change – solid, "indivisible" human values do not;

• there is an enduring area of human concern which is above and beyond politics and which informs the dignity and positive development of works; the leader ultimately is judged not only according to what he/she produces but also with respect to this area; and

• a sense of humor is crucial.

The Model

Many contemporary leaders have a highly political style as opposed to that of pure human relations. "Educational Leadership with CONSCIENCE" incorporates both styles. The appropriate blend is one of being collaborative/democratic and authoritative, but with justice and fairness as the bottom line.

Figure 7-4 depicts the components of Thom's "Educational Leadership with CONSCIENCE." The overall milieu is one in which the leader provides a subjective response to the collective needs and wants of the various education "publics" (e.g., students, parents, teachers, etc.)

Several realms/levels and frames are involved. First, the educational leader's activities are categorized under two realms: first-order and second-order. The first pertains to the more "routine," immediate things that the administrator/leader does. These are the day-to-day type things and, if the person truly likes administration, in these things he/she will find enjoyment, derive satisfaction, and generally will be able to "be his/herself." Appendix D contains material on specific routine activities. The second realm pertains to more serious, threatening activities. Associated with such are such terms as "playing hardball," and "covering your own A—." Certain individuals will thoroughly enjoy activities in the second realm, but many would prefer to avoid them. Risktaking, uncertainty, and principled, increased toughness enter in. In the most intense situations of applying justice and fairness, knowing the history of one's organization – the characters, and who has done what to whom – emerges as crucial. So does the ability to speak well, e.g., possessing outstanding dialectical (logical disputation) skills.

Boulding (1962) states, "[m]omentum has to be taken into account in most social behaviour systems; this is the element of habit, custom and resistance to change" (p. 22). In the Thom model, particularly the time frame and organizational knowledge factors accommodate this. Figure 7-4 outlines the bases for effectiveness in each realm and the feelings and characteristics which the leader will associate with each. One must be prepared. Overall, the root leadership style is one of Organization Development (O.D.).

Importance of Time-Frame

The critical core of "Educational Leadership with CONSCIENCE" is revealed when the longer term time frame is considered. Doing this projects to "the big, broader picture." This is the frame in which the true worth of the administrator/leader and the educational organization is assessed. Is the leader just and fair? Is the organization just and fair? One is talking here about the moral fibre of things. In this frame the administrator now "pays for" his/her poorly based decisions made in the first-order and second-order realm arenas. Winning battles unfairly leads to "losing the war." A good example is that of an incumbent administrator who seeks the renewal of a 5-year appointment. In the earlier years of the original appointment, the incumbent, in efforts to accomplish his/her goals, may have decided to often act with little regard for people. He/she may have been counting on the constituency members who were being served to have a short memory or, even if they remember, to forgive him/her later. Indeed, it does sometimes work this way. However, if too much disregard was shown, the administrator runs a risk and reappointment will be unlikely. The size of the organization, e.g., number of constituencies to satisfy, will be a factor here. James (1965) has stated emphatically that a schoolman's authority is a privilege that must be earned over and over again. This reinforces that *time* is an important factor in "Educational Leadership with CONSCIENCE."

Conscience, Justice, and Fairness Explained

In Thom's Conscience-based model justice and fairness form "the bottom line." This means that ultimately these are what is important for effectiveness as a leader. But just what is meant by "justice" and "fairness"? Moreover, how do these link to conscience?

Conscience is knowledge of one's own acts as right or wrong. Further, the informed conscience seeks justice, for justice is the basis for an ordered society. In this book, Judaeo-Christianity as informing the conscience and being the source of authority is presented – but more on this later.

In the Thom model the educational leader acts with conscience, performing deeds which are characterized by justice and fairness. Justice may be thought of as a universal view of what is right, and fairness as a subjective view of what should be. Justice affirms human worth and dignity and human rights; it means such things as caring, equality, and righteousness. Justice is what is right for the society.

In a primary sense everyone knows what fairness is. Even children know it (e.g., "It's not fair! - Jimmy got two more cookies than me!"). It has to do with what is correct, honest, appreciative, and according to the rules. Fairness is directly connected to one's character and value system – to one's ideas about what is right and wrong.

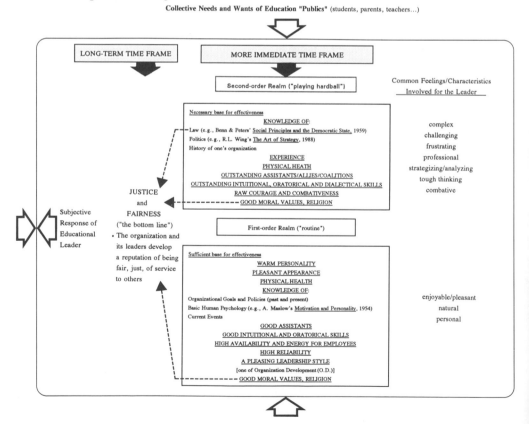

Figure 7-4
Thom's "Educational Leadership with CONSCIENCE" (TELC) Model

Fairness, in its most profound sense, is not completely appreciated by all as to its importance. Often, established, clear, social principles are ignored or confused in the problems of politics and social organization. "Fairness" (and "justice," "equality," "liberty") are such principles. The modern democratic/welfare state has evolved to a point where such principles need clarifying with respect to procedures and political practice. Philosophy is required for proper illumination.

"Fairness" as a legal concept has a long history and its original meaning, like other important social principles, still applies. The following comes from Giles and Proudfoot (1990) and is particularly appropriate for understanding fairness:

The Principles of Natural Justice

There exists a set of rules which usage, in our legal tradition, dictates must be applied in every situation where a person or body is charged with the duty of adjudicating disputes between people or adjudicating upon the rights of others. This set of rules is referred to as the rules of natural justice. They are written in many forms, pervade most of our rules of action, and are usually stated as follows. Those who adjudicate must act fairly and in good faith, without bias, and with a judicial temper. They must provide each party with an opportunity to understand what case has to be made and further, must provide them ample opportunity to state that case. (p. 113)

Gall (1990) explains that there are two fundamental rules of natural justice under which are many subrules:

1. *Audi Alteram Partem (Hear the Other Side) Rule*

This rule dictates that both parties to a dispute must be heard. There must be a fair hearing and each party must receive notice of the hearing. Moreover, during the course of the hearing each party must be allowed to rebut the evidence adduced, and to cross-examine witnesses – also, there is a right to counsel, but the courts generally have not extended the boundaries of the rule to include this right.

2. *Nemo Judex in Causa Sua Debet Esse (No One Ought to be a Judge in his Own Cause) Rule*

This rule requires the exclusion of all forms of bias from hearing proceedings. If actual bias is proven, or if there is a reasonable apprehension of bias, the invocation of this rule of natural justice renders a tribunal's decision null and void. The courts treat bias as an abuse of power.

For more detail one can consider the 1st McRver Report, Vol. 1, p. 137, which defines the Audi Alteram Partem Rule in terms of the following constituent elements:

1. Notice of the intention to make a decision should be given to the party whose rights may be affected.

2. The party whose rights may be affected should be sufficiently informed of the allegations against his interest to enable him to make an adequate reply.

3. A genuine hearing should be held at which the party affected is made aware of the allegations made against him and is permitted to answer.

4. The party affected should be allowed the right to cross-examine the party giving evidence against his interest.

5. A reasonable request for adjournment to permit the party affected to properly prepare and present his case should be granted.

6. The tribunal making the decision should be constituted as it was when the evidence and arguments were heard.

This McRver information is useful in analyzing justice and fairness in law Case 4 (concerning tenure) back in Part Two of this book. (In the final analysis the simple question to be answered on the case is this: on the facts of the particular case did the tribunal act justly and fairly toward the professor claiming to be aggrieved?)

So "fairness" can have a simpler or a more profound connotation. Both faces apply to Thom's "Educational Leadership with CONSCIENCE" Model (TELC) depending upon how complex the particular issue at hand is. When a leader "plays hardball" undoubtedly he/she will apply the concept in the most legal sense. This could involve a variety of other concepts associated with fairness such as arbitrary action, discrimination (usually by race, sex, religion, or nationality) and due process.

Administrative fairness is completely necessary within education. Many educators do not appreciate how important this is. The Canadian Charter of Rights and Freedoms was put into place in 1982. Sections 7 and 15 (see p. 17) speak to the doctrine of fairness and natural justice. Section 7 reads as follows:

> **7.** Everyone has the right to life, liberty and security of the person and the right not to be deprived thereof except in accordance with the principles of fundamental justice.

This Section and Section 15 (Equality Rights) provide a constitutional basis for cases in education ranging anywhere from the placing of students in special education classes to the expulsion of students. Often courts side with students against school authorities on the grounds that the students' constitutional rights have been denied. To understand the Charter's potential impact on educational policy, the reasonable limits clause (Section 1) is important. In *R. v. Oakes* (1986) the substantial government objective, the rational connection and the proportionality tests laid down by the Supreme Court of Canada form a basis for analysis of the complex value conflicts involved in cases. Suggested references for the implication of the Charter for education are Dickinson and

MacKay (1989), Hurlbert and Hurlbert (1992), and Confederation College's *The Charter and You* (videocassette).

"Due process" and administrative fairness have become very important. Basically, due process means that an individual has a right to be treated with fairness. For instance, a teacher who is in danger of losing his/her job should be informed of why his/her performance is deemed unsatisfactory, and be given time to do better. The powers given to principals and boards under education acts are limited by the need to provide for the minimum procedural rules outlined in the Statutory Powers Procedure Act. Further:

> Whether a hearing is or is not required by law, the rules of natural justice continue to apply. These require that the handling of any individual case should reflect the principles of fairness and justice. At the very least, this would involve the presence of an impartial decision maker or tribunal, a prior communication of the complaint with sufficient precision to enable the person to know what he or she faces, an opportunity for the person to communicate orally or in writing in his or her defence to the decision maker, and a decision that is consistent with the facts and evidence as they were known.

> The flexibility of due process permits the expansion of such proceedings into a true adversarial process, as in a court of law, including strict adherence to the rules of evidence, witnesses testifying under oath, a recording of evidence, and so on. However, as long as it can be perceived as fair, due process can also be so informal as to be virtually unrecognized as constituting a procedure. (Ontario Ministry of Education, *Discipline - Resource Guide*, 1986, p. 27)

The courts in interpreting the phrase "principles of fundamental justice" have looked to court decisions which have given meaning to the concepts of fairness and natural justice in administrative law.

With respect to education cases, it is worth noting that teachers and professors are also protected by tenure laws which make it difficult for them to be outright dismissed, and that often the courts (because of collective agreements and separation of powers at different levels) will refuse to hear cases involving purely educational decisions, leaving it to the educators involved to decide (Van Scotter, Haas, Kraft, & Schott, 1991, p. 17).

All of these ideas come to bear on conscience as incorporated into Thom's Model of Figure 7-4. The reader will be gaining an appreciation of how the model applies to "workplace disputes."

A Particular Thesis: Law, Moral Values, and Theology

> The true office of any faith is to give life a meaning which death cannot destroy.
>
> - Leo Tolstoy

A core thesis underlying this book and the conscience-based model is that in the culture of developed societies such as ours, law and moral values stem from theology. The dominant theology of our country is Judaeo-Christianity and this doctrine defines the standards. Figure 7-5 provides a basic depiction.

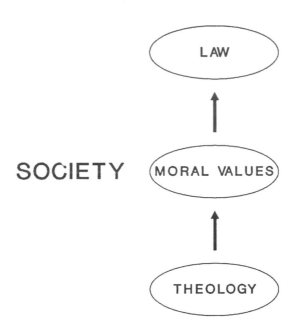

Figure 7-5
Law, Moral Values, and Theology

This gives rise to the "Thom Theorem" which associates with Thom's Model and is stated as follows – *Conscience drives behavior in mature individuals.* This recognizes that self-will may be at odds with conscience, as evidenced by guilt feelings.

Systematized principles (philosophy) of educational leadership have been developed with vigor in recent years and the discipline now has an emphasis of morality. Several scholars have been in the forefront of development but their work needs further extension. Hodgkinson and Sergiovanni have already been mentioned. Further, Codd (1989) stresses that "educational leadership is a form of moral action which can be meaningful only within a given cultural context. It is a form of cultural expression and negotiation deriving its meaning from the way in which social situations are cognitively appraised" (p. 176). Also, Schön has contributed the concept of reflective action and Evers and Lakomski (1991) their "coherentist view of knowledge" – based theory. However, from here there is a giant step forward which it is appropriate to take.

Educational leadership will be advanced when the praxis is "leading with conscience." Scholars have provided enlightenment on the importance of beliefs, moral values, and ethics within the administrator, but they have not "gone the distance" to specifically define the appropriate base for our culture. (Schön, 1989, goes further than some when he discusses the practice of law and the lawyer's "reflect-in-action" nature.) Justice and fairness represent ethical standards which find original definition in the Scriptures. Law stresses examining principles of morality, and theology provides individuals with the self-control and external standards which they naturally seek.

The appropriate step to take is to present a leadership model *based on law and theology*. Within this model, moral values and ethics are those of the Judaeo-Christian type. In other words, effectiveness is maximized if the educational leader follows Christian-type principles. The Jewish race is associated with "the observance of law," while Christians are associated with "faith." A combination (Judaeo-Christian) yields a law approach rooted in faith. Thom's "Educational Leadership with CONSCIENCE" has this underpinning. The approach includes going "beyond values and law" to the *theological* concept of justice.

Despite many media reports to the contrary, religion remains at the core of society and education for a multitude of people. The "Christian-type" leader believes in God and adheres to standards of behavior as in the Scriptures. The basics are accepted. This means observing the ten commandments, "doing unto others," forgiving, being patient and wise, and sacrificing for one's family. For some leaders this will involve a reprogramming of conscience from what was. Effective Christians are continually learning, listening, and accommodating. The assumption in the Thom model is that the leader is in a continual state of spiritual development. Interpreting the Scriptures in terms of metaphors and symbols which attest to the imaginative powers of human beings, as Northrop Frye (1982) suggests, is a useful means of developing one's spiritual component. Also, Ellul (1989) and Oden (1978) are good reading.

Many people suggest that within public education there should be teaching about all religions. This idea actually is not totally at odds with the promotion of Judaeo-Christian doctrine. Rather, teaching "Common Christianity," or Christian-type ideas (common to religions) about treating people nicely, is appropriate. Religion and morality broadly refer to "the general system of truth and morals taught in Holy Scriptures," without promoting any particular religious sect (Hodgins, 1899, p. 147). It seems that the apparent decline in Christianity's influence in society and education is detrimental, that Christians are willing to accept other religions, and educators who are Christian still are best attuned to our society's fabric. (See Gairdner, 1990.) Regardless, at least what is needed in the current situation is *some* spiritual/religious base for students – to promote the idea of a divine god who presents morals and truth along the lines of people being good to each other.

So too, at least these common elements of all religions should underlie leadership in education. Currently, in some provinces the catholic religion *per se* receives special recognition through separate school systems. Many citizens argue that this is unfair. In fact, many argue that religion is a personal thing which should be taught outside the school system. However, there is a need for *some* religion in the scheme of things. In any multicultural setting there will be people representing a variety of spiritual approaches. Jung (in Campbell, 1971), in discussing the difference between Eastern and Western thinking, contributes a valuable sensitivity to this.

To take a broader view of things, one might say that society and schools are in an advanced stage of accomplishment of the original goals which missionaries set in developing education in society. They desired to transmit Judaeo-Christian thought. The fact that we now have a multicultural emphasis, whereby there is tolerance of many different groups, could be interpreted as success in producing a Christian-based society. There can be true tolerance only if deeper beliefs are held. At this stage of development the distinction between tolerance and acceptance of different values must be recognized, lest society will become too fragmented. There can be tolerance without full-fledged acceptance. Christianity recognizes the value of all people/living things in the world. Any critics should consider that, as times have changed, flexibility in interpretation of any scriptures is required to accommodate such things as archaic views of the universe, sexist and racist inferences (Ellul, 1986; Mollenkott, 1988), and the inhumane treatment of animals.

So law, moral values, and theology are foundational in the Thom model. These entities fuel the leader's conscience which, when followed, develops solid reputations for educational organizations and their executives. A reputation of being just, fair, and of service to others can truly be obtained (depicted in the Thom model, left side). The leader draws on his/her religious base to weather difficulties.

A main reason for the apparent decline in Christianity's popularity and why scholars have not previously moved to the complete law and theology model, would seem to be secular humanism. Prior models have advanced to a basis of humanism (a Biblical concept) and a suggestion of faith, but our multicultural society dictates that to promote any *one* particular faith is intolerant and wrong. Secular humanists have been very vocal and their doctrine that there is no God and no evil is tempting to many; the doctrine gives an air of openness, equality, justice, and fairness. However, without God and *his* standards of justice and fairness. (God makes wrong right; man balances right and wrong), ultimately the secular humanist adopts nihilism and discovers that it is better to be a hedonist (pleasure seeker). Otherwise, one is always "doing" for someone else, something which takes tremendous energy at least. Logically, that does not make sense. (See "The Great Debate," 1990.) What is ignored is Judaeo-Christianity's recognition of the ultimate dialectic – good and evil. Secular humanism has a sociological basis, one where people come together and support a shared definition of reality. The danger is that the people become gods unto themselves, not entertaining the thought that there might be reality beyond human knowledge and experience; they develop many questions, but have few of the answers that the external reference of God provides. "New age deceptions" tend to be extensions of secular humanism, whereby the belief is that everyone is good and values are relative – all on a goodness scale. In this there is no bad. These deceptions pervade all areas of society – education, politics, environment, health, and so on.

Author Alan Bloom (see *Interchange*, 1991) and Bruce Wilshire in *The Moral Collapse of the University* (1990) challenge the current flow of secular humanism with a call for a return to some traditional values. Bloom's beginning claim is that a person has a soul. In the real world outside of the university, Christian justice is of utmost concern.

Summary

This book has overviewed approaches to educational leadership, past and present. The model entitled "Thom's Educational Leadership with CONSCIENCE" is proposed.

Key features of the model are as follows:

• The individual as the essential unit of culture is balanced with the group;

• Conscience is informed by Judaeo-Christian doctrine;

• Conscience is evidenced through the practice of justice and fairness;

• Justice may be thought of as a universal view of what is right and fairness as a subjective view of what should be;

• Two realms of leadership activity are involved, first-order ("routine") and second-order ("laying hardball");

•The "Thom Theorem"– *Conscience drives behavior in mature individuals* – is an underpinning.

Thom's approach is timely. These particular times are characterized by educational reform, beginning with the removal of purely autocratic leadership styles and the emergence of genuine collaboration between management and workers (as evidenced in collective bargaining and collective agreements). Both society and its institutions continue to grow through stages of the collaboration style. For instance, in Canadian universities in the 1970s collective agreements were introduced in an effort to remedy political corruption within. At the outset, once procedures, etc., were in black and white, many central administrators used a heavy-handed style of "laying-on" the agreement's terms with strong impersonality. Although this style is still somewhat evident in some settings, in most the top administrators increasingly practice democracy – listening carefully to, and then fairly and justly accommodating, the wishes of workers. It is the age in which we are (Murnighan, 1991), and these emphases will continue into the future.

Institution's collective agreements define relationships between management and workers and are viewed as "law" for the institutions. This "law" should not be applied without regard for societal law. With increasing external control vis-à-vis federal and provincial governments, institutions are finding that they cannot totally be "laws unto themselves." For instance, increasingly, external forces come to bear, e.g., lawyers are interfering in issues within – issues involving equity, bias, and natural justice generally.

On the one hand, there is a strong emphasis on *collectivism* or the wish of the workers (i.e., majoritarianism) yet, on the other hand, some thrust of *subjectivism* on the part of management (after all, management is accountable). Top leaders hold the formal power and authority. In effecting their mandate they need to be morally sound, action-oriented individuals who balance thinking with the head and the heart. They should be considerate and, then, decisive. Realistically, however, in many situations egos can grow too big. The application of justice and fairness is necessary to avoid a collision course between the subjectivism and collectivism – to head off the corruption (which is "only human") with objectivity. The Thom "Educational Leadership with CONSCIENCE" approach, with its Organization Development foundation and law and faith emphasis, is particularly appropriate.

As was discussed earlier there are many philosophies of management, administration and leadership. Robert Dahl (1961) hits on a core issue when he discusses the ambiguous relationship of leaders to those being led:

> Viewed from one position, leaders are enormously influential – so influential that if they are seen only in this perspective they might well be considered a kind of ruling elite. Viewed from another position, however, many influential leaders seem to be captives of their constituents. Like the blind men with the elephant, different analysts have meticulously examined different aspects of the body politic and arrived at radically different conclusions. To some, a pluralistic democracy with dispersed inequalities is all head and no body; to others it is all body and no head. (p. 89)

Again, the conscience-based approach speaks to this. It incorporates the many philosophies and basically suggests that, in the final analysis, *no matter what the leader's style and relation*, he/she must rise above the organizational culture, and with strong moral character, courage, and faith practice justice and fair play. Faith survives the power of politics, and inherent in Thom's model is that if the leader errors it should be on the side of mercy. One can see that conscience may involve breaking away from a party line. It may also entail one's self-will "giving in" to God's will.

Of justice and fair play in modern organizations, Mann says:

> Attitudes towards justice and fair play have shifted, with a move away from the individual towards the group. Nowhere is this more evident than in the way in which respect for individual rights of property has declined, and the value of the rights of the group has been enhanced. The group claims a loyalty

to-day which seems to transcend the value of individual conscience, and which brings extreme pressure upon the individual to comply.

Thus the emphasis is utilitarian – the moral and political rightness of an action being determined by its utility, defined as its contribution to the greatest good of the greatest number. However, this collective-welfare emphasis must be tempered with the notion of not restricting the initiative of an individual to too great a degree (Gairdner, 1990). A collective neurosis can develop and it can be harmful.

Clark and Meloy (1989) consolidate some of the foregoing ideas in their propositions with respect to a democratic structure for leadership in new schools (the sociological emphasis shows through):

1. A new school must be built on the assumption of the consent of the governed;

2. A new school must be built on shared authority and responsibility, not delegation of authority and responsibility;

3. The staff of a new school must trade assignments and work in multiple groups to remain in touch with the school as a whole;

4. Formal rewards to the staff – salary, tenure, forms of promotion – should be under the control of the staff of the new school as a whole; and

5. The goals of the new school must be formulated and agreed to through group consensus. The professional staff is responsible for negotiating the acceptability of the goals to the school community (pp. 291-292).

Also, Epp (1992) highlights teacher participation as a factor in reform, and Wilson (1992) explores the relevance of a "learning organization" construct.

In vogue are alternatives that consistently trade off control for freedom (or, as Evers and Lakomski explain, "administration for emancipation") built upon the principle of the consent of the governed. However, the administrator/leader must be allowed to retain some decision-making authority while following the laws of society and conscience. Perhaps the greater danger is that, in the enthusiasm for decentralization and devolution so as to effect new community schools, administration will give up control to a point where they become irresponsible.

Chapter 8, Conclusion, brings this book to a close. Main themes are reviewed and specific issues with respect to the effective application of "Educational Leadership with CONSCIENCE," are highlighted.

References

Baldridge, J.V. (1972, February). Organizational change: The human relations perspective versus the political systems perspective. *Educational Researcher, 1*(2), 4-10+.

Beck, C. (1986). Education for spirituality. *Interchange, 17*(2), 148-156.

Bennis, W., & Nanus, B. (1985). *Leaders: The strategies for taking charge.* New York, NY: Harper and Row.

Bereiter, C. (1972). Moral alternatives to education. *Interchange, 3*(1), 25-41.

Bloom, A. (1987). *The closing of the American mind.* New York, NY: Simon and Schuster.

Boulding, K.E. (1962). *Conflict and defense: A general theory.* New York, NY: Harper and Row.

Campbell, J. (Ed.). (1971). *The portable Jung.* (R.F.C. Hull, Trans.). New York, NY: Penguin Books.

Campbell, R.F., Fleming, T., Newell, J.L., & Bennion, J.W. (1987). *A history of thought and practice in educational administration.* New York, NY: Teachers' College Press.

Canadian Charter of Rights and Freedoms.

Clark, D.L., & Meloy, J.M. (1989). Renouncing bureaucracy: A democratic structure for leadership in schools. In Thomas J. Sergiovanni & John H. Moore (Eds.), *Schooling for tomorrow: Directing reforms to issues that count* (pp. 272-294). Boston, MA: Allyn and Bacon.

Coase, R. (1988). *The firm, the market, and the law.* Chicago, IL: University of Chicago Press.

Codd, J. (1989). Educational leadership as reflective action. In John Smyth (Ed.), *Critical perspectives on educational leadership* (pp. 157-178). Philadelphia, PA: The Falmer Press.

Cohen, D. (1976, November). Loss as a theme in social policy. *Harvard Educational Review, 46,* 553-571.

Confederation College of Applied Arts and Technology. (1985). *The charter and you: The Canadian charter of rights and freedoms* (videocassette, 59 min.). Thunder Bay, ON.

Dahl, R.A. (1961). *Who governs?: Democracy and power in an American city.* New Haven, CT: Yale University Press.

Dickinson, G.M., & MacKay, A.W. (1989). *Rights, freedoms and the education system in Canada: Cases and materials.* Toronto, ON: Edmond Montgomery.

Douglas, L.C. (1930). *Magnificent obsession.* London, England: George Allen and Unwin.

Dupuis, A.M. (1985). *Philosophy of education in historical perspective.* Lanham, MD: University Press of America.

Earle, R., Imrie, D., with Archbold, R. (1989). *Your vitality quotient.* Toronto, ON: Random House.

Ellul, J. (1986). *The subversion of Christianity* (G.W. Bromiley, Trans.). Grand Rapids, MI: Wm. B. Eerdmans.

Ellul, J. (1989). *What I believe* (G.W. Bromiley, Trans.). Grand Rapids, MI: Wm. B. Eerdmans.

Epp, J.R. (1992). Teacher participation in school governance: A central element in educational reform. Paper presented at the 1992 International Congress for School Effectiveness and Improvement, Victoria, BC.

Evers, C.W., & Lakomski, G. (1991). *Knowing educational administration: Contemporary methodological controversies in educational administration research.* Oxford, England: Pergamon.

Frye, N. (1982). *The great code: The Bible and literature.* Toronto, ON: Academic Press.

Gairdner, W.D. (1990). *The trouble with Canada: A citizen speaks out.* Toronto, ON: Stoddart.

Gall, G.L. (1990). *The Canadian legal system* (3rd ed.). Toronto, ON: Carswell.

Gardner, J. (1962). *Excellence: Can we be equal and excellent too?* New York, NY: Harper and Row.

Giles, T.E., & Proudfoot, A. (1990). *Educational administration in Canada* (4th ed.). Calgary, AB: Detselig.

The great debate: Christianity versus secular humanism (Professor William Craig and Dr. Henry Morgentaler). (1990). Held at the University of Western Ontario, London, ON, January 24th (on videocassette produced by Paragon Production Services, Vancouver, BC).

Greenewalt, C.H. (1959). *The uncommon man.* New York, NY: McGraw-Hill.

Greenfield, T.B. (1986). The decline and fall of science in educational administration. *Interchange, 17*(2), 57-80.

Greiff, B.S., & Munter, P.N. (1981). *Trade offs: Executive, family and organizational life.* Scarborough, ON: Mentor.

Haines, J., & Neeley, M. (1987). *Parents' work is never done.* Far Hills, NJ: New Horizon Press.

Hart, D. (1975, October). Conference report. *UCEA Review.*

Hesse, H. (1989). *Demian* (W.J. Strachan, Trans. from the German). London, England: Paladin.

Hodgins, J.G. (1899). *Documentary history of education in Upper Canada* (Vol. 6). Toronto, ON: Warwick Bros. and Rutter.

Hodgkinson, C. (1983). *The philosophy of leadership.* Oxford, England. Basil Blackwell.

Holy Bible, new international version (1984). East Brunswick, NJ: Zondervan Bible Publishers.

Hurlbert, E.L., & Hurlbert, M.A. (1992). *School law under the charter of rights and freedoms* (2nd ed.). Calgary, AB: University of Calgary Press.

Interchange (1991), Special issue on A. Bloom's *The closing of the American mind.* Toronto, ON: OISE.

James, H.T. (1965). The nature of professional authority. In W.G. Hack, J.A. Ramseyer, W.J. Gephart, & J.B. Heck (Eds.), *Educational administration: Selected readings* (pp. 17-24). Boston, MA: Allyn and Bacon.

Klassen, D. (1991a). A model for successful change in organizations. Paper, School of Education, Lakehead University, Thunder Bay, ON.

Klassen, D. (1991b). [Review of *Harvard diary: Reflections on the sacred and the secular* (by Robert Coles, 1988)]. *Canadian Journal of Counselling, 25*(3), 371-372.

Koestenbaum, P. (1991). *Leadership: The inner side of greatness.* San Francisco, CA: Jossey-Bass.

Mann, M. (1986). The human spirit in leadership. *Journal of the Royal Society of Arts, CXXXIV* (5358), 396-407.

McRver, 1st report, Vol. 1.

Mitchell, B., & Cunningham, L.L. (Eds.) (1990). *Educational leadership and changing contexts of families, communities, and schools.* Eighty-ninth yearbook of the National Society for the Study of Education, Part II. Chicago, IL: The National Society for the Study of Education.

Mollenkott, V.R. (1988). *Women, men, and the Bible*. New York, NY: Crossroad.

Murnighan, J.K. (1991). *The dynamics of bargaining games*. Englewood Cliffs, NJ: Prentice-Hall.

Oden, T.C. (Ed.). (1978). *Parables of Kierkegaard*. Princeton, NJ: Princeton University Press.

Ontario Ministry of Education. (1986). *Discipline: Intermediate and senior divisions. Resource guide*. Toronto, ON: Queen's Printer.

Parsons, T. (1958). Some ingredients of a general theory of formal organization. In A.W. Halpin (Ed.), *Administrative theory in education* (pp. 40-72). Chicago, IL: Midwest Administration Center, University of Chicago.

Postman, N., & Weingartner, C. (1969). *Teaching as a subversive activity*. New York, NY: Dell Publishing.

"R. v. Oakes". (1986). *Dominion Law Reports* (4th). 26.

Ripple, R.E. (1986). Machines: The human dimension. *New Horizons*.

Roszak, T. (1986). *The folklore of computers and the true art of thinking*. Cambridge, England: Lutterworth Press.

Schlechty, P.C. (1990). *Schools for the twenty-first century: Leadership imperatives for educational reform*. San Francisco, CA: Jossey-Bass.

Schön, D.A. (1989). Professional knowledge and reflective practice. In Thomas J. Sergiovanni & John H. Moore (Eds.), *Schooling for tomorrow: Directing reforms to issues that count* (pp. 188-206). Boston, MA: Allyn and Bacon.

Sergiovanni, T.J. (1990). *Value-added leadership: How to get extraordinary performance in schools*. New York, NY: Harcourt Brace Jovanovich.

Sergiovanni, T.J. (1992). *Moral leadership: Getting to the heart of school improvement*. San Francisco, CA: Jossey-Bass.

Thom, D.J. (1986). On improving society and schools. *Comment on Education, 17*(1), 7-12.

Toffler, A. (1990). *Powershift: Knowledge, wealth, and violence at the edge of the 21st century*. New York, NY: Bantam Books.

Tubesing, D.A., & Tubesing, N.L. (1991). *Seeking your healthy balance*. Duluth, MN: Whole Person Press.

Van Scotter, R.D., Haas, J.D., Kraft, R.K., & Schott, J.D. (1991). *Social foundations of education* (3rd ed.). Englewood Cliffs, NJ: Prentice-Hall.

Weber, M. (1958). *The protestant ethic and the spirit of capitalism* (T. Parsons, Trans., with a foreword by R.H. Tawney). New York, NY: Scribner's.

Wilshire, B. (1990). *The moral collapse of the university: Professionalism, purity, and alienation*. Albany, NY: State University of New York Press.

Wilson, K. (1992). Developing a learning organization. Presentation at the Seventh Regional Conference of the Commonwealth Council for Educational Administration, "Educational Administrators – Facing the Challenges of the Future," Hong Kong, August 21st.

8

Conclusion

... political democracy. . . is an innovation in human history that is less than fifty years old. It came into existence through a series of constitutional amendments and judicial measures that began in the second decade of this century and continued through successive decades until the very recent past. With these legal advances in the direction of political equality and with the expansion of human rights to include economic as well as political rights, social, economic, and political democracy gradually emerged on paper, but it still has not been fully implemented.

Alder, 1983, p. 10.

Original Goal of the Book

The main goal of this book is to provide an understanding of education and effective educational leadership, now and for the future. Its complexion is sociological and its audience is all interested persons but, particularly, those in education – students, teachers, consultants, professors, and administrators. Canada is emphasized but much of the contents has wide applicability.

The goal was accomplished by first discussing the changing order in society and education, a situation of turbulence as things move into a fully multicultural, just vision. Next, goals and some history of education were covered. Then, results from research on teacher professionalism, sociological theory, and, in particular, an updated theory of bureaucracy which incorporates growing collectivist action were critically applied to the turbulence within education itself. Then, the theory and practice of educational management and leadership – past and present – were outlined. Law and finance were an initial focus. It would appear that the quest for a general theory, which began many years ago, has gone full cycle to arrive at a focus on the importance of values, beliefs, and attitudes, and redefinition of educational administration and leadership as a moral science and art within a critical knowledge context. Elaboration of this focus and a discussion of challenges culminated in the presentation of Thom's "Educational Leadership with CONSCIENCE" (TELC) Model, where conscience is Christian-shaped.

Thom's original model is rooted in concepts from Organization Development and law, and is informed by the originator's particular thesis which interrelates law, moral values, and theology within a milieu of politics and power realities. The importance of administrative law and especially a working knowledge of "justice" and "fairness" within today's educational organizations cannot be stressed enough. Education and its leaders are trailing developments in society at large. The Thom model is characterized by a blend of "applied ethics" and "administrative law," appropriate to the contemporary and future scene. Finance equity and equality issues are part of the situation. Ultimately the model and the book address the desirability of balancing the scientific and the spiritual in coming to grips with leadership, and the willingness of the leader to commit to that portion of existence which is acknowledged as unknown.

Issues

With respect to the "leading with conscience" concept, there are issues which are worth highlighting.

Currently within organizations there are several recurring issues to which "Educational Leadership with CONSCIENCE" can be applied. Such issues include women's equity, age discrimination, race discrimination, conflict of interest, and freedom of information and protection of individual privacy. The understanding of these is not "cut and dried"; each specific case must be considered by itself. McKeown (1983) and Mullan (1975) reflect this in their provocative articles, "It May Be Legal But Is It Fair?" and "Fairness, the New Natural Justice," respectively. With reference to Thom's model, depending on the specific case the resultant activity may be of a first-order realm ("routine") or second-order realm ("playing hardball") nature.

The arguments by Benn and Peters (1959) concerning "equality" illustrate the deeper complexity which is ever latent:

> . . .'Equality' as an ideal is intelligible only in a given context; that it is negative, in the sense of denying the legitimacy of certain kinds of discrimination grounded on differences held to be irrelevant. A positive egalitarianism, demanding similar treatment for all, irrespective of *any* difference, would clearly lead to absurdities. To sweep away all distinctions would be to commit injustices as inexcusable as any under attack. Moral progress is made as much by making new and justifiable distinctions as by eliminating established but irrelevant 'inequalities.' This is no less true of law than of other aspects of social organization. 'Equality before the law' is not a single ideal; its intention changes with the criteria under attack. But if we demand that legislators remove the disabilities of Roman Catholics, negroes, or women, we take it for granted nevertheless that judges should elaborate legal distinctions, create new categories with appropriate rights and duties, wherever there are reasonable and relevant differences not obviously provided for in the rules. (p. 133)

With respect to women's equity, for example, it is not just a question of removing existing criteria which restrict opportunities for women and creating a situation whereby just "being a woman" is the basis for opportunity. Once the old criteria are discarded they need to be replaced by a logical, new set which provide opportunity according to *true competence*/merit, with females and males being considered alike. To not do so is an injustice. Some employers do play an "equity game" in hiring women who are less qualified than men applicants, with a view to enhancing their organization's image. A "partnership" approach involving both men and women (Eisler, 1987) is a good beginning in attempts to resolve these types of things.

Gender, class, and race issues are becoming increasingly prevalent. They tend to form the basis of what are being termed "workplace disputes." There is growing complexity as to the jurisdiction, structure, and operation of adjudicative machinery regarding these. One can expect more and more of the same.

Several other issues are important to consider in the conscience-based approach. First, educational organizations, like all organizations, are complex social systems. Sociology, psychology, political science, economics, and related social and behavioral science disciplines all deal with such systems (Kuhn, 1974). The educational leader needs knowledge in these disciplines and a personal notion of how they combine in a unified social science for practical application in understanding one's organization. In essence, the system should be viewed as one with a variety of interacting sociological groups ("publics") with particular needs and wants. In leading with conscience the administrator must be sensitive to all the groups. Further, groups should be sensitive to each other. For example, students should be expected to follow the principle of natural justice in dealing with their teachers and professors, just as their teachers and professors should be in dealing with them. Thus, to be fair, a student with a grievance with respect to an instructor should discuss it before "going over the instructor's head" to a higher authority.

One sociological group of great importance in all of this is the young student. This was earlier mentioned, and W.R. Wees in *Nobody Can Teach Anyone Anything* (1971) reminds us as to how impressionable and precious children are. He laments that education systems are set up for adults more than they are for young students. The students are viewed as objects and teachers really believe that they are learning the information which they espouse. In reality, Wees says, "Whatever the child learns, he learns on his own . . ." The child chooses from the information provided that which integrates into his/her person. The child makes it happen.

Wees' brilliance can be summarized in his following thoughts:
- faith in children is faith in humanity;
- education is the pursuit of truth in the company of friends;
- "I have set out steps toward professionalism [in teaching] . . .

    Teacher accepts child.

    Child accepts teacher.

    Child talks, paints, cuts up, copies, and so reveals himself.

    Teacher knows child.

    Teacher provides what the child's mind needs.

    Child's mind grows;"
- nurturing the power of thought is the most important job that a person can undertake; and
- nourishing the mind means providing the child with things to think about and then encouraging him/her to think about them on his/her own.

He has the following to say about values:

> Studying man's search for what is good, philosophers identify three sets of values. The first set they call the psychological values, which turn out to be biological, the life preservers such as nourishment, security, sleep, and sex. The second set – logical, aesthetic, ethical, economic, and religious values – they call the historical values. The third set are the axioms – the triad of goodness, beauty, and truth, which from ancient times, have been the *axioma*, forms of worthiness that are self-evident.

> Within these sets of categories the child must eventually find his values. At the start, however (except for the life-preserving values), they aren't there. The children can make them live only as they formulate their own value systems, as they grow. (p. 197)

Also of interest is Coles' book on children's spiritual life (1990). In leading, the educator must have sound values – must avoid having politics overshadow such basic elements as genuine understanding, support, friendship, and learning and growth with respect to all groups being led. However, young students are terribly important and one needs to pay added attention to the treatment of this particular group. Further, a great need in society and schools, now, is for students to learn sound moral values. This would improve discipline problems. Administrators and teachers should lead by example.

One might surmise that educational leadership is becoming increasingly more difficult. The frequency of workplace disputes is just one indication. Many systems are too large and cumbersome. In recent years there has been somewhat of a moral collapse in society and institutions. Technology more and more tends to be dehumanizing. Professions seem to be stagnating. More and more, people and organizations seem to be holding few values beyond economics – money seems to be the highest ranking goal. Considering the state of affairs, it is difficult to blame administrators for becoming extremely political and for staying just a few years in one position.

Not surprisingly, a concern for law and its basis has gained new prominence. (The concern began in the U.S.) In the early 1980s the Charter of Rights and Freedoms was instituted to meet our society's wishes and it has since fueled our growth toward the multicultural, just goal. However, the journey is problematic – varied interpretations have been put on the Charter. Immigration policies are being affected. Oftentimes it appears that those who benefit the most are the lawyers and judges handling cases, often lengthy and involving large legal fees. Those in legal circles sometimes seem more interested in cases than in people. But, in the long run things should work out. For one thing, other countries seem to be following our lead with respect to the rights and freedoms theme (Germany, the Soviet Union, Hong Kong, for example). The author presented and tested his ideas in Hong Kong (Thom, 1992).

The law concern is entering a new phase. Things are settling down now that the Charter has been in place for several years. We are closer to a plateau than previously. As the yuppie generation becomes middle aged, society is witnessing a return to traditional ideas about moral values. The thesis of the association of law, moral values, and theology can ignite renewed interest in religion and family. Some individuals are calling for a redefinition of the Charter of Rights and Freedoms as the Charter of *Responsibility* (re more responsible personal expectations and behavior). This is in the conservative vein of "working for what one gets" and thinking of comforts more as privileges than as rights. The important point here is that there needs to be balance. In many cases of individuals asking for their rights and the application of fairness, things are improper. The individual becomes greedy and loses perspective. Demands can overshadow a more appropriate "asking for permission" (e.g., in abortion cases). Conscience, law, justice, and fairness are high profile terms (Meindl, 1989). With scrutiny, a just society is quite possible.

Concern for justice and fairness to prevent the abuse of managerial power is growing and will continue to grow in educational institutions. Of note is a growing interest in different emphases between female and male administrators with respect to this concern (Fennell, 1992; Young et al., 1992). Unfair/arbitrary measures of law are being heavily scrutinized. Many organizations are naive as to how the law is being broken. In-house policies may be incongruent with labor laws of general society. From all perspectives, workers and management alike are seeking legal protection, to a point where there is a danger of being "lawed to death." Those working within education need law knowledge. (References such as McCormack, 1987, are useful.) Decision-making surrounding the financial management of education, a theme which clearly is impacted by the changing social order and equity concerns, is particularly important.

In this Part Three, Educational Leadership with CONSCIENCE, the following have been presented:

• advancing leadership in education, and

• conclusion.

This book hopefully meets its original goal and through Thom's Conscience-based model plants the seed for future thought, research, publication, and development. On the horizon is a great need for the leader to understand justice and fairness and, with conscience and faith, to employ these at every level in both the enjoyable and not-so-enjoyable parts of one's work. All the while, one balances wishes of the collective with one's decision-making authority, in a changing social order. And through it all the leader must take "one day at a time" and never lose a sense of humor.

How can the "Educational Leadership with CONSCIENCE" (TELC) Model be developed from this point? Discussion of its legal and theological base can be extended in consideration of the use of knowledge, understanding, wisdom, righteousness, faith, and truth. This will further enrich a balance of both the scientific and spiritual dimensions in shaping leadership.

Both multiculturalism and Christianity are prevalent and widely supported throughout the world. This facilitates the elaboration of the Thom model and testing of "Thom's Theorem." For those who are open to God, the world is maturing. In "the big picture," Christian fellowship and patience continually place hope and faith above fear and hate.

The purpose of further development will be to increase understanding of the essence of great educational leadership. At last, through research, publication, and development such leadership is being "revealed." The structure of things is that "knowledge with understanding leads to wisdom," and the result of wisdom is righteousness and truth. Knowledge is attained through study, understanding through patience, and wisdom flowers with reflection and time. Is Christianity perhaps the ultimate paradigm which theorists are seeking?

In a just society, education, management, and leadership have many faces. The unfolding quest for greatness in such must go beyond outward manifestations of the likes of policy, politics, restructuring, and values to serious engagement with destiny, faith, and an unknown inner side.

References

Alder, M.J. (1983). *Paideia: Problems and possibilities.* New York, NY: Macmillan.

Benn, S.I., & Peters, R.S. (1959). *Social principles and the democratic state.* London, England: George Allen and Unwin.

Canadian Charter of Rights and Freedoms.

Coles, R. (1990). *The spiritual life of children.* Boston, MA: Houghton Mifflin.

Eisler, R. (1987). *The chalice and the blade.* San Francisco, CA: Harper & Row.

Fennell, H.A. (1992). Leadership for change: Two cases from the feminist perspective. Presentation at the Canadian Association for Studies in Educational Administration/Canadian Society for the Study of Education Conference, University of Prince Edward Island, Charlottetown, PEI, June 7th.

Kuhn, A. (1974). *The logic of social systems.* San Francisco, CA: Jossey-Bass.

McCormack, M.H. (1987). *The terrible truth about lawyers.* London, England: Collins.

McKeown, E.N. (1985). It may be legal but is it fair? Paper presented at the Ontario Teachers' Federation and the Ontario Association of Deans of Education Conference, Toronto, ON.

Meindl, J.R. (1989). Managing to be fair: An exploration of values, motives and leadership. *Administrative Science Quarterly, 34*(2), 252-276.

Mullan, D.J. (1975). Fairness, the new natural justice. *University of Toronto Law Journal, 25.*

Thom, D.J. (1992). The Hong Kong council for educational administration (HKCEA): Conscience and leadership. Invited address to the Seventh Regional Conference of the Commonwealth Council for Educational Administration, "Educational Administrators – Facing the Challenges of the Future," Hong Kong, August 21st.

Wees, W.R. (1971). *Nobody can teach anyone anything.* Toronto, ON: Doubleday Canada.

Young, B., Joly, L., McIntyre, S., & Staszenski, D. (1992). Care and justice in educational leadership. Presentation at the Canadian Association for Studies in Educational Administration/Canadian Society for the Study of Education Conference, University of Prince Edward Island, Charlottetown, PEI, June 7th.

Appendix A

The Context of Education

Section 93 (Education) of
the *British North America Act* (BNA Act), 1867
[renamed the *Constitution Act*, 1867, in 1982]

THE BRITISH NORTH AMERICA ACT, 1867

Education

93. In and for each Province the Legislature may exclusively make Laws in relation to Education, subject and according to the following Provisions:--

(1)   Nothing in any such Law shall prejudicially affect any Right or Privilege with respect to Denominational Schools which any Class of Persons have by Law in the Province at the Union;

(2)   All the Powers, Privileges, and Duties at the Union by Law conferred and imposed in Upper Canada on the Separate Schools and School Trustees of the Queen's Roman Catholic Subjects shall be and the same are hereby extended to the Dissentient Schools of the Queen's Protestant and Roman Catholic Subjects in Quebec;

(3)   Where in any Province a System of Separate or Dissentient Schools exists by Law at the Union or is thereafter established by the Legislature of the Province, an Appeal shall lie to the Governor General in Council from any Act or Decision of any Provincial Authority affecting any Right or Privilege of the Protestant or Roman Catholic Minority of the Queen's Subjects in relation to Education,

(4)   In case any such Provincial Law as from Time to Time seems to the Governor General in Council requisite for the due Execution of the Provisions of this Section is not made, or in case any Decision of the Governor General in Council on any Appeal under this Section is not duly executed by the proper Provincial Authority in that Behalf, then and in every such Case, and as far only as the Circumstances of each Case require, the Parliament of Canada may make remedial Laws for the due Execution of the Provisions of this Section and of any Decision of the Governor General in Council under this Section. (43)

From   *The Constitution Acts 1867 to 1982* by Department of Justice, Canada, 1986, Ottawa, ON: Ministry of Supply and Services.

Note: Canada's written constitution is called The Canada Act, 1982. It consists of five sections: The Constitution Act, 1867 (The British North America Act, 1867); The acts bringing British Columbia, Manitoba, Prince Edward Island, Alberta, Saskatchewan, and Newfoundland into Confederation; The Statute of Westminster, 1931; All amendments to the British North America Act, 1867; and The Constitution Act, 1982. The fifth section provides the Charter of Rights and Freedoms.

CANADIAN CHARTER OF RIGHTS AND FREEDOMS

Whereas Canada is founded upon principles that recognize the supremacy of God and the rule of law:

Guarantee of Rights and Freedoms

1. The *Canadian Charter of Rights and Freedoms* guarantees the rights and freedoms set out in it subject only to such reasonable limits prescribed by law as can be demonstrably justified in a free and democratic society.

Fundamental Freedoms

2. Everyone has the following fundamental freedoms: (*a*) freedom of conscience and religion; (*b*) freedom of thought, belief, opinion and expression, including freedom of the press and other media of communication; (*c*) freedom of peaceful assembly; and (*d*) freedom of association.

Democratic Rights

3. Every citizen of Canada has the right to vote in an election of members of the House of Commons or of a legislative assembly and to be qualified for membership therein. 4. (1) No House of Commons and no legislative assembly shall continue for longer than five years from the date fixed for the return of the writs at a general election of its members. (2) In time of real or apprehended war, invasion or insurrection, a House of Commons may be continued by Parliament and a legislative assembly may be continued by the legislature beyond five years if such continuation is not opposed by the votes of more than one-third of the members of the House of Commons or the legislative assembly, as the case may be. 5. There shall be a sitting of Parliament and of each legislature at least once every twelve months.

Mobility Rights

6. (1) Every citizen of Canada has the right to enter, remain in and leave Canada. (2) Every citizen of Canada and every person who has the status of a permanent resident of Canada has the right (*a*) to move to and take up residence in any province; and (*b*) to pursue the gaining of a livelihood in any province. (3) The rights specified in subsection (2) are subject to (*a*) any laws or practices of general application in force in a province other than those that discriminate among persons primarily on the basis of province of present or previous residence; and (*b*) any laws providing for reasonable residency requirements as a qualification for the receipt of publicly provided social services. (4) Subsections (2) and (3) do not preclude any law, program or activity that has as its object the amelioration in a province of conditions of individuals in that province who are socially or economically disadvantaged if the rate of employment in that province is below the rate of employment in Canada.

Legal Rights

7. Everyone has the right to life, liberty and security of the person and the right not to be deprived thereof except in accordance with the principles of fundamental justice. 8. Everyone has the right to be secure against unreasonable search or seizure. 9. Everyone has the right not to be arbitrarily detained or imprisoned. 10. Everyone has the right on arrest or detention (*a*) to be informed promptly of the reasons therefor; (*b*) to retain and instruct counsel without delay and to be informed of that right; and (*c*) to have the validity of the detention determined by way of *habeas corpus* and to be released if the detention is not lawful. 11. Any person charged with an offence has the right (*a*) to be informed without unreasonable delay of the specific offence; (*b*) to be tried within a reasonable time; (*c*) not to be compelled to be a witness in proceedings against that person in respect of the offence; (*d*) to be presumed innocent until proven guilty according to law in a fair and public hearing by an independent and impartial tribunal; (*e*) not to be denied reasonable bail without just cause; (*f*) except in the case of an offence under military law tried before a military tribunal, to the benefit of trial by jury where the maximum punishment for the offence is imprisonment for five years or a more severe punishment; (*g*) not to be found guilty on account of any act or omission unless, at the time of the act or omission, it constituted an offence under Canadian or international law or was criminal according to the general principles of law recognized by the community of nations; (*h*) if finally acquitted of the offence, not to be tried for it again and, if finally found guilty and punished for the offence, not to be tried or punished for it again; and (*i*) if found guilty of the offence and if the punishment for the offence has been varied between the time of commission and the time of sentencing, to the benefit of the lesser punishment. 12. Everyone has the right not to be subjected to any cruel and unusual treatment or punishment. 13. A witness who testifies in any proceedings has the right not to have any incriminating evidence so given used to incriminate that witness in any other proceedings, except in a prosecution for perjury or for the giving of contradictory evidence. 14. A party or witness in any proceedings who does not understand or speak the language in which the proceedings are conducted or who is deaf has the right to the assistance of an interpreter.

Equality Rights

15. (1) Every individual is equal before and under the law and has the right to the equal protection and equal benefit of the law without discrimination and, in particular, without discrimination based on race, national or ethnic origin, colour, religion, sex, age or mental or physical disability. (2) Subsection (1) does not preclude any law, program or activity that has as its object the amelioration of conditions of disadvantaged individuals or groups including those that are disadvantaged because of race, national or ethnic origin, colour, religion, sex, age or mental or physical disability.

Official Languages of Canada

16. (1) English and French are the official languages of Canada and have equality of status and equal rights and privileges as to their use in all institutions of the Parliament and government of Canada. (2) English and French are the official languages of New Brunswick and have equality of status and equal rights and privileges as to their use in all institutions of the legislature and government of New Brunswick. (3) Nothing in this Charter limits the authority of Parliament or a legislature to advance the equality of status or use of English and French. 17. (1) Everyone has the right to use English or French in any debates and other proceedings of Parliament. (2) Everyone has the right to use English or French in any debates and other proceedings of the legislature of New Brunswick. 18. (1) The statutes, records and journals of Parliament shall be printed and published in English and French and both language versions are equally authoritative. (2) The statutes, records and journals of the legislature of New Brunswick shall be printed and published in English and French and both language versions are equally authoritative. 19. (1) Either English or French may be used by any person in, or in any pleading in or process issuing from, any court established by Parliament. (2) Either English or French may be used by any person in, or in any pleading in or process issuing from, any court of New Brunswick. 20. (1) Any member of the public in Canada has the right to communicate with, and to receive available services from, any head or central office of an institution of the Parliament or government of Canada in English or French, and has the same right with respect to any other office of any such institution where (*a*) there is a significant demand for communications with and services from that office in such language; or (*b*) due to the nature of the office, it is reasonable that communications with and services from that office be available in both English and French. (2) Any member of the public in New Brunswick has the right to communicate with, and to receive available services from, any office of an institution of the legislature or government of New Brunswick in English or French. 21. Nothing in sections 16 to 20 abrogates or derogates from any right, privilege or obligation with respect to the English and French languages, or either of them, that exists or is continued by virtue of any other provision of the Constitution of Canada. 22. Nothing in sections 16 to 20 abrogates or derogates from any legal or customary right or privilege acquired or enjoyed either before or after the coming into force of this Charter with respect to any language that is not English or French.

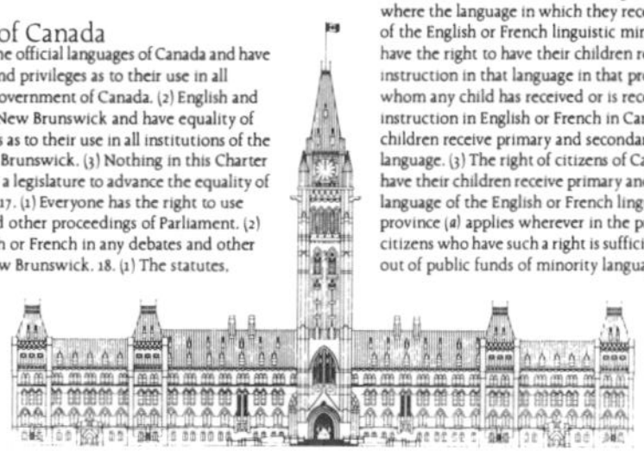

Minority Language Educational Rights

23. (1) Citizens of Canada (*a*) whose first language learned and still understood is that of the English or French linguistic minority population of the province in which they reside, or (*b*) who have received their primary school instruction in Canada in English or French and reside in a province where the language in which they received that instruction is the language of the English or French linguistic minority population of the province, have the right to have their children receive primary and secondary school instruction in that language in that province. (2) Citizens of Canada of whom any child has received or is receiving primary or secondary school instruction in English or French in Canada, have the right to have all their children receive primary and secondary school instruction in the same language. (3) The right of citizens of Canada under subsections (1) and (2) to have their children receive primary and secondary school instruction in the language of the English or French linguistic minority population of a province (*a*) applies wherever in the province the number of children of citizens who have such a right is sufficient to warrant the provision to them out of public funds of minority language instruction; and (*b*) includes, where the number of those children so warrants, the right to have them receive that instruction in minority language educational facilities provided out of public funds.

Enforcement

24. (1) Anyone whose rights or freedoms, as guaranteed by this Charter, have been infringed or denied may apply to a court of competent jurisdiction to obtain such remedy as the court considers appropriate and just in the circumstances. (2) Where, in proceedings under subsection (1), a court concludes that evidence was obtained in a manner that infringed or denied any rights or freedoms guaranteed by this Charter, the evidence shall be excluded if it is established that, having regard to all the circumstances, the admission of it in the proceedings would bring the administration of justice into disrepute.

General

25. The guarantee in this Charter of certain rights and freedoms shall not be construed so as to abrogate or derogate from any aboriginal, treaty or other rights or freedoms that pertain to the aboriginal peoples of Canada including (*a*) any rights or freedoms that have been recognized by the Royal Proclamation of October 7, 1763; and (*b*) any rights or freedoms that may be acquired by the aboriginal peoples of Canada by way of land claims settlement. 26. The guarantee in this Charter of certain rights and freedoms shall not be construed as denying the existence of any other rights or freedoms that exist in Canada. 27. This Charter shall be interpreted in a manner consistent with the preservation and enhancement of the multicultural heritage of Canadians. 28. Notwithstanding anything in this Charter, the rights and freedoms referred to in it are guaranteed equally to male and female persons. 29. Nothing in this Charter abrogates or derogates from any rights or privileges guaranteed by or under the Constitution of Canada in respect of denominational, separate or dissentient schools. 30. A reference in this Charter to a province or to the legislative assembly or legislature of a province shall be deemed to include a reference to the Yukon Territory and the Northwest Territories, or to the appropriate legislative authority thereof, as the case may be. 31. Nothing in this Charter extends the legislative powers of any body or authority.

Application of Charter

32. (1) This Charter applies (*a*) to the Parliament and government of Canada in respect of all matters within the authority of Parliament including all matters relating to the Yukon Territory and Northwest Territories; and (*b*) to the legislature and government of each province in respect of all matters within the authority of the legislature of each province. (2) Notwithstanding subsection (1), section 15 shall not have effect until three years after this section comes into force. 33. (1) Parliament or the legislature of a province may expressly declare in an Act of Parliament or of the legislature, as the case may be, that the Act or a provision thereof shall operate notwithstanding a provision included in section 2 or sections 7 to 15 of this Charter. (2) An Act or a provision of an Act in respect of which a declaration made under this section is in effect shall have such operation as it would have but for the provision of this Charter referred to in the declaration. (3) A declaration made under subsection (1) shall cease to have effect five years after it comes into force or on such earlier date as may be specified in the declaration. (4) Parliament or a legislature of a province may re-enact a declaration made under subsection (1). (5) Subsection (3) applies in respect of a re-enactment made under subsection (4).

Citation

34. This Part may be cited as the *Canadian Charter of Rights and Freedoms*.

"We must now establish the basic principles, the basic values and beliefs which hold us together as Canadians so that beyond our regional loyalties there is a way of life and a system of values which make us proud of the country that has given us such freedom and such immeasurable joy."

P.E. Trudeau 1981

Ontario
Human Rights Commission

Declaration of Management Policy

We observe and uphold the

HUMAN RIGHTS CODE, 1981

It is public policy in Ontario to recognize the dignity and worth of every person and to provide for equal rights and opportunities without discrimination that is contrary to law.

The Human Right Code, 1981, provides for equal treatment in the areas of services, goods and facilities, accommodation, contracts, employment, and membership in vocational associations and trade unions without discrimination on the grounds of race, ancestry, place of origin, colour, ethnic origin, citizenship, creed, sex, sexual orientation, handicap, age, family status, marital status, the receipt of public assistance (in accommodation only), and record of offences (in employment only).

The Code provides for freedom from harassment or other unwelcome comments and actions in employment, services and accommodation on all of the grounds.

It is the privilege and the responsibility of every person in Ontario to honour and adhere to the letter and spirit of the Code, and to support its aim of creating a climate of understanding and mutual respect for the dignity and rights of each individual.

We recognize that this applies to all employers, employees, employment agencies, trade unions, professional associations, landlords, tenants, realtors, those entering into a contract, and those providing goods, services and facilities.

ONTARIO HUMAN RIGHTS COMMISSION
400 University Avenue, Toronto, Ontario M7A 2R9

Offices in Hamilton, Kenora, Kingston, Kitchener, London, Mississauga,
Ottawa, Sault Ste. Marie, St. Catharines, Scarborough, Sudbury, Thunder Bay, Timmins, Windsor.

reprinted with permission.

Legal Rights of Young Offenders
(re the Schools)

11.(1) A young person has the right to retain and instruct counsel without delay, and to exercise that right personally, at any stage of proceedings against the young person and prior to and during any consideration of whether, instead of commencing or continuing judicial proceedings against the young person under this Act, to use alternative measures to deal with the young person.

(2) Every young person who is arrested or detained shall, forthwith on his arrest or detention, be advised by the arresting officer or the officer in charge, as the case may be, of his right to be represented by counsel and shall be given an opportunity to obtain counsel.

56.(1) Subject to this section, the law relating to the admissibility of statements made by persons accused of committing offences applies in respect of young persons.

(2) No oral or written statement given by a young person to a peace officer or other person who is, in law, a person in authority is admissible against the young person unless
a) the statement was voluntary;
b) the person to whom the statement was given has, before the statement was made, clearly explained to the young person, in language appropriate to his age and understanding, that
i) the young person is under no obligation to give a statement,
ii) any statement given by him may be used as evidence in proceedings against him,
iii) the young person has the right to consult another person in accordance with paragraph (c), and
iv) any statement made by the young person is required to be made in the presence of the person consulted, unless the young person desires otherwise;
c) the young person has, before the statement was made, been given a reasonable opportunity to consult with counsel or a parent, or in the absence of a parent, an adult relative, or in the absence of a parent and an adult relative, any other appropriate adult chosen by the young person; and
d) where the young person consults any person pursuant to paragraph (c), the young person has been given a reasonable opportunity to make the statement in the presence of that person.

(3) The requirements set out in paragraphs (2)(b), (c) and (d) do not apply in respect of oral statements where they are made spontaneously by the young person to a peace officer or other person in authority before the person has had a reasonable opportunity to comply with those requirements.

(4) A young person may waive his rights under paragraph (2)(c) or (d) but any such waiver shall be made in writing and shall contain a statement signed by the young person that he has been apprised of the right that he is waiving.

(5) A youth court judge may rule inadmissible in any proceedings under this Act a statement given by the young person in respect of whom the proceedings are taken if the young person satisfies the judge that the statement was given under duress imposed by any person who is not, in law, a person in authority.

(6) For the purpose of this section, an adult consulted pursuant to paragraph 56(2)(c) shall, in the absence of evidence to the contrary, be deemed not to be a person in authority.

From   "Young Offenders Act (1988)" in E.L. Greenspan, 1988, *Martin's Annual Criminal Code 1989*. Aurora, ON: Canada Law Book.

Child Abuse Reporting

7.(1) A person who has reasonable grounds to believe that a child is in need of protection shall forthwith report the circumstances to the superintendent of a person designated by the superintendent to receive such reports.

(2) The duty under subsection (1) overrides a claim of confidentiality of privilege by a person following any occupation or profession, except a claim founded on a solicitor and client relationship.

(3) No action lies against a person making a report under this section unless he makes it maliciously or without reasonable grounds for his belief.

(4) A person who contravenes subsection (1) commits an offence.

From   "Family and Child Service Act (1980)" in *Statutes of the Province of British Columbia*. Victoria, BC: Queen's Printer.

3.(1) Any person who has reasonable and probable ground to believe and believes that a child is in need of protective services shall forthwith report the matter to a director.

...

(5) Notwithstanding and in addition to any other penalty provided by this Act, if a director has reasonable and probable grounds to believe that a person has not complied with subsection (1) and that person is registered under an Act regulating a profession or occupation prescribed in the regulations, the director shall advise the appropriate governing body of that profession or occupation of the failure to comply.

(6) Any person who fails to comply with subsection (1) is guilty of an offence and liable to a fine of not more than $2000 and in default of payment to imprisonment for a term of not more than 6 months.

From   "Child Welfare Act (1984)" in *Statutes of Alberta*. Edmonton, AB: Queen's Printer.

Legal Framework of a Provincial System

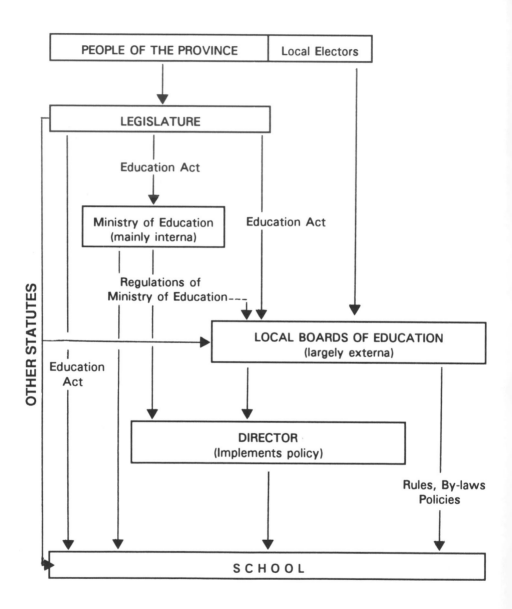

Education Organization (Ontario)

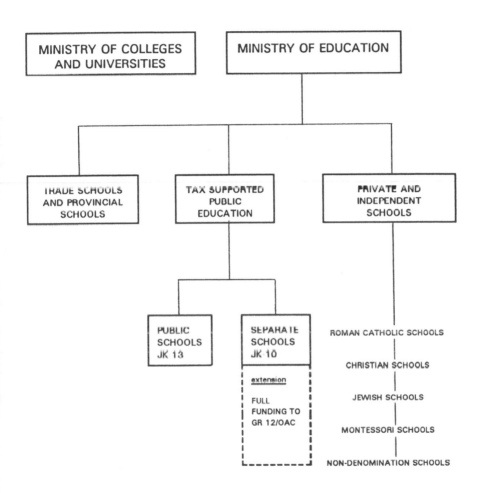

MINISTRY OF COLLEGES AND UNIVERSITIES

MINISTRY OF EDUCATION

TRADE SCHOOLS AND PROVINCIAL SCHOOLS

TAX SUPPORTED PUBLIC EDUCATION

PRIVATE AND INDEPENDENT SCHOOLS

PUBLIC SCHOOLS JK 13

SEPARATE SCHOOLS JK 10

extension

FULL FUNDING TO GR 12/OAC

ROMAN CATHOLIC SCHOOLS

CHRISTIAN SCHOOLS

JEWISH SCHOOLS

MONTESSORI SCHOOLS

NON-DENOMINATION SCHOOLS

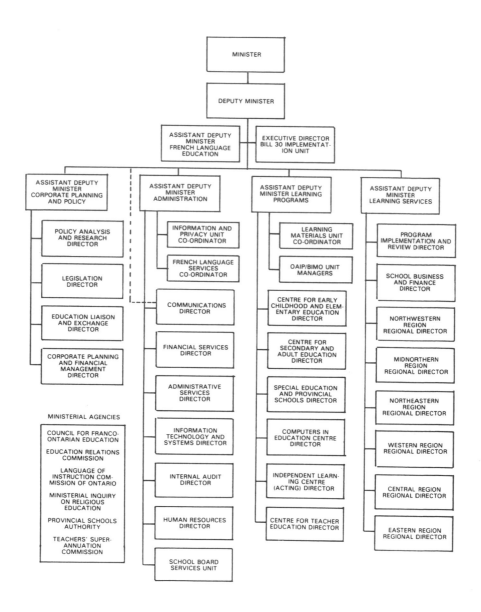

**MINISTRY OF EDUCATION
ORGANIZATION CHART
APRIL 1989**

Reproduced with the permission of the
Ministry of Education, Ontario

Note: In February 1993 it was announced that Ontario would structure a new super-Ministry for Education and Training.

BOARD OF EDUCATION

1. ADMINISTRATION

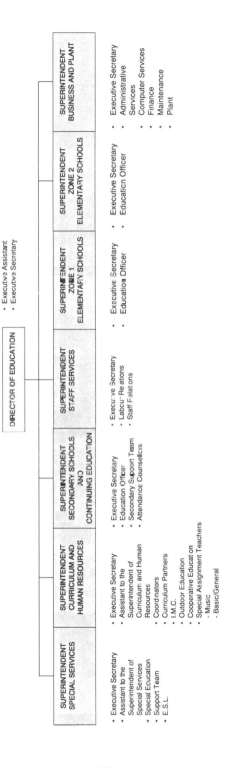

- Executive Assistant
- Executive Secretary

DIRECTOR OF EDUCATION

SUPERINTENDENT SPECIAL SERVICES
- Executive Secretary
- Assistant to the Superintendent of Special Services
- Special Education
- Support Team
- E.S.L.

SUPERINTENDENT CURRICULUM AND HUMAN RESOURCES
- Executive Secretary
- Assistant to the Superintendent of Curriculum and Human Resources
- Coordinators
- Curriculum Partners
- I.M.C.
- Outdoor Education
- Cooperative Education
- Special Assignment Teachers
  - Music
  - Basic/General

SUPERINTENDENT SECONDARY SCHOOLS AND CONTINUING EDUCATION
- Executive Secretary
- Education Officer
- Secondary Support Team
- Attendance Counsellors

SUPERINTENDENT STAFF SERVICES
- Executive Secretary
- Labour Relations
- Staff Relations

SUPERINTENDENT ZONE 1 ELEMENTARY SCHOOLS
- Executive Secretary
- Education Officer

SUPERINTENDENT ZONE 2 ELEMENTARY SCHOOLS
- Executive Secretary
- Education Officer

SUPERINTENDENT BUSINESS AND PLANT
- Executive Secretary
- Administrative Services
- Computer Services
- Finance
- Maintenance
- Plant

2. SCHOOL TRUSTEES

Varying number elected by the community to serve that community's educational interests

193

Table 2
Duties of school boards

Schools	Officers and employees	Ministry	Board
☐ Run in accordance with the Act and regulations and keep open for the whole school year	☐ Appoint a secretary and a treasurer or a secretary-treasurer for the board	☐ Transmit to the minister all information required by the act and regulations	☐ Fix time and place for meetings; keep records of proceedings
☐ Provide instruction and adequate accommodation for pupils	☐ Take proper security from the treasurer	☐ Report once per year the names of all children of compulsory school age in its jurisdiction who are not attending school or in private schools – plus the reasons for lack of attendance	☐ Establish and maintain a head office and notify the ministry of any change in address
☐ Keep buildings in repair and insured	☐ Order treasurer to pay moneys for school purposes		
☐ Appoint adequate number of qualified principals and teachers	☐ Issue statement of sick leave credits to employees on termination of employment		
☐ Provide without charge texts required by regulations			
☐ Provide special-education programs for exceptional children			

Source: Education Act, RSO 1980: various sections.

From: *A Hard Act to Follow* (rev. 13th ed.) by V.K. Gilbert, R.A. Martin, and A.T. Sheehan, 1990, pp. 26-27. Copyright © 1990 by Guidance Centre, OISE, Toronto, ON. Reprinted by permission.

The Goals of Education

The family is one of the prime forces in the total education and development of most children. Further influences come from the church, the community, the media, and a variety of other social groups. The Ministry of Education and the school boards in the Province of Ontario share the responsibility for public education, that is, for formal schooling. When these groups are in harmony in their beliefs and practices, the goals of education, forged from the needs of society and the wealth of accumulated knowledge about teaching and learning, can be pursued with vigor and confidence.

The Ministry of Education in Ontario strives to provide in the schools of the province equal educational opportunity for all. In its contribution to programs, personnel, facilities, and resources, the Ministry has the overall purpose of helping individual learners achieve their potential in physical, intellectual, emotional, social, cultural, and moral development. The goals of education, therefore, consist of HELPING EACH STUDENT DEVELOP:

1 A RESPONSIVENESS TO THE DYNAMIC PROCESS OF LEARNING

Processes of learning include observing, sensing, inquiring, creating, analysing, synthesizing, evaluating, and communicating. The dynamic aspect of these processes springs from their source in many instinctive human activities, their application to real-life experiences, and their systematic interrelation within the curriculum.

2. RESOURCEFULNESS, ADAPTABILITY, AND CREATIVITY IN LEARNING AND LIVING

These attributes apply to modes of study and inquiry, to the management of personal affairs such as career plans and leisure activities, and to the ability to cope with challenge and change.

3. THE BASIC KNOWLEDGE AND SKILLS NEEDED TO COMPREHEND AND EXPRESS IDEAS THROUGH WORDS, NUMBERS, AND OTHER SYMBOLS

Such knowledge and skills will assist the learner in applying rational and intuitive processes to the identification and solution of problems by
a) using language aptly as a means of communication and an instrument of thought;
b) reading, listening, and viewing with comprehension and insight;
c) understanding and using mathematical operations and concepts.

4. PHYSICAL FITNESS AND GOOD HEALTH

Factors that contribute to fitness and good health include regular physical activity, and understanding of human biology and nutrition, the avoidance of health hazards, and concern for personal well-being.

5. SATISFACTION FROM PARTICIPATING AND FROM SHARING THE PARTICIPATION OF OTHERS IN VARIOUS FORMS OF ARTISTIC EXPRESSION

Artistic expression involves the clarification and restructuring of personal perception and experience. It is found in the visual arts, music, drama, and literature, as well as in other areas of the curriculum where both the expressive and receptive capabilities of the learner are being developed.

6. A FEELING OF SELF-WORTH

Self-worth is affected by internal and external influences. Internally it is fostered by realistic self-appraisal, confidence and conviction in the pursuit of excellence, self-discipline, and the satisfaction of achievement. Externally it is reinfrorced by encouragement, respect, and supportive evaluation.

7. AN UNDERSTANDING OF THE ROLE OF THE INDIVIDUAL WITHIN THE FAMILY AND THE ROLE OF THE FAMILY WITHIN THE SOCIETY

Within the family the individual shares responsibility, develops supportive relationships, and acquires values. Within society the family contributes to the stability and quality of a democratic way of life.

8. SKILLS THAT CONTRIBUTE TO SELF-RELIANCE IN SOLVING PRACTICAL PROBLEMS IN EVERYDAY LIFE

These skills relate to the skilfull managment of personal resources, effective participation in legal and civic transactions, the art of parenthood, responsible consumerism, the appropriate use of community agencies and services, the application of accident prevention techniques and a practical understanding of the basic technology of home maintenance.

9. AN ACCEPTANCE OF PERSONAL RESPONSIBILITY IN SOCIETY AT THE LOCAL, NATIONAL, AND INTERNATIONAL LEVELS

Awareness of personal responsibility in society grows out of knowledge and understanding of one's community, one's country, and the rest of the world. It is based on an understanding of social order, a respect for the law and the rights of others, and a concern for the quality of life at home and abroad.

10. ESTEEM FOR THE CUSTOMS, CULTURES, AND BELIEFS OF A WIDE VARIETY OF SOCIETAL GROUPS

This goal is related to social concord and individual enrichment. In Canada it includes regard for
a) the native peoples;
b) the English and French founding peoples;
c) multiculturalism;
d) national identity and unity.

11. SKILLS AND ATTITUDES THAT WILL LEAD TO SATISFACTION AND PRODUCTIVITY IN THE WORLD OF WORK

As well as the appropriate academic, technical, and interpersonal skills, this goal relates to good work-habits, flexibility, initiative, leadership, the ability to cope with stress, and regard for the dignity of work.

12. RESPECT FOR THE ENVIRONMENT AND A COMMITMENT TO THE WISE USE OF RESOURCES

This goal relates to a knowledgeable concern for the quality of the environment, the careful use of natural resources, and the humane treatment of living things.

13. VALUES RELATED TO PERSONAL ETHICAL OR RELIGIOUS BELIEFS
AND TO THE COMMON WELFARE OF SOCIETY

Moral development in the school depends in part on a consideration of ethical principles and religious beliefs, a respect for the ideals held by others, and the identification of personal and societal values.

The preceding goals are not arranged in any hierarchical order, nor are they discrete categories from which a checklist should be made. The integrated nature of learning and the complex pattern of human development preclude such a sequential or fragmented approach. The translation of the goals into classroom objectives, however, will undoubtedly result in sequences of learning appropriate to the particular level and stages of development of the students for whom a program is being planned. To the extent that these goals of education are achieved through endeavors inside and outside the schools of this province, to that extent will the future citizens of Ontario be lifelong learners who can think clearly, feel deeply, and act wisely.

From: *Issues and Directions* by Ministry of Education and Ministry of Colleges and Universities, Ontario, 1980, pp. 4-7, Toronto, ON: Queen's Printer.

Typical School Board Statement of Goals

Whereas Board of Education X is charged with the responsibility of providing the best possible educational services for the students under its jurisdiction, it is, therefore, the intent of this document to state the goals which will provide direction to those associated with Board of Education X.

The student, as a person and a learner, is the focus of concern in the schools.

> The schools will nurture the development of the individual's self-worth, self-respect, self-discipline, and pride in personal achievement.

> The schools will foster the development of social responsibility, respect for others and their rights, and an appreciation of the democratic process.

> The schools will encourage the development of inquiring, critical minds, and the ability to adapt to change.

> The schools will strive to provide for individual and collective interests, abilities, and needs.

> The schools will provide opportunities for the development of competence and the achievement of excellence in the basic skills, and a variety of academic, aesthetic, vocational, and special education programs.

> The schools will produce learning environments conducive to the development of physical and mental well-being and moral sensitivity.

> The schools will provide opportunities for students to grow and learn through individual and cooperative experiences.

> Board of Education X, and its schools, will provide for the continuous development of the student as he or she progresses through a coordinated program.

> Board of Education X will provide an organizational climate characterized by openness and trust.

> Board of Education X will strive to provide, within the limits of its resources, equal access to educational opportunities for all of its students.

> Board of Education X will foster a process of community-school involvement.

Board of Education X recognizes the professional teachers as the key element in the formal educational process. The students, parents, and the community share responsibility with Board of Education X and its staff in the attainment of the above stated goals.

Table 1
Provincial Arrangements re Choice in Schooling*

		Separate System	Allows for private schools	Direct funding for private schools	Other Benefits	Special Arrangements
1.	British Columbia	no	yes	yes	$500 grant per pupil in 1979	private schools may have their own inspectors
2.	Alberta	yes	yes (four categories)	up to 75% of per pupil grant for Category I	–	Minister of Education may inspect schools
3.	Saskatchewan	yes	yes	yes, for secondary schools only	may charge extra fees for students from public systems	subject to provincial inspection
4.	Manitoba	no	yes	yes, since 1979	free textbooks, and shared services with public, e.g. transportation	public boards may enter into tuition agreements
5.	Ontario	yes	yes	no	free curriculum materials	secondary private schools may ask for inspection to become accredited
6.	Quebec	yes	yes, five types	yes	private school body may meet with minister	provincial inspection required periodically
7.	New Brunswick	no	yes	only for handicapped	–	–
8.	Nova Scotia	no	yes	no	private schools may buy materials through public offices wholesale	
9.	Prince Edward Island	no	not really	no	–	students need special permission from the Minister to attend other than public schools
10.	Newfoundland	yes	yes, but none exist	yes, but only if they are the only school available to a community	–	private schools are subject to provincial approval and inspection

Appendix B
Teachers and Administrators

Nature of the Teaching Profession –
Policy Statement, Canadian Teachers' Federation

The following statement was adopted at the Annual General Meeting of the Canadian Teachers' Federation in 1976 as a statement of policy of the Federation concerning the teaching profession. This statement serves in place of a National Code of Ethics for Canadian Teachers, as a result of the position taken by the Canadian Teachers' Federation at its Annual Meeting in 1968 which established the principle of provincial right and responsibility to develop, approve and implement provincial codes of ethics and/or standards of conduct. In Canada, then, there is no national Code of Ethics, but rather, the 1976 statement of the nature of the teaching profession, which reads:

The teacher provides a personal service to each student, based on the specialized application of the teacher's understanding of the learning process and designed to meet the educational needs of each individual within the individual's society. Society, of which teachers are a part, establishes the goals of education, and the organizational frame, within which formal education occurs. Teachers (and, ultimately, each teacher) determine the strategies, the techniques, and the materials by which these goals are achieved. The general purpose of education is the full development of the potential of each individual, the full cultivation of the learning capacity of each individual, and the full expression of the creative skills of each individual.

A. It is the responsibility of the teacher:

(a) constantly to review her/his own level of competence and effectiveness, and to seek necessary improvements as part of a continuing process of professional development;

(b) to perform her/his professional duties according to an appropriate code of ethics, and appropriate standard of professional conduct;

(c) to recognize that teaching is a collective activity, and to seek the most effective means of consultation and of collaboration with her/his professional colleagues;

(d) to support, and to participate in, the efforts of her/his professional association to improve the quality of education and the status of the teaching profession.

B. It is the responsibility of the teaching profession:

(a) to participate in defining the specific goals of education;

(b) to devise appropriate sets of learning programs, and remedies for specific difficulties;

(c) to develop instruments for the evaluation of the educational process;

(d) to assist in the design and the production of resource materials for the learning process;

(e) to participate in the design of systems, facilities, organizational patterns, and the administrative structures for the educational process.

C. It is the responsibility of the teaching profession:

(a) to promote the continuous improvement of professional competence, and of conditions of learning, and of teaching;

(b) to establish its own code of ethics, and standard of professional conduct, its own criteria for professional qualifications, and its own procedures for the assessment of professional competence;

(c) to strive to attain, for each teacher, a level of status and of economic standing appropriate to the education and responsibilities of the professional teacher;

(d) to protect each teacher from interference in the proper discharge of professional duties.

D. It is the responsibility of the teaching profession:

(a) to cooperate with institutions of teacher education to establish entry qualifications and educational programs suitable to such institutions;

(b) to cooperate with institutions of teacher education to provide appropriate practical experience for teachers-in-training;

(c) to cooperate with institutions of teacher education to evaluate potential graduates of such institutions.

E. It is the responsibility of organizations of the teaching profession:

(a) to assume, to administer, and to discharge effectively the collective responsibility of the profession;

(b) to maintain autonomous status and effective democratic self-government within the organization;

(c) to maintain the principle of professional unity and collegial relationship among all certified teachers within the jurisdiction of the organization.

From: *An Introduction to Educational Administration in Canada* (2nd ed.) by Leslie R. Gue, 1985, pp. 259-261. Copyright © 1985 by McGraw-Hill Ryerson Ltd., Toronto, ON. Reprinted by permission.

Canadian Teachers' Federation (CTF) Structure

Member Organizations

British Columbia Teachers' Federation
The Alberta Teachers' Association
Saskatchewan Teachers' Federation
The Manitoba Teachers' Society
Ontario Teachers' Federation
*Federation of Women Teachers'
Associations of Ontario
*Ontario Secondary School Teachers'
Federation
*The Ontario English Catholic Teachers'
Association
*L'Association des Enseignants Franco
-Ontariens
*Ontario Public School Teachers'
Federation
Provincial Association of Catholic
Teachers (Quebec)
Provincial Association of Protestant
Teachers of Quebec
New Brunswick Teachers' Association
L'Association des Enseignants
Francophones du Nouveau-Brunswick
New Brunswick Teachers' Federation
Nova Scotia Teachers' Union
Prince Edward Island Teachers'
Federation
The Newfoundland Teachers' Association
Northwest Territories Teachers'
Association
Yukon Teachers' Association

Executive Committee

Board of Governors

Annual
General Meeting

*Technically, these are not member organizations in that the members hold CTF membership only through their OTF membership.

Ontario Teachers' Federation (OTF)

In Ontario all teachers teaching in publicly supported schools must, by provincial statute, belong to the Ontario Teachers' Federation. This professional organization has five affiliated organizations, each of which will be described following the OTF description. The OTF members are allocated membership in one of these five affiliates according to the OTF by-laws. Thus OTF membership is mandatory, as is membership in the appropriate affiliate. The Board of Governors votes on the fee, as requested by an affiliate, which then needs to be approved by the Lieutenant Governor in Council. The fees, which include the affiliate fee, a fee for the Canadian Teachers' Federation and a fee for the OTF, are collected by the OTF and distributed accordingly.

The OTF, which was formed in 1944, is governed by a 50 member Board of Governors, with each affiliate appointing ten members. The Board meets at least three times a year dealing primarily with matters which affect all the teachers of the province. A policy developed in this manner may be reconsidered at the request of at least one affiliate. The Federation Executive, consisting of eleven members elected by the Board of Governors, meets once per month. Standing committees and special committees of the Board of Governors report to the Board of Governors.

The OTF is the official liaison between the teachers of the province and the Minister of Education. They meet with the Ministry frequently during the year to discuss matters of an educational and professional nature. The OTF names representatives to committees set up by the Ministry of Education. Breaches of the Code of Ethics are dealt with by the OTF, with the right of appeal to the Federation Executive or Board of Governors. The OTF concerns itself with activities which contribute to the further professional improvement of education in the province.

At least three times a year the OTF, through its official publication, *Interaction,* reports to the members on the Federation's activities and other matters of concern. The address of the OTF is 1260 Bay Street, Toronto. In addition to the secretary-treasurer... there is a senior staff of seven persons each with a major responsibility such as teacher education, educational finance, superannuation, acts and regulations, professional education, communications.

Ontario Teachers' Federation –

Approximately 105,000 members; five affiliated bodies

Ontario Secondary School Teachers' Federation –
Approximately 35,000 members; 55 districts; districts divided into branches of one school staff each

Federation of Women Teachers' Association of Ontario –

Approximately 30,000 members; 5 Regions divided into 78 Associations; Associations by inspectorates; some Associations divided into units

Ontario Public School Teachers' Federation –

Approximately 15,000 members; 72 districts divided into branches

Ontario English Catholic Teachers' Association –
Approximately 20,000 members; 49 units

L'Association des Enseignants Franco-Ontariens –

Approximately 5,300 members; 28 Regional Districts; Districts divided into locals

From: *Educational Administration in Canada* (3rd ed.) by T.E. Giles and A.J. Proudfoot, 1984. Copyright © 1984 by Detselig Enterprises Ltd., Calgary, AB.

Ontario

This is to certify that
Nous, soussignés, certifions que

having complied with the
regulations made under The
Education Act, 1974 is
hereby granted an

_yant satisfait aux exigences
des règlements établis selon
la loi sur l'Éducation de 1974
reçoit par la présente un

SAMPLE ONLY

Ontario Teacher's Certificate
Brevet d'enseignement de l'Ontario

valid in the schools of
Ontario in accordance with
the regulations made under
The Education Act, 1974

valable dans les écoles de
l'Ontario d'après les
règlements établis selon la
loi sur l'Éducation de 1974

Number
Numéro _____

Dated at Toronto this _____ day of
Fait à Toronto ce _____ jour du mois de _____ 19 ____

DEPUTY MINISTER
OF EDUCATION

LE SOUS-MINISTRE
DE L'ÉDUCATION

MINISTER
OF EDUCATION

LE MINISTRE
DE L'ÉDUCATION

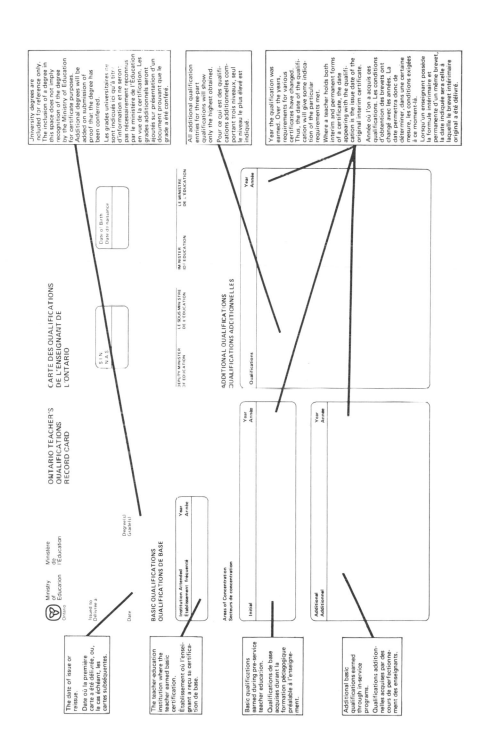

ONTARIO TEACHER'S QUALIFICATIONS RECORD CARD

CARTE DES QUALIFICATIONS DE L'ENSEIGNANT DE L'ONTARIO

Ministry of Education — Ministère de l'Éducation — Ontario

Issued to / Délivré à

Date

Degree(s) / Grade(s)

Date of Birth / Date de naissance

S I N / N A S

DEPUTY MINISTER OF EDUCATION / LE SOUS-MINISTRE DE L'ÉDUCATION

MINISTER OF EDUCATION / LE MINISTRE DE L'ÉDUCATION

BASIC QUALIFICATIONS
QUALIFICATIONS DE BASE

Institution Attended / Établissement fréquenté — Year / Année

Areas of Concentration / Secteur de concentration

Initial — Year / Année

ADDITIONAL QUALIFICATIONS
QUALIFICATIONS ADDITIONNELLES

Qualifications — Year / Année

Additional / Additionnel — Year / Année

University degrees are included for reference only. The inclusion of a degree in this space does not imply recognition of the degree by the Ministry of Education for certificate purposes. Additional degrees will be added on submission of proof that the degree has been conferred.

Les grades universitaires ne sont indiqués ici qu'à titre d'information et ne seront pas nécessairement reconnus par le ministère de l'Éducation en vue de la certification. Les grades additionnels seront ajoutés sur présentation d'un document prouvant que le grade a été conféré.

All additional qualification entries for three-part qualifications will show only the highest obtained.

Pour ce qui est des qualifications additionnelles comportant trois niveaux, seul le niveau le plus élevé est indiqué.

Year the qualification was earned. Over the years, requirements for various certificates have changed. Thus, the date of the qualification will give some indication of the particular requirements met.

Where a teacher holds both interim and permanent forms of a certificate, the date appearing with the qualification is the issue date of the original interim certificate.

Année où l'on a acquis ces qualifications. Les conditions d'obtention des brevets ont changé avec les années. La date permettra donc de déterminer, dans une certaine mesure, les conditions exigées à ce moment-là.

Lorsqu'un enseignant possède la formule intérimaire et permanente d'un même brevet, la date indiquée sera celle à laquelle le brevet intérimaire original a été délivré.

The date of issue or reissue.

Date où la première carte a été délivrée, ou, le cas échéant, les cartes subséquentes.

The teacher-education institution where the teacher earned basic certification.

Établissement où l'enseignant a reçu sa certification de base.

Basic qualifications earned during pre-service teacher education.

Qualifications de base acquises durant la formation pédagogique préalable à l'enseignement.

Additional basic qualifications earned through in-service programs.

Qualifications additionnelles acquises par des cours de perfectionnement des enseignants.

How OSSTF Certification Works

The OSSTF Certification Plan is designed to assist individual members by providing a systematic and consistent method for improving qualifications.

Ministry of Education

Authorization to teach is the responsibility of the Ontario Ministry of Education. The Ministry issues Ontario Teacher's Certificates (OTC) and Ontario Teacher's Qualifications Record Cards (OTQRC).

Certification Department

Members of the Department include trained evaluators and appropriate support staff. The Department evaluates teacher qualifications according to the regulations of the OSSTF Certification Plan and then issues Certification Rating Statements. These Statements are used in OSSTF - Board Collective Agreements for salary placement.

Certification Council

Council is comprised of up to 10 members from across Ontario who are participating teacher members of OSSTF. Council formulates and interprets the OSSTF Certification Regulations and is responsible for recommending any changes to the Regulations to the Annual Meeting of the Provincial Assembly.

Certification Appeal Board

The Certification Appeal Board has a minimum of three teacher members who are appointed by the Provincial Executive. The Board is responsible for hearing member appeals.

Certification: Where You Start

1. Begin by obtaining an application form for an OSSTF Certification Rating Statement from your Branch President, your Principal, or the Certification Department (address below).

2. Enclose with the application form copies of your Ontario Teacher's Certificate, Ontario Teacher Qualifications Record Card, originals of official university transcripts, originals of any additional information pertaining to courses taken, and your membership card number.

3. Mail to: OSSTF Certification, 60 Mobile Drive, Toronto, Ontario M4A 2P3.

4. Applications are evaluated by evaluators in the Certification Department using the Regulations of the current Certification Plan.

5. Allow approximately six weeks for processing.

6. Be sure to inform your Board that you have applied for a Certification Rating Statement.

> Avoid calling the Certification Department for progress reports on your file. This merely slows down the processing. The Certification Department normally receives about 14,000 pieces of correspondence annually.

Certification: The Flow Chart

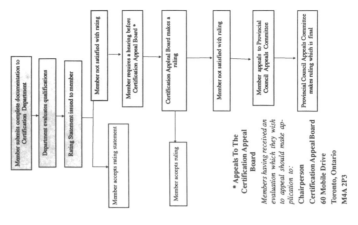

Member submits complete documentation to Certification Department

Department evaluates qualifications

Rating Statement issued to member

Member accepts rating statement

Member not satisfied with rating

Member requires a hearing before Certification Appeal Board *

Certification Appeal Board makes a ruling

Member accepts ruling

Member not satisfied with ruling

Member appeals to Provincial Council Appeals Committee

Provincial Council Appeals Committee makes ruling which is final

* Appeals To The Certification Appeal Board

Members having received an evaluation which they wish to appeal should make application to:

Chairperson
Certification Appeal Board
60 Mobile Drive
Toronto, Ontario
M4A 2P3

Reprinted by permission of Ontario Secondary School Teachers' Federation (OSSTF)

Probationary Teacher's Contract

This Agreement made in duplicate this . . . . day of . . . . , 19 . . . ., between

. . . . hereinafter called **the "Board"**

and . . . . of the . . . . of

. . . . in the County (or as the case may be) / Territorial District } of . . . .

hereinafter called **the "Teacher".**

1. The Board agrees to employ the Teacher as a probationary teacher for a probationary period of
. . . . years and the Teacher agrees to teach for the Board commencing the . . . .
day of . . . ., 19 . . . . . , at a yearly salary of . . . . Dollars,
subject to any changes in salary mutually agreed upon by the Teacher and the Board, payable in . . . .
(not fewer than ten)
payments, less any lawful deduction, in the following manner:

    i.   Where there are ten payments, one-tenth on or before the last teaching day of each teaching month.

    ii.   Where there are more than ten payments, at least one-twelfth on or before the last teaching day of each teaching month, any unpaid balance being payable on or before the last teaching day of June, or at the time of leaving the employ of the Board, whichever is the earlier.

2. This Agreement is subject to the Teacher's continuing to hold qualifications in accordance with the Acts and regulations administered by the Minister.

3. The Teacher agrees to be diligent and faithful in his duties during the period of his employment, and to perform such duties and teach such subjects as the Board may assign under the Acts and regulations administered by the Minister.

4. Where the Teacher attends an educational conference for which the school has been legally closed and his attendance thereat is certified by the supervisory officer concerned or by the chairman of the conference, the Board agrees to make no deductions from the Teacher's salary for his absence during that attendance.

5. Where an Act of Ontario or a regulation thereunder authorizes the Teacher to be absent from school without loss of pay, the Board agrees that no deduction from his pay will be made for the period of absence so authorized.

6. Notwithstanding anything in this contract this Agreement may be terminated,

    (a)   at any time by the mutual consent in writing of the Teacher and the Board; or

    (b)   on the 31st day of December in any year of the Teacher's employment by either party giving written notice to the other on or before the last preceding 30th day of November; or

    (c)   on the 31st day of August in any year of the Teacher's employment by either party giving written notice to the other on or before the last preceding 31st day of May.

7. The Teacher agrees with the Board that in the event of his entering into an agreement with another board he will within 48 hours notify the Board in writing of the termination of this Agreement unless the notice has already been given.

8. Where this Agreement is not terminated under paragraph 6 at the conclusion of the probationary period in paragraph 1, the Teacher is deemed to be employed as a permanent teacher by the Board.

In witness whereof the Teacher has signed and the Board has affixed hereto its corporate seal attested by its proper officers in that behalf.

. . . .
(signature of Chairman of the Board)

. . . .
(signature of Secretary of the Board)

. . . .
(signature of Teacher)

Permanent Teacher's Contract

This Agreement made in duplicate this . . . . day of . . . . , 19 . . . . . between

. . . . hereinafter called **the "Board"**

and . . . . of the . . . . of

                                  County (or as the case

. . . . in the may be)   of . . . .

                                  Territorial District

hereinafter called **the "Teacher"**

1. The Board agrees to employ the Teacher as a permanent teacher and the Teacher agrees to teach for the Board commencing the . . . . day of . . . . 19 . . . . . . ,

at a yearly salary of . . . . Dollars, subject to any changes in salary mutually agreed upon by the Teacher and the Board, payable in . . . . payments,

                             (not fewer than 10)

less any lawful deduction, in the following manner:

    i.   Where there are ten payments, one-tenth on or before the last teaching day of each teaching month.

    ii. Where there are more than ten payments, at least one-twelfth on or before the last teaching day of each teaching month, any unpaid balance being payable on or before the last teaching day of June, or at the time of leaving the employ of the Board, whichever is the earlier.

2. This Agreement is subject to the Teacher's continuing to hold qualifications in accordance with the Acts and regulations administered by the Minister.

3. The Teacher agrees to be diligent and faithful in his duties during the period of his employment, and to perform such duties and teach such subjects as the Board may assign under the Acts and regulations administered by the Minister.

4. Where the Teacher attends an educational conference for which the school has been legally closed and his attendance thereat is certified by the supervisory officer concerned or by the chairman of the conference, the Board agrees to make no deductions from the Teacher's salary for his absence during that attendance.

5. Where an Act of Ontario or a regulation thereunder authorizes the Teacher to be absent from school without loss of pay, the Board agrees that no deduction from his pay will be made for the period of absence so authorized.

6. This Agreement may be terminated,

    (a) at any time by the mutual consent in writing of the Teacher and the Board; or

    (b) on the 31st day of December in any year of the Teacher's employment by either party giving written notice to the other on or before the last preceding 30th day of November; or

    (c) on the 31st day of August in any year of the Teacher's employment by either party giving written notice to the other on or before the last preceding 31st day of May.

7. The Teacher agrees with the Board that in the event of his entering into an agreement with another board he will within 48 hours notify the Board in writing of the termination of this Agreement unless the notice has already been given.

8. Where the Teacher is to be transferred by the Board from a school in one municipality to a school in another municipality, the Board agrees to notify the Teacher in writing on or before the 1st day of May immediately prior to the school year for which the transfer is effective, but nothing in this paragraph prevents the transfer of a teacher at any time by mutual consent of the Board and the Teacher.

9. This Agreement shall remain in force until terminated in accordance with any Act administered by the Minister or the regulations thereunder.

In witness whereof the Teacher has signed and the Board has affixed hereto its corporate seal attested by its proper officers in that behalf.

                        . . . .

                                (signature of Chairman of the Board)

                        . . . .

                                (signature of Secretary of the Board)

                        . . . .

                                  (signature of Teacher)

Duties of Teachers

235.(1) It is the duty of a teacher and a temporary teacher:

a. to teach diligently and faithfully the classes or subjects assigned to him by the principal;

b. to encourage the pupils in the pursuit of learning;

c. to inculcate by precept and example respect for religion and the principles of Judaeo-Christian morality and the highest regard for truth, justice, loyalty, love of country, humanity, benevolence, sobriety, industry, frugality, purity, temperance and all other virtues;

d. to assist in developing cooperation and coordination of effort among the members of the staff to the school;

e. to maintain, under the direction of the principal, proper order and discipline in his/her classroom and while on duty in the school and on the school ground;

f. in instruction and in all communications with the pupils in regard to discipline and the management of the school,

   i) to use the English language, except where it is impractical to do so by reason of the pupil not understanding English, and except in respect of instruction in a language other than English as one of the subjects in the course of study, or

   ii) to use the French language in schools or classes in which French is the language of instruction except where it is impractical to do so by reason of the pupil not understanding French, and except in respect of instruction in a language other than French when such other language is being taught as one of the subjects in the course of study;

g. to conduct his/her class in accordance with a timetable which shall be accessible to pupils and to the principal and supervisory officers;

h. to participate in professional activity days as designated by the board under the regulations;

i. to notify such person as is designed by the board if he/she is to be absent from school and the reason therefore.

From: *Education Act,* Ontario, 1991, Toronto, ON: Queen's Printer for Ontario. Reprinted by permission. Note: s.235 is now s.264.

DUTIES OF TEACHERS

In addition to the duties assigned to the teacher under the Act and by the board, a teacher shall,

a. be responsible for effective instruction, training and evaluation of the progress of pupils in the subjects assigned to the teacher and for the management of the class or classes, and report to the principal on the progress of pupils on request;

b. carry out the supervisory duties and instructional program assigned to the teacher by the principal and supply such information related thereto as the principal may require;

c. where the board has appointed teachers under sections 15, 16 or 18, co-operate fully with such teachers and with the principals in all matters related to the instruction of pupils;

d. unless otherwise assigned by the principal, be present in the classroom or teaching area and ensure that the classroom or teaching area is ready for the reception of pupils at least fifteen minutes before the commencement of classes in the school in the morning and, where applicable, five minutes before the commencement of classes in the school in the afternoon;

e. assist the principal in maintaining close co-operation with the community;

f. prepare for use in the teacher's class or classes such teaching plans and outlines as are required by the principal and the appropriate supervisory officer and submit the plans and outlines to the principal or the appropriate supervisory officer, as the case may be, on request;

g. ensure that all reasonable safety procedures are carried out in courses and activities for which the teacher is responsible; and

h. co-operate with the principal and other teachers to establish and maintain consistent disciplinary practices in the school. O.Reg. 617/81, s. 17; O.Reg. 785/81, s.3

Duties of Principals

Duties of principal,   **236.** It is the duty of a principal of a school, in addition to his duties as a teacher,

discipline   a) to maintain proper order and discipline in the school;

co-operation   b) to develop co-operation and co-ordination of effort among the members of the staff of the school;

register pupils and record attendance   c) to register the pupils and to ensure that the attendance of pupils for every school day is recorded either in the register supplied by the Minister in accordance with the instructions contained therein or in such other manner as is approved by the Minister; '

pupil records   d) to establish and maintain, and to retain, transfer and dispose of, in the manner prescribed by the regulations, a record in respect of each pupil enrolled in the school;

timetable   e) to prepare a timetable, to conduct the school according to such timetable and the school year calendar or calendars applicable thereto, to make the calendar or calendars and the timetable accessible to the pupils, teachers and supervisory officers and to assign classes and subjects to the teachers;

examinations and reports   f) to hold, subject to the approval of the appropriate supervisory officer, such examinations as he considers necessary for the promotion of pupils or for any other purpose and report as requested by the board the progress of the pupil to his parent or guardian where the pupil is a minor and otherwise to the pupil;

promote pupils   g) subject to revision by the appropriate supervisory officer, to promote such pupils as he considers proper and to issue to each such pupil a statement thereof;

textbooks   h) to ensure that all textbooks used by pupils are those approved by the board and, in the case of subject areas for which the Minster approves textbooks, those approved by the Minister;

reports   i) to furnish to the Ministry and to the appropriate supervisory officer any information that it may be in his power to give respecting the condition of the school premises, the discipline of the school, the progress of the pupils and any other matter affecting the interests of the school, and to prepare such reports for the board as are required by the board;

care of pupils and property   j) to give assiduous attention to the health and comfort of the pupils, to the cleanliness, temperature and ventilation of the school, to the care of all teaching materials and other school property, and to the condition and appearance of the school buildings and grounds;

215

report to MOH	k)	to report promptly to the board and to the municipal health officer or to the school medical officer where one has been appointed, when he has reason to suspect the existence of any infectious or contagious disease in the school, and of the unsanitary condition of any part of the school building or the school grounds;
persons with communicable diseases RSO 1980, c.409	l)	to refuse admission to the school of any person who he believes is infected with or exposed to communicable diseases requiring quarantine and placarding under regulations made pursuant to the *Public Health Act* until furnished with a certificate of a medical officer of health or of a legally qualified medical practitioner approved by him that all danger from exposure to contact with such person has passed;
access to school or class	m)	subject to an appeal to the board, to refuse to admit to the school or classroom a person whose presence in the school or classroom would in his judgment be detrimental to the physical or mental well-being of the pupils; and
visitor's book	n)	to maintain a visitor's book in the school when so determined by the board. **RSO 1980, c. 129, s. 236.**

From: *Education Act,* Ontario, 1991, Toronto, ON: Queen's Printer for Ontario. Reprinted by permission. Note: s.236 is now s.265.

The Job of the Principal

AREAS OF RESPONSIBILITY	FUNCTIONS OF THE PRINCIPALSHIP	SOME ILLUSTRATIVE DUTIES
IMPROVING THE EDUCATIONAL PROGRAM	Operating the program as it exists	Develop efficient schedules, reasonable workload, coordination, communication, integration
	Evaluation	Coordinate periodic staff evaluation, student surveys, standardized tests, and other surveys
	Revision	Stimulate and coordinate work of lay and professional committees; provide material and resources for curriculum study
	Selection and dismissal	Survey staff needs and possible candidates; provide sound evaluative techniques
SELECTING AND DEVELOPING PERSONNEL	Personnel policies	Take an active part in developing system policies; fairly apply the policies in the building units
	Personal relationships	Recognize teacher achievement; encourage teachers to participate in school planning
	Orientation and in-service growth	Provide necessary background information on new teachers; develop a program of professional experiences
	Pupil personnel problems	Coordinate pupil personnel activities with other educational activities

WORKING WITH THE COMMUNITY	Knowing the community	Utilize study techniques of social science and education; survey community resources
	Participating in community life	Be available as speaker, consultant, civic worker; plan to allow staff members to be active in community affairs
	Community participation in the school	Initiate parent workshops, school visitations, organizations for parents and teachers; plan for community use of school facilities
	Interpreting the school	Develop contacts with mass media outlets; provide direct releases to parents - i.e., newsletters
MANAGING THE SCHOOL	Organizing the staff	Define job, authority and responsibility; develop a purpose-based administrative organization
	Determining needs	Plan cooperative budget by school units; work with the central staff on the total budget
	Use and maintenance of facilities	Make schedules -- opening and closing school; establish an efficient system of plant maintenance
	Keeping records	Provide for staff and pupil personnel file; establish a system of requisitioning, classifying and accounting

Appendix C
School Order, Discipline, and Student Rights

School Order and Discipline Preferred over Students' Rights: R. v. G. (J.M.)

Bruce E. Thom, Q.C. and Douglas J. Thom*

Since the advent of the *Canadian Charter of Rights and Freedoms*,[1] many areas of the law have been examined and reexamined to determine whether or not they comply with the various *Charter* standards. Public education has not escaped scrutiny during this process, although it certainly has not been in the forefront of challenged activities.

Legal experts in the area of education law pondered whether or not education would change with the *Charter*. In pre-*Charter* days, judges were not disposed to enter the arena of educational decision-making. As an example, in *Ward v. Blaine Lake School Board*,[2] a boy was suspended for having his hair too long for the rules established by the Board and Principal. The Court dismissed the case without considering the merits of the boy's arguments by deferring to the judgment of the administration.

One major area of educational authority that was being monitored with care was the power to search lockers and students. It has been of uniform concern across Canada and opposing views on how it should be resolved abound.

In March 1986, for example, one school district in Alberta passed "Policy 915," which attempted to bring school policy in line with existing rights as guaranteed by the *Charter*. While the policy was prefaced by a statement that the schools have a responsibility to act in loco parentis (as a reasonable and prudent parent would) toward the students they serve, opponents on the School Board protested. One commented as follows:

> I have difficulties with this [policy] in that a 13 year old could get into trouble without parents knowing. Who is protecting the rights of the student?

This example illustrates the tension that exists between school authority and pupil rights and the confusion that undoubtedly reigns in the minds of school administrators as they struggle to cope with conflicting state agent and in loco parentis roles.

The main *Charter* provision which has been considered in this field is section 8: "Everyone has the right to be secure against unreasonable search and seizure."

In the 1986 case *R. v. G. (J.M.)*,[3] the Ontario court of Appeal gave some important guidance on the issue of school searches. Since leave to appeal to the Supreme Court of Canada was refused,[4] the Court of Appeal's comments constitute the highest legal authority.

The case arose in Thunder Bay, Ontario. The accused, a 14-year-old Grade 7 pupil, was summoned to the principal's office after the principal received information that the student had been seen outside the school placing drugs in his socks. In the office, in the presence of the vice-principal, the principal advised the accused that he had reason to suspect that the accused was in possession of drugs and asked him to remove his shoes and socks. The student managed to eat a rolled cigarette that he had taken out of his pant cuff, but the principal did secure some tinfoil containing butts from the student's

From: *Education and Law Journal,* vol. 3, no. 1 (August, 1990), pp. 105-109.

sock. A policeman subsequently arrived and charged the student with possession of marijuana. (It is interesting that the student's father was himself a policeman.)

At trial, the accused was convicted and fined, but on appeal he was acquitted. On further appeal to the Court of Appeal, the conviction was restored.

The Court first indicated that it did not need to decide the difficult question of whether or not a principal was governed by the *Charter* (since he derived his authority from provincial legislation) or was exempt as simply a delegate of parental authority who, as the parents' alter ego, could discipline as could any parent. The Court simply assumed the Charter applied (which was, of course, the easiest decision to make).

Mr. Justice Grange, writing for the Court, then pointed out that "there is no Canadian authority that deals directly with the situation." He therefore reviewed a recent United States Supreme Court decision on point. In *New Jersey v. T.L.O.*,[5] a student's purse was searched based on suspicion that the student was smoking tobacco, and traces of marijuana were found. The court found that students could claim the protection of the Fourth Amendment and had legitimate expectations of privacy. But against that was set the school's equally legitimate need to maintain an environment in which learning can take place.

The U.S. decision went on to set the following interesting standards for student searches as it tried to balance the competing interests:

> [T]he legality of a search of a student should depend simply on the reasonableness, under all the circumstances, of the search. Determining the reasonableness of any search involves a twofold inquiry: first, one must consider "whether the ... action was justified at its inception" ... second, one must determine whether the search as actually conducted "was reasonably related in scope to the circumstances which justified the interference in the first place". . . . Under ordinary circumstances, a search of a student by a teacher or other school official will be "justified at its inception" when there are reasonable grounds for suspecting that the search will turn up evidence that the student has violated or is violating either the law or the rules of the school. Such a search will be permissible in its scope when the measures adopted are reasonably related to the objectives of the search and not excessively intrusive in light of the age and sex of the student and nature of the infraction.[6]

Mr. Justice Grange utilized the above tests and held that the principal's action was "not only justified at its inception but indeed was dictated by the circumstances."[7]

Referring next to the principal's duty under the *Education Act*[8] "to maintain proper order and discipline in the school," the Court held that, given that the principal had received information about criminal conduct, it was

> not unreasonable that the student should be required to remove his socks in order to prove or disprove the allegation. . . . Moreover, the search was not excessively intrusive.[9]

As to the accused's suggestion that the principal should have simply turned the whole matter over to the police, the Court disagreed and again adopted the reasoning in the

New Jersey case regarding what type of information an educator needs to justify a search:

> By focussing attention on the question of reasonableness, the standard will spare teachers and school administrators the necessity of schooling themselves in the niceties of probable cause and permit them to regulate their conduct according to the dictates of reason and common sense.[10]

The court next discussed what, if any, prior authorization a principal needs to conduct a search:

> First, the principal has a substantial interest not only in the welfare of the other students but in the accused student as well. Secondly, society as a whole has an interest in the maintenance of a proper educational environment, which clearly involves being able to enforce school discipline efficiently and effectively. It is often neither feasible nor desirable that the principal should require prior authorization before searching his or her student and seizing contraband.[11]

Finally, the court reviewed the argument that the accused was detained by the principal within the meaning of section 10(b) of the *Charter*, and was deprived of his right to counsel. Mr. Justice Grange ruled as follows:

> The search here was but an extension of normal discipline such as, for example, the requirement to stay after school or to do extra assignments or the denial of privileges.[12]

Hence, the Court ruled that there was no "detention" in this case within the meaning of section 10(b). In obiter dicta, however, Grange J.A. suggested that in instances where a student is held under circumstances where "significant legal consequences appear inevitable, and the principal appears to be acting as an agent of the police, section 10 Charter rights might well accrue.[13]

The *G. (J.M.)* case is a welcome outline for educators to follow. It appears that the courts in general are prepared to continue to view school discipline as an area in which they will rarely intervene. It is obvious that judges recognize that school administrators have a broad duty to enforce school rules, and that the rules and their exercise are best left to the common sense of the administration rather than courts of law.

As a final note, since the *G. (J.M.)* case supported a personal search of a student, it appears that a locker search, which involves access to what is ultimately school property,[14] is even further removed from the niceties of Charter interpretation.

---

*Bruce E. Thom, Q.C., City Solicitor, Mississauga, Ontario; Douglas J. Thom, Associate Professor, Educational Administration, Lakehead University, Thunder Bay, Ontario.

[1]Part I of the *Constitution Act, 1982*, being Schedule B of the *Canada Act 1982* (U.K.), 1982, c. 11.

[2][1971] 4 W.W.R. 161 (Sask. Q.B.).

[3](1986), 56 O.R. (2d) 705, 33 D.L.R. (4th) 277 (C.A.)

[4](1987), 59 O.R. (2d) 286 (note) (S.C.C.).

[5]105 S.Ct. 733 (1985).

[6]Ibid. at 743-744 (S.Ct.).

[7]Above, note 3 at 709 (O.R.).

[8]R.S.O. 1980, c. 129.

[9]Above, note 3 at 709 (O.R.).

[10]Above, note 5 at 744 (S.Ct.).

[11]Above, note 3 at 710-711 (O.R.).

[12]Ibid. at 712.

[13]Ibid.

[14]This conclusion could be open to debate, however, under circumstances where school locker policies give students reason to believe they have a right of privacy concerning their lockers: see, for example, G. Dickinson and A. MacKay, eds., *Rights, Freedoms and the Education System in Canada* (Toronto: Emond Montgomery, 1989) at 390.

Appendix D
Leadership and Teambuilding Research Materials

Tools for Measuring Leadership Behavior

1.

Continuum of Leadership Behavior

(Tannenbaum & Schmidt)

2 versions

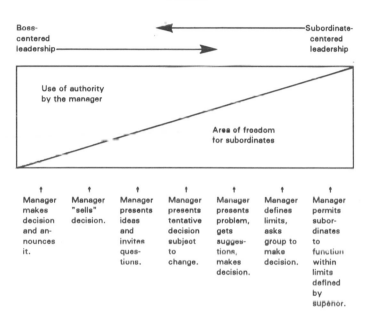

↑	↑	↑	↑	↑	↑	↑
Manager makes decision and announces it.	Manager "sells" decision.	Manager presents ideas and invites questions.	Manager presents tentative decision subject to change.	Manager presents problem, gets suggestions, makes decision.	Manager defines limits, asks group to make decision.	Manager permits subordinates to function within limits defined by superior.

and

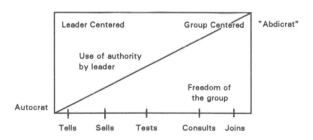

If we extend the continuum at either extreme we get autocracy or abdication. The autocrat violates our traditional values and our self image as people who are open and sensitive. The abdicrat is irresponsible and violates concepts of leadership which gets work done.

2.

Leader Behavior Description Questionnaire (LBDQ)

(Halpin & Winer, 1952)

The following 30 items are used to describe the practices and policies of an administrator. Each item describes a specific kind of behavior. Opposite each item, please indicate the frequency with which the administrator in question behaves as described in the item.

A = Very Frequently or Always

B = Often

C = Occasionally

D = Seldom

E = Very Rarely or Never

		For Scoring (I = Initiating Structure) (C = Consideration)
1.	He lets his staff members know what is expected of them.	A B C D E I
2.	He is friendly and approachable.	A B C D E C
3.	He encourages the use of uniform procedures.	A B C D E I
4.	He does little things to make it pleasant to be a member of his staff.	A B C D E C
5.	He tries out new ideas with his staff.	A B C D E I
6.	He puts suggestions made by his staff into action.	A B C D E C
7.	He makes his attitudes clear to his staff.	A B C D E I
8.	He treats all staff members as his equals.	A B C D E C

9. He assigns his staff members to particular tasks.   A B C D E   I

10. He keeps to himself.   A B C D E   *C

11. He makes sure that his part in the organization is understood by all members.   A B C D E   I

12. He looks out for the personal welfare of individual staff members.   A B C D E   C

13. He sees to it that the work of his staff members is coordinated.   A B C D E   I

14. He is willing to make changes.   A B C D E   C

15. He maintains definite standards of performance.   A B C D E   I

16. He refuses to explain his actions.   A B C D E   *C

17. He asks that his staff members follow standard rules and regulations.   A B C D F   I

18. He acts without consulting his staff.   A B C D E   *C

19. He sees to it that his staff members are working up to capacity.   A B C D E   I

20. He rules with an iron hand.   A B C D E   *I

21. He criticizes poor work.   A B C D E   I

22. He speaks in a manner not to be questioned.   A B C D E   I

23. He works without a plan.   A B C D E   *I

24. He emphasizes the meeting of deadlines.   A B C D E   I

25. He does personal favours for his staff members.   A B C D E   C

26. He is easy to understand.   A B C D E   C

27. He finds time to listen to his
    staff.   A B C D E   C

28. He is slow to accept new
    ideas.   A B C D E   *C

29. He makes his staff members
    feel at ease when talking with
    them.   A B C D E   C

30. He gets staff approval on
    important matters before
    going ahead.   A B C D E   C

                                        *SCORED NEGATIVELY

2. TASK STRUCTURE RATING SCALE -- PART 1

Circle the number in the appropriate column.	Usually True	Sometimes True	Seldom True
Is the Goal Clearly Stated or Known?			
1. Is there a blueprint, picture, model or detailed description available of the finished product or service?	2	1	0
2. Is there a person available to advise and give a description of the finished product or service, or how the job should be done?	2	1	0
Is There Only One Way to Accomplish the Task?			
3. Is there a step-by-step procedure, or a standard operating procedure which indicates in detail the process which is to be followed?	2	1	0
4. Is there a specific way to subdivide the task into separate parts or steps?	2	1	0
5. Are there some ways which are clearly recognized as better than others for performing this task?	2	1	0
Is There Only One Correct Answer or Solution?			
6. Is it obvious when the task is finished and the correct solution has been found?	2	1	0
7. Is there a book, manual, or job description which indicates the best solution or the best outcome for the task?	2	1	0
Is It Easy to Check Whether the Job Was Done Right?			
8. Is there a generally agreed upon understanding about the standards the particular product or service has to meet to be considered acceptable?	2	1	0

9. Is the evaluation of this task gener-   2   1   0
    ally made on some quantitative
    basis?

10. Can the leader and the group find   2   1   0
    out how well the task has been
    accomplished in enough time to
    improve future performance?

    SUBTOTAL   _____

3.

Leader Match Scales - Matching Style and Situation

(Fiedler & Chemers)

1. LEADER-MEMBER RELATIONS SCALE

Circle the number which best represents your response to each item.	strongly agree	agree	neither agree nor disagree	disagree	strongly disagree
1. The people I supervise have trouble getting along with each other.	1	2	3	4	5
2. My subordinates are reliable and trustworthy.	5	4	3	2	1
3. There seems to be a friendly atmosphere among the people I supervise.	5	4	3	2	1
4. My subordinates always cooperate with me in getting the job done.	5	4	3	2	1
5. There is friction between my subordinates and myself.	1	2	3	4	5
6. My subordinates give me a good deal of help and support in getting the job done.	5	4	3	2	1
7. The people I supervise work well together in getting the job done.	5	4	3	2	1
8. I have good relations with the people I supervise.	5	4	3	2	1

Total Score [ ]

From   *Improving Leadership Effectiveness: The Leader Match Concept* (2nd ed.) by Fred E. Fiedler and Martin M. Chemers, 1984, pp. 261-265. Copyright (c) 1984 by John Wiley & Sons, Inc., New York, NY. Reprinted by permission of John Wiley & Sons, Inc.

3. TASK STRUCTURE RATING SCALE -- PART 2

Training and Experience Adjustment

NOTE: Do not adjust jobs with task structure scores of 6 or below.

a. Compared to others in this or similar positions, how much **training** has the leader had?

3	2	1	0
No training at all	Very little training	A moderate amount of training	A great deal of training

b. Compared to others in this or similar positions, how much **experience** has the leader had?

6	4	2	0
No experience at all	Very little experience	A moderate amount of experience	A great deal of experience

Add lines (a) and (b) of the training and experience adjustment, then **subtract** this from the subtotal given in Part 1.

Subtotal from Part 1.

Subtract training and experience adjustment.

Total Task Structure Score

4. POSITION POWER RATING SCALE

Circle the number which best represents your answer.

1. Can the leader directly or by recommendation administer rewards and punishments to subordinates?

2	1	0
Can act directly or can recommend with high effectiveness	Can recommend but with mixed results	No

2. Can the leader directly or by recommendation affect the promotion, demotion, hiring or firing of subordinates?

2	1	0
Can act directly or can recommend with high effectiveness	Can recommend but with mixed results	No

3. Does the leader have the knowlege necessary to assign tasks to subordinates and instruct them in task completion?

2	1	0
Yes	Sometimes or in some aspects	No

4. Is it the leader's job to evaluate the performance of subordinates?

2	1	0
Yes	Sometimes or in some aspects	No

5. Has the leader been given some official title of authority by the organization (e.g., foreman, department head, platoon leader)?

2	0
Yes	No

Total [ ]

5. SITUATIONAL CONTROL SCALE

Enter the total scores for the Leader-Member Relations dimension, the Task Structure scale, and the Position Power scale in the spaces below. Add the three scores together and compare your total with the ranges given in the table below to determine your overall situational control.

1. Leader-Member Relations Total

2. Task Structure Total

3. Position Power Total

Grand Total

Total Score	51 - 70	31 - 50	10 - 30
Amount of Situational Control	High Control	Moderate Control	Low Control

Tools for Measuring the Growth of a Group

1.

As a group begins its life and at several points during its growth, the leader and members might individually fill out the following scales and then spend some time sharing the data that is collected. Through these scales, it is possible to get a general picture of the perceptions which various members have about the group and how it is growing. It is also possible to pick up areas in which there may be some difficulties which are blocking progress.

1. How clear are the group goals?

1.	2.	3.	4.	5.
No apparent goals	Goal confusion, uncertainty, or conflict	Average goal clarity	Goals mostly clear	Goals very clear

2. How much trust and openness in the group?

1.	2.	3.	4.	5.
Distrust, a closed group	Little trust, defensiveness	Average trust and openness	Considerable trust and openness	Remarkable trust and openness

3. How sensitive and perceptive are group members?

1.	2.	3.	4.	5.
No awareness or listening in the group	Most members self-absorbed	Average sensitivity and listening	Better than usual listening	Outstanding sensitivity to others

4. How much attention was paid to process? (The way the group was working?)

1.	2.	3.	4.	5.
No attention to process	Little attention to process	Some concern with group process	A fair balance between content and process	Very concerned with process

5. How were group leadership needs met?

1.	2.	3.	4.	5.
Not met, drifting	Leadership concentrated in one person	Some leadership sharing	Leadership functions distributed	Leadership needs met creatively and flexibly

6. How were group decisions made?

1.	2.	3.	4.	5.
No decisions could be reached	Made by a few	Majority vote	Attempts at integrating minority vote	Full participation and tested consensus

7. How well were group resources used?

1.	2.	3.	4.	5.
One or two contributed, but deviants silent	Several tried to contribute, but were discouraged	Average use of group resources	Group resources well used and encouraged	Group resources fully and effectively used

8. How much loyalty and sense of belonging to the group?

1.	2.	3.	4.	5.
Members had no group loyalty or sense of belonging	Members not close but some friendly relations	About average sense of belonging	Some warm sense of belonging	Strong sense of belonging among members

A MATURE GROUP POSSESSES:

1. **Adequate mechanisms for getting feedback:**

Poor feedback mechanisms	1	2	3	4	5	Excellent feedback mechanisms
			Average			

2. **Adequate decision making procedure:**

Poor decision making procedure	1	2	3	4	5	Very adequate decision making
			Average			

3. **Optimal cohesion:**

Low cohesion	1	2	3	4	5	Optimal cohesion
			Average			

4. **Flexible organization and procedures:**

Very inflexible	1	2	3	4	5	Very flexible
			Average			

5. **Maximum use of member resources:**

Poor use of resources	1	2	3	4	5	Excellent use of resources
			Average			

6. **Clear communications:**

Poor communication	1	2	3	4	5	Excellent communication
			Average			

7. **Clear goals accepted by members:**

Unclear goals -- not accepted	1	2	3	4	5	Very clear goals -- accepted
			Average			

8. **Feelings of interdependence with authority persons:**

No interdependence	1	2	3	4	5	High interdependence
			Average			

9. Shared participation in leadership functions:

No shared   1   2   3   4   5   High shared participation
participation

Average

10. Acceptance of minority views and persons:

No acceptance   1   2   3   4   5   High acceptance
mechanisms

Average

From: *Process Consultation,* volume I: Its Role in Organization Development by E.H. Schein, 1988, pp. 81-82. Copyright © 1988 by Addison-Wesley Pub. Co., reading, MA. Reprinted by permission.

Index

equity, 60, 67-68, 70, 76, 84-85, 172, 178, 181
ethics, 10, 95-96, 101-102, 109, 123, 160-161, 169, 177
ethnography, 10
Etzioni, A., 36, 49, 97
European countries, 153
Evers, C., 33, 49, 98, 116, 160, 168, 173-174
evil, 126, 145, 155, 159, 170-171
"executive privilege," 135
external regulation, 156, 172

Fair Tax Commission, 91
fairness (natural justice) defined, 165-167
  audi alteram partem rule, 165
  nemo judex in causa sua debet esse rule, 165-166
faith, 100-101, 123, 125-126, 167, 169-170, 172, 181-182
family
  importance of, 127, 145, 151-153, 169, 181
  "dysfunctional," 18, 152-153
Family and Child Service Act (British Columbia), Appendix A
Farquhar, R., 21, 30, 96-98, 104, 116-117
Fayol, H., 97
Federal government role in education, 22-23, 40, 57, 68-69, 83
feminism, 124, 170, 181
Fennell, H., 181-182
Feuerstein, R., 105-106, 117
Fiedler, F., 95, 117, Appendix D
Financial Post, 131, 147
"fishbowl," 131, 136, 142
Fleming, T., 174
"floating paranoia," 44
Flower, G., 96, 117
force field analysis (unfreezing, changing, refreezing), 139-140
Foster, W., 96, 117
Foucault, M., 45, 49
Frankl, V., 103-104, 109, 117
Free Trade, 89, 152
freedom of information, 59-60, 178
Froebel, 110
Fromm, E., 104-105, 117
Frye, N., 169, 175

Frymier, J., 40, 49
Fullan, M., 26, 30, 97, 127, 147
Fullan and Connelly report, 26, 30

Gairdner, W., 17, 30, 104, 117, 169, 173, 175
Gall, G., 66, 165, 175
"gambare," 158
Gardner, J., 152, 175
gender equity, 178-179
Gerth, H., 34, 49
Getzels, J., 41, 97
Gibb, J., 95, 117
Gilbert, V., 97, Appendix A
Giles, T., 15, 25, 30, 66, 97, 165, 175, Appendix B
Girling, R., 98, 118
global educational market, 153
goals of education, 21-24, 33-34, 42, 46, 153-155, 173, 179, Appendix A
God, 108, 110, 123-125, 160-161, 169-172, 181
  and physics, 124
Goldhammer, K., 97
good and evil, 145, 159, 170-171
Goodwin, B., 145
Gouldner, A., 34, 49, 97
"Govan" case, 59, 66
government educational jurisdictions, 68-69
Government Sales Tax (GST), 18, 83, 89, 152
Greenewalt, C., 152, 175
Greenfield, T., 10, 96-98, 117, 143, 147, 160-161, 175
Greenspan, E., Appendix A
Greiff, B., 160, 175
Greiner, L., 96, 117, 143-144, 147
grievance, 20, 61-65, 166
  avenues of appeal in, 63-64
Griffin, P., 27
Griffith, F., 39, 49, 95, 117, 129, 147
Griffiths, D., 10, 97
Gross, M., 45, 49
"groupthink," 141
Guba, E., 41, 97
Gue, L., 98, 117

Haas, J., 167, 176
Hage, J., 97
Haines, J., 153, 175

246